D0523620

HARRY,
A HISTORY

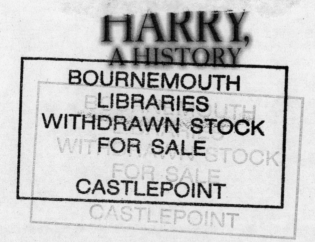

HARRY,
A HISTORY

THE TRUE STORY OF A BOY WIZARD,
HIS FANS, AND LIFE INSIDE
THE HARRY POTTER PHENOMENON

MELISSA ANELLI

POCKET
BOOKS

LONDON • SYDNEY • NEW YORK • TORONTO

First published in the USA by Pocket Books, an imprint of
Simon & Schuster, Inc, 2008
First published in Great Britain by Pocket Books, an imprint of
Simon & Schuster UK Ltd, 2008
A CBS COMPANY

Designed by Elliott Beard

1 3 5 7 9 10 8 6 4 2

Simon & Schuster UK Ltd
222 Gray's Inn Road
London
WC1X 8HB

www.simonsays.co.uk

Simon & Schuster Australia
Sydney

A CIP catalogue record for this book is available
from the British Library

ISBN: 978-1-84739-458-3

Printed by CPI Cox & Wyman, Reading, Berkshire RG1 8EX

For my fellow Harry Potter fans,
who know that a good story
never dies

CONTENTS

Contents

FOREWORD

J. K. Rowling

Over and over again they asked me the same question, with tiny variations. "What is it that makes Harry Potter so popular?" "What's the magic formula?" "What advice would you give anyone wanting to write a children's bestseller?"

And I always gave them non-answers. "It's not me you should ask." "This has taken me by surprise as much as anyone." "It's hard for the author to be objective. . . ."

As Somerset Maugham said, "There are three rules for writing a novel. The trouble is, nobody knows what they are." Harry just happened. The idea slid into my mind on a train journey from Manchester to London, and I wrote it the way I thought I would like to read it. I then had the immense good fortune to find an agent who liked it. After a lot of rejections, Chris found a publisher prepared to take a chance on an overlong novel (45,000 words was considered about the right length for nine-year-olds then; *Philosopher's Stone* was 95,000), set in a boarding school (a horribly unfashionable subject), by a completely unknown author.

When I started writing the Potter series I was aiming to please nobody but myself, and the more I was asked, the more I was sure that I ought not to try and analyse the reasons for its gathering popularity. I knew that if I tried to find this formula everyone was talking about, I would become self-conscious, start "doing" J. K. Rowling rather than being her. I was concerned for the safety of the fragile glass bubble within which I wrote, and which was still bobbing along intact on the swirling tide of madness that was gathering around Harry Potter, the still centre of the storm.

For similarly self-protective reasons, I kept myself as ignorant as possible about the degree of fan activity that was taking place both on the Internet and off it. Occasionally friends or journalists would impart some startling piece of information about what was going on out there; it tended to harden my resolve not to know. If that sounds bizarre or, worse, ungrateful, then I can only say that a day in my shoes would have convinced you otherwise. The letters I received daily made it perfectly clear how invested in the characters' futures my readers had become. "Please don't kill Fred or George, I LOVE THEM!" "If Hermione becomes Harry's girlfriend that will show that you can be smart and still team up with the hero!!! This would be a really good message!!!!" "Why didn't you let Harry go and live with Sirius and be happy?" "I read somewhere that you are going to make Draco and Harry become friends and fight evil together, I think this would be a good thing and show that Draco is not all bad." "Ms. Rowling, your books are a safe place in a dangerous world. May I urge you to resist commercial pressure: *let your characters keep their innocence.*" "DON'T KILL HAGRID. DON'T KILL HAGRID. DON'T KILL HAGRID" (repeated hundreds of times over ten sides of A4 paper).

Not until some time in 2002 did I finally crack and do the thing that people assumed I did daily. I googled Harry Potter.

I knew, of course, that there were fan sites out there. My postbag was full of mentions of them, my readers assuming that I was au fait with what was happening online. My PA, Fiddy, had had contact with a few of the webmasters. But I was still utterly unprepared for what I found during that first, mammoth trawling session.

The fan sites were so professional looking; easily up to the standard of any of my publishers' sites. And they had tens of thousands of visitors. They had forums, message boards, editorials, rolling news, fan art, fan fiction, quotes of the day from my books . . . and the shipping wars . . . my God, the shipping wars . . .

I had already heard of the Leaky Cauldron; it was one of the biggest and most popular Harry Potter sites on the Net, and I had been told about a couple of great things they had done (freeing the already-free Dobby got my attention). But I had never seen it for myself, never realised exactly what went on there. I sat and read editorials, predictions, theories that ranged from strange to wild to perfectly accurate. I was, frankly, stunned . . . and I remain stunned.

Reading the book you now have in your hands has been an astonishing experience for me. It is as though I have, at last, achieved the ambition I held for years: to go along to a bookshop at midnight on Harry Potter publication night, in disguise, and simply watch and listen.

At long last I understand what was going on while I was holed up writing, trying to filter my exposure to Potter hysteria. A great chunk of my own life has been explained to me; Melissa has filled in an enormous number of blanks, taken me to places I wish I could have visited with her (like the House of Pancakes, to meet the United States's most prominent anti–Harry Potter campaigner); explained jokes that fans assumed I understood; introduced me to people they thought I knew; filled me in on arguments I had inadvertently started. She has reminded me of incidents I had half forgotten in the furore surrounding every publication from 2000 onwards—the stolen truck full of copies of *Order of the Phoenix*, that irksome "Green Flame Torch," and the endless War on Spoilers. . . .

The online Harry Potter fandom has become a global phenomenon with its own language and culture, its own wars and festivals, its own celebrities, of which Melissa is certainly one. She was a fan who ended up with her own fan club, one of the online fandom's most tireless champions and representatives, endeavouring, always, to be fair and honest and impartial.

So this book is a history of a community, written by an insider, and I have found it inspiring, moving, humbling, amusing, and, on occasion, downright alarming. It can be read as a warts-and-all exposé of fan mentality or as a story of the world's biggest book group or as the personal journey of a group of people who would never otherwise have met. The tale of the online fandom is every bit as extraordinary as Harry's own, and it has left me with a feeling of awe and gratitude. At last, I know what was really happening out there—and it is wonderful.

CHAPTER ONE

Release

ithin twenty-four hours, everyone would know. They'd read about it on their computer screens or in the newspaper; they'd find out on their way to work or over morning coffee, listening to the radio or watching television. The news would be shouted into their cell phones or overheard on the train. They'd talk about it at the watercooler and on coffee breaks. There'd be group e-mails, message-board postings, hastily scribbled notes. They'd call grandchildren, and grandparents, to share and discuss.

The news would race around an electronic ribbon in Times Square and on billboards in London and news tickers all over the world. It would break into regular broadcasts and be teased on the morning shows. It would be whispered behind cupped hands in classrooms and screamed across playgrounds. Some would laugh and others would cry, but all would be affected. The news would skitter at light speed, unstoppable, through land lines and fiber-optic cables and over airwaves until it reached workplaces and houses and playgrounds, multiplying until it could weave itself into a blanket and cover the world.

I was barely conscious when I found out. I was on my bed, fully dressed, lying on my stomach and trying to keep my head from lolling right onto the keys of my laptop. When my phone rang, my head hit the keys like a dropped melon. I groaned and rubbed the new indentations on my nose while fumbling for the Talk button.

"Whagugh?"

"It's up!"

It was Sue Upton shrieking at me, and I let the phone fall so I could use my remaining free hand to rub what now felt like a punctured eardrum. At this rate I'd end up comatose before breakfast.

Sue was still yelling, the sound muffled from the dropped phone, but now completely unnecessary. Clarity broke upon me and I knew exactly what she was yelling about. It was why I was lying next to my keyboard, the reason I had been awake in the first place. The last few hours replayed themselves in my mind in a blink. Barely 10:00 p.m., sitting at my friend Julie's house, watching television after a light news day, chatting during commercials. Reaching for my cell phone out of unbreakable habit, as natural a motion as blinking. Tapping my Web browser, waiting for my e-mail to load, all without interrupting the flow of conversation—in fact, barely showing I was holding a phone at all. Flicking my eyes down to the screen, just to check that everything was all right online while I was away from a computer. No important e-mails, good. No emergencies, no broken servers, good. Pausing. One, two, three, four e-mails. Four of the fifty e-mails I'd received over the past hour were eerily alike and seemed to come from different parts of the country with the same news—like witnesses who chose the same man from a police lineup.

"I work in a bookstore and we just got an e-mail from Scholastic . . ."

". . . it said something big is coming . . ."

". . . said it's what we've been waiting for . . . Do you think this is *that*?"

I did, but didn't know if I wanted to. It had been such a calm, slow day, for a change, which meant I should have known it would be followed by a crazy parade. Six years on this beat had taught me to shake out the news from the rubbish, and this—this felt real. This felt like everything had just changed. Those short and simple e-mails had effects on me far disproportionate to their size—my heart seemed to sneak up into my throat and stick, pounding through me with the same rush I got when I reached the top of a roller coaster—about to get to the best part, the part I'd been waiting for, but still panicky and unsure I was ready to plummet.

Julie asked what was wrong but I was already gathering my stuff, making my apologies, telling her to check the Web site the next morning, bowing my way out of the apartment and calling Sue, the site's senior editor.

"I know," Sue said, instead of "hello." A clear thrill trembled under her words.

"They look real, Sue," I said. "Is this happening right now?"

"I think it is!" There it was again, that squeal of happiness threatening to break free. I denied myself my own flourish of giddiness, which was squirming around in my chest. No way. There was an announcement to be made in mere hours, and we'd be helping bring it to millions, and we were not ready, there were things to do and lists of things we had *wanted* to do and all these things we had planned to do, and now . . .

"I have to call John. And D. H. And Nick, and Alex, and Doris, and everyone, and make sure we're going to stay up tomorrow and get a low-bandwidth page ready and get home, and, and . . . a lot of things."

Sue made a squeaking sound. She was going to burst. T-minus thirty seconds and counting.

"See you online at five a.m.? Podcast right after?" I asked. No answer. "Sue?"

A high-pitched squeal exploded out of the phone and assaulted my eardrums. I held the phone at arm's length. *Oh my God, Melissa it's coming NOW!*"

"Yeah, I think it is," I said, and with that she had infected me. The words wavered as though I'd rattled them, and I danced a little on the spot.

Five minutes later I was on my way home. I called John on my car phone as I hit the Staten Island Expressway, which was thick with late-January mush. He answered thickly and it sounded like I was distracting him from something more important.

"So, are you ready for this?" I asked, and told him what I thought was about to happen.

"Are you *kidding* me?" John yelled. "Now? Holy—" and he let loose a stream of obscenities. "That's it? We're on a six-month timer?"

"Looks like."

"I'll be damned. What am I going to do with *school*?" John worked on a trimester basis, which meant he didn't get the same summer breaks as every other student, and the idea that he might not be able to take part in whatever celebrations were going on this summer was already causing a tightness in my chest. "I'm going to need about a month off."

"We'll work it out," I told him.

He promised to be awake and alert at 7:00 a.m. to record a podcast, and to stay up afterward to create a countdown for the site, and we hung up. I paused before calling Alex; genius programmer or not, he was in high school, and it was late; I could send him an e-mail when I got home, and he'd be up in time to act on it. Nick would be sleeping; it was nearly 4:00 a.m. his time.

Out of people to call, I drove in silence, worried for a moment that this was all an elaborate scam. No, it couldn't be—what would the plan be, to send e-mails from all corners of the country to convince people to wake up early on a specific day, realize there was no news to be had, and go back to bed? That wasn't even a scam, it was a complicated and pointless prank. This had to be real. Scholastic had informed bookstores to be on the alert tomorrow for a huge announcement. And there was no reason for them to do that, except—

The phone rang, and I laughed upon seeing the caller ID. It was Paul. Was word spreading so fast inside this community that it had already gotten to the rock stars?

"Yo, DeGeorge."

"Yo, Anelli," he said, as always sounding slightly bemused. I waited for him to ask me if the rumors were true. "I've got news."

"So do I."

"I'm announcing the EP of the Month Club tomorrow!"

He might as well have said, "I'm going to the moon tomorrow!" I'd have the same reaction. "*Such* a bad idea, man."

"What? Why?!"

I filled him in. No announcement of any kind in our community would get any play tomorrow except one. Not even if Bruce Springsteen decided to cover Britney Spears for Paul's charity compilation would it get any attention tomorrow. To my surprise, Paul wasn't annoyed—he just started talking more swiftly than his usual sauntering pace allowed.

"When do you think it will be? Joe and I are betting on July 31. We're planning our whole tour around it, I've got it all mapped out, we'll be back in Boston for the release. The birthdays, you know?"

"But that's not a Saturday. They always come out on Saturdays," I offered, then yawned and exited the highway at my stop. "All right. I have to get home and e-mail everyone in the world. Check the site when you get up. If it's even working."

Helplessness while driving made me twitchy. I thought briefly about calling Cheryl, but that would be pointless; she wouldn't be able to tell me anything anyway, and to press her wouldn't be fair. And besides, she'd just lie. In fact, I realized, laughing grimly, she had lied to me less than a week ago. We'd had dinner and she'd said . . . Oh, I was going to get her back, and soon.

There was nothing left to do, not until I got to my computer. I tapped the steering wheel impatiently and tried to obey the speed limit. Tomorrow was it; this frigid final day of January was the last day of sanity, at least for a while. What had started seventeen years ago would now end in six months. After a year and a half of waiting, a year and a half of preparation, a year and a half of knowing that this announcement was only a breath away, I now felt like my own breath had been stolen. For me this journey had lasted seven years, and it had changed me, and now it was time to say good-bye. If I could, I would have put out my hands and pushed back against the oncoming train.

But morning was coming despite my wishes, so I parked the car in front of my building and dragged myself upstairs to my shoddy apartment. I fired off a storm of e-mails: to programmers, to tell them to be ready to defend our Web site against the onslaught; to our hosting company, to ask them to monitor our bandwidth and give us more when we needed it; to John, to describe what the site countdown should look like; to editors; to all the senior staff; and to friends and family warning them I'd be out of touch. David and

Kathleen got texts of warning. I prepared our links and wrote a draft post, and fell asleep with my laptop next to my head.

At 5:00 a.m. on February 1, Sue was waiting for me, with an IM conversation already flashing on my computer screen. We had, no doubt, overshot our time frame—announcements usually came at 7:00 a.m.—by waking at 5:00, but better safe than sorry. We stared at the only Web site that mattered, which wasn't ours, and tried to use our knowledge of code to see which files changed, to try and get a few minutes up on the news, try to get ahead of it just a little. A few more e-mails like the first four had trickled in overnight, slow and steady, confirming that this was not a drill.

Everything was set. Our post was ready, just waiting for one crucial piece of information, and I had, in my early-morning stupor, nearly hit Publish prematurely. My hands shook while we waited. I checked news sites religiously. I put on NBC in the background. I fended off my cat, who seriously wanted my attention, but with my luck the news would hit in the minute it took me to fill her bowl with water.

And then waiting overtook me. I succumbed to a little nap, my fingers still poised in the air over my keyboard. Sue's phone call, and her shrieks, woke me back up, and when I had shaken the stiffness out of my fingers and willed them to work again, it was to refresh the site that had been my main focus all night: JKRowling.com. The words I'd been waiting for all these years were now there for me to see, and I barely even registered what they were as I typed them into my own site and hit Publish.

It took only moments for others to do the same: the news started breaking widely. Behind me, on my television screen, someone handed the anchorwoman a folded white piece of paper, as though they were announcing a war had broken out. My phone started buzzing with text messages, and then calls.

In the next few hours all the news outlets would pick up the story; the announcement would run all around the world. Schoolchildren in Ireland would write the date on pieces of white paper and post them all over their schools' walls. At a university in Australia, one student would shriek and fall off her chair. The news would go no faster around the Times Square ticker than through passed notes in high school classes.

Later, the mingled joy and sadness at the date, and at the end of it all, would start to spread over the fandom. Cheryl would finally call me and shout, "We know something you don't know!" through her speakerphone, and I'd swear to get my revenge at an undetermined date and time; Paul would e-mail me with expletive-enhanced declarations about having to reschedule his whole tour; JKRowling.com would update with further news; and the Leaky Cauldron would groan and crack under the traffic, leaving us to hold the site together with the digital equivalent of Silly String and a Band-Aid. But all that would come later. For now, all I could do was stare at the words I had just written on my screen, words that would shape the next several months of my life, that signified the end of an extraordinary time, a time that had given me confidence and purpose and independence, an era in which millions of people found fun and community and enchantment under one boy wizard's thrall.

"*Harry Potter and the Deathly Hallows* will be published on July 21, 2007."

CHAPTER TWO

The Beginning and the End

t quickly became clear that we were in for the most intense few months of being a Potter fan that had ever been: If the release of the most hotly anticipated book in recent history wasn't enough, Warner Bros. had decided to release the fifth film in the series, *Harry Potter and the Order of the Phoenix,* just eight days before the publication of *Deathly Hallows.* Already we were getting questions about what we were going to do for the release, and as we treated the Leaky Cauldron as a fan's Harry Potter news service, it was going to be hard enough to keep up with everything, never mind celebrate it properly. The prospect of the sheer volume of work that was going to be required over the next few months, together with the notion that after ten years of waiting and wondering, we had only 169 days, 15 hours, 14 minutes, and 42 seconds before the release of the final book, added touches of panic and nostalgia to what was otherwise supposed to be a joyous day.

By 7:15 a.m. Sue, John, and I were recording a podcast, still trying to process the news and shake off the shock enough to talk about it

coherently while juggling the rapidly intensifying stream of responses from all corners of Harry Potter fandom. John was already hard at work on a graphic countdown to add to the front page of the site, and even as he tinkered we received at least ten e-mails from people asking why it wasn't up already. "Real life" friends and colleagues who knew of our special interest in the series would, without fail, call or e-mail to see if we had gotten the news, thinking they were being helpful. My in-box was on fire, and every few minutes another reporter would call for a quote about the fans' excitement over the release; for one crazy second I started speaking an answer to my e-mail and typing a response to the person on the phone.

John was trying to talk at the same time he was finishing designing our countdown: it was a two-book-releases-strong tradition at Leaky by now to post the big, ticking reminder of the book's due date on the site as soon as we were able to calculate it, so that the global salivating could begin. Usually fans bemoaned the slow passage of time as the clock ticked down; once we put this one up, however, it started to serve opposite purposes. To some, it was a tease; to others, it more closely resembled a ticking time bomb. To me, it was both.

The reporters were all asking the same questions. How were we planning on celebrating the release? Were we happy or sad when we heard the news? And my favorite question, the one that, had I still been working at a newspaper, I'd be asking, too: What happens to Leaky after the last Harry? Will the Web site just close up?

Perhaps I imagined it, but I always felt an aftershock to that question, the secret nudge of the real question underneath: they were really asking me what we as Harry Potter fans planned on doing after Harry Potter. Whether we had anything in our lives besides a children's book series—how we planned to gather up the fragments of our lives—whether we had even existed before there were Harry books to read. I was tempted to tell them I hadn't. That before I read Harry Potter I was composed of magic dust and fairy breath, and reading the first book had been what brought all my particles together. That Harry Potter was my personal Big Bang.

But the truth was, that was exactly what I was wondering. Harry Potter had been a huge part of my life for so long I wasn't sure what came next, or even what I had *actually* been doing since the turn of the century. How had I ended up twenty-seven years old and the webmistress of one of the largest Harry Potter fan sites on the Net? It wasn't an answerable question. I avoided thinking about it altogether until I got an e-mail from Sarah Walsh. I hadn't heard from her in a year and a half.

> I saw the headline on Leaky and as excited as I am, I think I'm more sad to know that it's really, finally, wildly, gloriously and heartbreakingly coming to an end. What on earth are we going to do? My students are going to laugh when I tell them that I cried when I first read the publish date! Keep up the good work—I'm reading *Goblet of Fire* aloud to my sixth-graders and they're obsessed and now check Leaky religiously!

Meanwhile, the podcast, where people usually came to hear intelligent and thoughtful discussion on the Harry Potter series, was quickly turning into a display of how many ways we could find to say, "Wow," or "Oh my God."

"Golly!" Sue said, and then instantly laughed at herself. "Man, I sound so hokey. *'Golly!'* But, what do you say?"

"I wish we had more time, honestly," I said.

"Well, it's a good thing that I just made a new friend named Hiro Nakamura," John said, referring to the television show *Heroes'* character with supernatural powers. "He's coming over today to stop time for me for a little bit. So, you guys are screwed. I feel bad for you guys."

I was grateful for the joke, the way I was always grateful for John's jokes, because everything about today was turning into a sappy nostalgia-fest. Cheryl called, and I thought back to the first time we met, when all I knew about her was that she worked on the editing team for Harry Potter, read Leaky, and was about my age. David, Kathleen, and I spoke about July 21 with an absolute assumption that we'd be together for it, and I thought how much we owed Harry Potter, and how remarkable it was for an aspiring actor from Michigan, a kindergarten teacher from Washington, D.C., and a reporter from New York to still be so close. My mother came over unprompted, just to help me manage the day, and I thought back to the hairy eyeball she used to give me every time I mentioned the series by name. And every person who wrote to me with their thoughts about the announcement, and especially the e-mail from Sarah, made it impossible not to spend the day remembering when Harry Potter was, to me, just an inexplicable focus of pop culture, like Cabbage Patch Kids or Vanilla Ice.

Like most things upon which I fixate, Harry Potter came to me via my big sister. It was August 2000, the day before my last semester at Georgetown started, and she had come with my parents to Washington, D.C., to help get me set up. We had just finished shopping for my massive pile of textbooks when she slammed a copy of *Harry Potter and the Sorcerer's Stone* on top.

"You need something light to read," she insisted, gesturing to my stack of books, which included *Through a Glass Darkly*, Truffaut's

Hitchcock, and a history text that looked just about as boring as it ended up being.

I read the first Harry Potter in the first week of school. By the end of the month I'd started on the second. I liked the books a lot, but that was as far as it went. They were charming and funny, and I knew I would read them all. When I finished each of the first two, I simply put them on a shelf, where they stayed, perhaps never to be touched again, while I moved rapaciously through other books and furiously through my classwork.

I got to the third book, *Prisoner of Azkaban*, on a break between classes that September, a day I found myself alone in the *Hoya*'s office. It was Tuesday, one of the Georgetown newspaper's two weekly publish days, which meant a fresh edition was on campus newsstands and everyone involved in its creation was home sleeping off the long, hard production night. Perfect. As much as I enjoyed working as an arts editor, I was still relatively new to the higher levels of *Hoya* staff, having only joined the editing ranks in my junior year right after I decided I would become a journalist instead of a doctor. By that point, strong friendships had already formed between staffers, and it seemed I was always missing the meaning of some inside joke. Outside the newsroom and newspaper parties, I didn't socialize with the staff much. And I especially didn't relish the idea of being scoffed at for my new Harry Potter interest by people who had the power to make *The Brothers Karamazov* seem like *Romper Room* storytime material.

Yet the newsroom felt like my natural home; I spent almost every free period between classes there. With an hour to spare and feeling confident that no one would disturb me, I tucked myself into a corner of the sofa and pulled *Harry Potter and the Prisoner of Azkaban* from my bag.

"Ohh, I envy you."

It was Sarah Walsh, a bright-eyed and genial editor with whom I'd only spoken with casually. I hadn't heard her come in, so I emitted a surprised squeal and shut the book, trying not to look like I'd been caught playing with dolls. "I'm sorry, what?"

"I envy you—that's the first time you're reading it, right?"

I followed her gaze down to my book, which suddenly felt lighter in my lap. "I—yes."

Sarah had spent several semesters as the *Hoya*'s senior sports editor and had done the job better than most of the boys. She was never unkind or immature, and had a humor-and-play-with-the-guys tough side that earned her respect from all corners of the newsroom. We had the same loose kind of friendship I had with almost everyone else at the paper and had never had a real or long conversation. I'd certainly never pegged her as a Harry Potter fan.

She made a tiny, emphatic grunt and threw herself into the chair across from me. "And?"

"Oh, I like it a lot," I said, not quite yet able to say "love," like I suspected she wanted me to. "It's really absorbing, and—"

"Oh, no no no. No, wait," she said conspiratorially, eyes twinkling, nodding her head as if to confirm her own supposition. "You're not there yet. I can tell. Just wait—oh, I can't wait to talk to you about it!" She rubbed her hands together in a kind of glee I thought a little odd for having to do with children's books. "We'll have to have lunch."

Egged on by her excitement, I powered through the rest of *Azkaban*, starting to fall in love with it, starting to love Harry himself. As he tussled with his likeness to his father and the memory of his mother's horrifying last moments, I felt myself sinking in more deeply. The book rarely left my side; I sat reading in the hallways, hoping class wouldn't start.

The day I reached the final chapters, I sat sprawled on the grass, hunched over the pages, unable to believe what I was reading. When I was done, I snapped the book shut and marched from my spot on the campus lawn to the *Hoya*'s office in our student center. I planted myself in front of Sarah.

"You didn't tell me," I accused, brandishing the book.

"What? I didn't tell you what?" she asked, too innocently.

"That it was all connected." I opened a page to show Sarah what I meant. "Look—SIRIUS. Sirius! He's mentioned in the first book, in the very *first chapter* of the very first *book,* and now he's all over *this* book and I never noticed he was mentioned right in the beginning of book one! She has a master plan; it's all connected!"

Sarah started to snicker. "Told you."

"And—and, Harry—and his father, and his Patronus—how *sad* was that? And now Wormtail's off back to *Voldemort* and J. K. Rowling just let it happen, and that's not how books end!" I exclaimed, ignoring my sniggering comrades. "It's all one big huge story and I have to *read these all again now!*"

"You have no idea," Sarah teased, laughing at my hysterics. "You have absolutely no idea of the extent." She drummed her hands on the tabletop. "Lunch, when you're done. You tell me when you're done; I can't wait to talk to you about it."

It took two weeks, thanks to schoolwork, for me to gobble up *Harry Potter and the Goblet of Fire.* I sat on my bed, a quarter of a mile away from my Gothic Conventions in Media class, battling the need to go to school against the need to finish my real reading.

Harry, in book four, was locked in a showdown with Voldemort. He'd just watched a friend die and had been forced to help bring Voldemort back to full power. Fate and circumstance had intervened, and Voldemort's wand began emitting shadows of all his past victims. Smoky figures in the likeness of Harry's parents and the just-killed Cedric Diggory issued forth, offering whispered help and pleas.

"Harry . . ." whispered the figure of Cedric, "take my body back,
will you? Take my body back to my parents . . ."

"I will," said Harry, his face screwed up with the effort of
holding the wand.

I could barely see the pages. Poor little Harry—severely out-
matched, broken and alone, was finally starting to understand the
enormity of evil in the world, and his role in fighting it.

Screw class. I marched into the newsroom and grabbed Sarah by
the shoulders.

"I finished," I said, my eyes still glistening from the read.

She beamed and dropped her page proof on the table. "Let's go."

We walked to Darnall Hall, a campus cafeteria. On the way I
didn't say anything: If I started I wouldn't stop, and I didn't want to
have to stop talking to get our food and get settled. But once we were
all set up, I launched right into it.

"What is up with that gleam in Dumbledore's eye?" I asked, referring to the way that the headmaster had looked triumphant at the
end of book four while being told the story of Voldemort's return.

"It doesn't mean he's evil," said Sarah, as if J. K. Rowling had told
her this herself. "I think it means there's something about the way he
came back to life that will be Voldemort's undoing."

I quickly appreciated how intricate the story was, even outside
my own current understanding, for Sarah kept coming up with scenarios and theories that only time to ponder could have produced. It
seemed as though the more you thought about the series, the more
complicated it became, and though my head started to spin while we
sat there over our cafeteria food, I couldn't wait to dive back into it
and start making those discoveries myself.

CHAPTER THREE

Near Misses

s my staff woke to e-mails from me that threatened to break all rules of grammar and decency (the subject line on the one to Nick Poulden, my programmer, read simply, "NIIIIIIIIIIIIIIIIIIIIIIIIICK!" I was also already booking plane tickets: not for the *Deathly Hallows* release date, but for my trip to England with John Noe later that month to see and report back on the battery of plays in which Harry Potter actors were starring. We were staying near London with my friends Theresa Waylett and John Inniss, the latter of whom had little-to-no reaction to the release date except, "Bought your tickets yet?" I had to laugh; his life was as entangled with Potter as mine, since Theresa's son, Jamie, plays Vincent Crabbe in the films. But knowing John, his only reaction was to shrug, take a long drag of his cigarette, and use the same smoking hand to scratch his head. The entire Warner Bros. side of the Harry Potter franchise would be just as quiet today, even though a lot of the fan discussion online centered around the unusual proximity of the two July releases. The two worlds hardly ever connected except when it was inescapable, which was by design and why release dates usually stayed far away from each other, and why there's never been a Harry Potter novel with Daniel

Radcliffe or any other actor's image on the front beside a "Now a major motion picture!" starburst.

Not that either sector needs the publicity. By the time the final Harry book hit shelves, the series had been in print for ten years and in J. K. Rowling's brain for seventeen. There are now 400 million books in print worldwide, in sixty-five languages and two hundred territories. Five movies have been made and released, and by the end of 2007 made up a quarter of the top twenty grossing films worldwide, ever. Harry Potter as a franchise had been estimated to be worth $15 billion, most of which has funded a worldwide enterprise that has been crammed into every crevice of popular culture—it has spawned video games, films, playing cards, toys, parodies, and even an entire music genre, and has become so absorbed in pop culture that it appears inside other pop culture references. When a character in Dan Brown's *The Da Vinci Code*, the phenomenally successful novel about a Holy Grail quest, speaks of a lie that is coded into the "ultimate best-selling book of all time," he is referring to the Bible. The character to whom he's speaking, however, says, "Don't tell me Harry Potter is actually about the Holy Grail."

A newcomer to the series, someone who had never read one of the books or seen one of the films or even heard of Harry Potter by 2007—in other words, someone from outer space—might easily look on the franchise and assume it was pieced together by cunning businessmen, deployed via market data, and carefully contrived to give people exactly what they wanted at exactly the moment they wanted it most, using tested formulas, celebrity horsepower, and the kind of advertising push that fuels mega-industries like Coca-Cola, McDonald's, and Microsoft. The past ten years has seen an almost clockworklike release schedule of books and films that has given the phenomenon an endless feel—sometimes it intensifies, but it never quite disappears. It is very easy to believe that Harry Potter's prolonged hold on world consciousness can be blamed on strategy, or that it has been crosshatched into the fabric of culture by people who intended to do just that from day one.

But Harry Potter has actually been a very intimate phenomenon, the story of small groups of people acting in ways they shouldn't, doing things they usually wouldn't, and making the kind of history that, without Harry, they pretty much couldn't. There's been one woman, a handful of small companies, and one multibillion-dollar corporation—which has, at times, operated like an independent movie studio—at work. They sold things that aren't supposed to sell, at a time when fantasy books weren't supposed to appeal to a generation of people who weren't supposed to care. At almost every step of Harry's early journey, things occurred in ways they shouldn't, confounded expectations, and nearly didn't happen at all.

It might have all been different if J. K. Rowling had remembered a pen. The Harry Potter story begins (where else?) on a train, and though Joanne Rowling had been writing since she could form letters, she didn't have so much as a pencil to record her thoughts. She wasn't writing on that fated 1990 commute from Manchester to London. She wasn't even thinking about writing.

This part of the story is now legend, told a billion times in a million ways: A woman on a crowded train, lucky to have a seat, stares out the window, thinking—and boom, into her head comes Harry Potter, a then-unnamed boy wizard who doesn't know he's a wizard, but who will soon go off to wizard school. Those three things—boy, unknown wizard, school—came together, like a gift in a box with a bow, and Jo would later refer to the idea itself as luck. But the rush, the breath of inspiration, that followed, was what fanned luck and the whisper of an idea into reality.

She rummaged in her bag, tried to get started right away—she would have settled for an eyeliner to write with, but didn't have it. The train was delayed and she was forced to spend hours staring out the window just thinking about her idea, holding all the new details in her head as fast as she could think of them, and that uninterrupted time to think would give way to the fundamentals of the series. She answered her own questions quickly; of course, this boy was an orphan—but why? His parents were murdered. How and why were they murdered? And what about the magic school? Immediately it had four houses, which had yet to be named; she saw ghosts streaming through them, and classes, and subjects, and teachers, and more questions came on the heels of each answer until it became the most prolific nonwriting train trip she'd ever taken.

She was about twenty-five years old, and had just finished her longest-ever job working at Amnesty International, a worldwide human rights group, as a secretary. She'd been writing since she was six, and the boy who'd fallen into her head, who was soon to be called Harry Potter, became an all-consuming project, and for all she knew only she would ever care about it.

The children's book industry in Britain, meanwhile, was undergoing an increasingly politically correct era, producing stories that were purposefully devoid of the traditional fairy-tale whimsy driving Jo Rowling's new work. The trend was partly fueled by a similar movement in America, and it wasn't the only one; afraid of turning off potential customers west of the Atlantic, U.K. publishers would excise particularly British elements, such as cars that drive down the left side of the street, or double-decker buses, or milk bottles on doorsteps. It seemed incredibly important not to trip the American political-correctness censors, who had a tendency to screech whenever children recognized that they had hormones or digestive bodily functions.

While Jo Rowling was first fleshing out Harry, bookstore owners weren't hot-selling fantasy books to children; the perennial favorites were books about ponies for girls and sports stories for boys. Parents snapped up the old classics out of nostalgia; Roald Dahl, Elinor Brent-Dyer, and Enid Blyton, a much-referenced favorite of Jo Rowling's (whose stories also feature drafty old castles and run-amuck children who, by working together, can outsmart adults), still sold, but by the early to mid-1990s, new children's fiction was all about real life, about "message" books. In 1993, Britain's big children's book award winners were stout but hardly whimsical: the winner of the coveted Nestlé Smarties Book Prize, an award chosen by a panel of children (who are, in turn, chosen by adults), was *War Game*, a picture book about young soldiers in World War I (for kids aged six to eight). The Whitbread Children's Book of the Year went to *Flour Babies*, a lighthearted morality lesson in which bad-mannered schoolchildren became better people by playing parents to bags of white flour.

The prevailing wisdom held that a children's book should teach the child something about life, and boarding schools were too elite or classist to fulfill such a purpose. There was no sense of adventure, or mysticism, or violence. Young adult fiction delivered inoffensive lessons about being inoffensive adults.

"Parents and godparents who wander into children's book departments or bookshops in search of Christmas presents can be forgiven for feeling at a loss," Christina Hardyment wrote in the *Independent* in London in November of that year. "Unfamiliar titles line the walls. Those formerly reliable volumes of fairy tale are now lurid cartoons in which the princess saves the prince, and the frog has to get fair species recognition in a sage-green eco-home."

The children's market was considered a side job for the authors, to whom came very small advances and even smaller royalty checks.

Children's authors didn't get stopped on the street for autographs, and they didn't do the morning talk shows.

"There are none of the swings in fashion which can take a new adult writer of fiction into stardom after a single title," said Hardyment. "Children grow up too fast to stay loyal readers for long."

Children's book publishers saw more lucrative results by the mid-1990s, owing to developments in computers, DVDs, television, video, and related merchandising; by 1995 *The Lion King* and *Thomas the Tank Engine* were selling videos by the barrel. Short horror stories were also in vogue among teens and young adults, thanks to R. L. Stine, who published the massively popular *The New Girl*, the first book in the Fear Street series, in 1989 and followed it with other quick and scary tales like *Hit and Run* and *The Girlfriend*.

Then came Goosebumps, Stine's teen-centric horror series. Originally published by Scholastic in America, the horror books were about a hundred pages in length and were more fantastical than the usual fare, typically featuring an isolated location and a twist ending. The books lived on the paperback best-seller list, and became inbred in teen culture, though they were (mostly) critically ignored.

Scholastic published sixty-two Goosebumps books between 1992 and 1997. The books inspired two board games, three comic books, a video game, a handful of direct-to-video movies, and a television series, and enjoyed large popularity on the Internet. From 1996 to 1997, right before the first Harry Potter book was born, finance magazine *Forbes* estimated that Stine had reaped $41 million for his efforts. Stine was a celebrity author in a time when celebrity young adult authors were alien, and by then some were even bemoaning his rise, saying it was impossible for single-title authors to survive in a market that wanted "instant horror or romance."

The possibility of the celebrity author had been reimagined and reestablished before Harry Potter was published, and the idea of a cross-platform children's book success wasn't new. But on the cusp of Harry, just a few months before he was in print for the first time, perhaps to try to capitalize on an increasingly cross-platform industry, the number of children's book titles grew, doubling what it had produced in 1990 and swelling until there were well over eight thousand books published. Picture books were becoming more prevalent, with print runs pushing into the hundreds of thousands, and sales to libraries were on the decline thanks to shrinking budgets. "Never have so many books been produced for so few consumers," said author Hilary Macaskill in the *Independent* in March 1997, hinting that the glut meant fewer translations and the potential for overlooking a classic. "*Grimm's Fairy Tales, Heidi, Pippi Longstocking* would probably never have made it into English if published now."

Two years later I'd almost forgotten about Harry, myself; I spent my last semester in college supernaturally busy. Most nights I would hole up in the office after class, doing assignments and making layouts for the arts section of the paper until after midnight, sleep for a few hours on the office sofa, then catch the earliest shuttle home to get a few more hours of sleep and a shower before going to class and starting all over again. On Friday afternoons I'd go straight home, crawl into bed, and sleep as long as my body let me. One Saturday my housemate banged on my door with a portable phone in hand. My mother had called and was worried I'd died, and when I saw that I had slept twenty-four hours straight, I was concerned she was right.

I barely knew Harry Potter existed, except for the few pockets of spare time I spent talking about it with Sarah. During production nights, while others were blaring music or slopping down fast food, we would send each other one-liner e-mails with Potter plot questions, and soon our friendship was blossoming outside the books as well. When I wanted to procrastinate, the Internet was willing to help, offering up endless arrays of information. I quickly discovered that almost anything I wanted to know about Harry Potter was on fan sites and message boards. Once, I downloaded and installed AOL on a *Hoya* computer, violating newspaper rules, to participate in a J. K. Rowling chat. I'd be teased mercilessly, and our tech guy would claim it was my crazy Potter downloads, and not the thousands of daily downloads from Napster or the 3:00 a.m. visits some male students made to adult sites, that had clogged up and virtually destroyed our entire network. Totally worth it: that download led to my first-ever interaction with the author, when one of my questions was chosen in the online chat.

Somehow I managed to complete all my courses and even achieve high grades in my major and minor. I graduated with accolades and recommendations and a feeling that everything I wanted was within reach—even carefully planned. I'd pay my dues in the news media for a few years, then transition over to entertainment journalism, just like that.

When I graduated, that bubble of excitement, energy, and activity burst. I got sick in June. I slept a lot. I sent out résumés at a snail's pace. Something was lost without the *Hoya*'s urgency or Georgetown's air of promise. Back in Staten Island, I spent a lot of time in my green paisley pajamas; college seemed a pleasant memory and my real life was one in which I had little chance of doing anything with my English degree besides giving it a nice spot on my mother's living room wall.

The job market seemed to feel the same way. My first few efforts at employment (including an interview at the *Staten Island Advance* that began—and ended—in, "We thought you were applying for an internship, not a job") sunk like stones, and I lost heart just as quickly.

By late July I had the routine down pat; by the time the sun started to cook me through the window, I rose, threw a robe over the green paisley pajamas, and padded down to the kitchen. The house was silent: no clinking coffee mugs, no muffled phone chatter, no hum from the downstairs television set.

A cold pot of coffee and the cheery note—*Please empty the dishwasher—love, Mom!*—awaited me. I huffed a little at the chore and ignored it. I nuked my morning coffee and wandered absently over to the plate-glass door leading to the backyard, where an oppressively hot day preened. My microwaved coffee had grown cold by the time a loud honk snapped me out of my stupor. The clock said twenty minutes had gone by; a familiar flash of fright at my own inertia shot through me. The distinct pattern of toots meant my mother was home and that I should come help her bring her stuff from the car. Morse code at its worst.

Plastic bags lined our concrete steps when I got outside, and I wordlessly set myself about bringing them into the kitchen. I was pretty good at it, I thought, as I balanced a bag on each finger and one in my elbow. Maybe I could get a job as a grocery clerk.

My mom balanced her pocketbook, Dunkin' Donuts coffee, and keys perfectly as she brought her share of the goods inside, swinging the front door closed with a push of her hip and clattering everything onto the table. We made small talk for a few minutes, and then I could have spoken her next phrase along with her as it came out of her mouth: "Did you send out any résumés?"

She said it the same way as she always did, innocently, but a little too carefully. I was just as practiced in deflection, having done this every day for the past two months. Though my whole posture instantly changed—I looked away, crossed my arms, and tightened my jaw—I'd become schooled in dispensing smidgens of truth: I'd found some great listings online, I'd say. I'd polished a few things—changed my cover letter a bit. Or I'd just lie.

But there were some days—days when perhaps the heat had gotten to me, or I was just itching for a fight—when only the truth would do.

"No."

"Why?"

"I just haven't. I just woke up—leave me alone," I shot back, as if she were rude for just asking the question.

Silence swelled between us like a balloon.

"Did you at least empty the dishwasher?"

Crap. "I forgot," I said. If she was searching for a reason to complain about my laziness, then I had just handed it to her on a stainless-steel platter. I counted two seconds before the speech began.

"I don't ask much of you, Melissa."

And we were off. I slammed my hands down on the table and used them to push me up.

"Yes, I know, I know, look, I'm doing it now," I spat as I walked. "Look at me doing it now!"

"I don't ask you for rent," she said. "I don't ask you for anything but a few little favors every day. You sleep late, you laze around, you don't even do the tiniest of things I ask you to do—all you do is sit here."

"I do not!" I snapped, turning with a dish in hand.

My mother had lit a cigarette and thrown the lighter casually onto the table out of exasperation. At my exclamation she flicked her wrist slowly, in a manner that might be confused for waving away smoke but which really meant, *Whatever you're about to say, I've heard before.*

I slammed the dish down on the counter just hard enough not to break it. "It's summer! God, just leave me alone already!"

"You will not sit around all summer."

"Why *not?*" I finally yelled. I always yelled first, but never yelled alone. "I need a break!" I shouted. "You don't run my life anymore!"

My mother straightened and pointed at me. "We paid good money for Georgetown and you will not sit here and do nothing. You are going to work at your father's office—"

"*I—will—not!*" I exploded. "I'm sick of that place. I'm not going back to be a secretary! What is so wrong with me having a summer off? I'm *tired,* do you get that? I need a *break.* I'm going to be working for the rest of my life!"

I could feel rationality swirling away. I had no power to pull it back. All I could think to do was scream loud enough and say enough things that the fight would swerve my way. This was a tactic that hadn't worked in all twenty-one years of its use.

"At least, if . . ." my mother started, and her thoughts were as plain to me as if they were written on her forehead.

"At least . . . if . . . what?" I asked slowly, icily. "At least if I was going to medical school?"

She looked like I'd slapped her, and opened her mouth to answer, but an answer wasn't desired or necessary.

"If I was going to med school you wouldn't be pushing me to work, is that it?" I charged. "Well, sorry, Ma. I'm *sorry.*"

"That is not what I said, Melissa."

"No, forget it, just forget it. I swear, I will never, *never,* forget what *hell* you made this summer for me!"

I stormed off to my room, slamming my door so hard the house seemed to shake. I sank down onto my beige carpeting and lay flat on my back, my face crumpling. I lay there for hours, surveying the ceiling, feeling fat and useless, and wondering how this had become my life.

The next week I was back at my father's office, performing the same secretarial work I did at age twelve. Now, I saw the job listings as deliverance. Résumés and cover letters winged into the void and were never heard from again.

One day in August, bored and out of self-addressed return envelopes, I started rifling through the boxes of books I'd brought home from school. After a few minutes of sifting through organic chemistry workbooks and abandoned physics practice tests, I pried loose a rose-colored book with a textured cover, and stared again at *Harry Potter and the Sorcerer's Stone.*

I ran a hand across the cover in the cheesy way people do when they look at albums in Hallmark commercials, then scurried back to sit against the wall, and opened the book for a second time.

> *Mr. and Mrs. Dursley, of number four, Privet Drive, were proud to say that they were perfectly normal, thank you very much.*

I sighed aloud, as if I'd sunk into a down comforter. The ho-hum tone of the opening sentence was a complete lie, and it felt great to know it. There were giants and dragons and spells and witches and battles and friendship and magic to come, and it was all funny and warm and loving and powerful, and I hadn't realized how much I missed it.

By that afternoon I was through book one and onto book two. I traveled everywhere with a book affixed to my hands, sneaked it into my bag for reading at work and snapped at people who came between me and the next page.

More than anything, I found myself revisiting portions of the books that featured the bonds of friendship and difficulty of courage.

When, under extreme stress, Hermione suggests using wood to start a fire and Ron bellows, "ARE YOU A WITCH OR NOT?" I guffawed so loudly I woke my snoring father. When Neville, poor downtrodden Neville, strides forward in the third book to finish off a spell, in his first show of determination and talent and skill and confidence in the books thus far, I burst into tears. And above all, I renewed my love for Harry himself, the forlorn orphan who fights a mighty enemy with kid-sized fists, just because he should.

When I turned the last page of the fourth book, my hand kept repeating the motion in air. Surely there was more. It was completely unacceptable that almost a year had passed since I read these books and there wasn't more available. Someone, somewhere, knew the whereabouts of the next book, and I was going to find that person.

Feeling as able to find the publication date of that book as I was of getting a turkey sandwich for lunch, I went to the Internet. It was uncooperative. I searched for days in every single permutation of terms I could produce: "Harry Potter Book Five," "Harry Potter five," "J. K. Rowling," "next Harry Potter," "Potter five," "Order of the Phoenix." All I got were news articles with key phrases like "much-anticipated," and "long-awaited." Fan sites had speculation but no fact. There seemed to be no solid information on the book whatsoever.

In my searching I had stumbled across probably every Web site imaginable that focused on Potter, but I kept going back to one: a small news blog called the Leaky Cauldron. A tan Web page with black accents and a badly pixilated picture of Hermione Granger in the top corner, it was about the most rudimentarily designed site I'd ever seen. It listed every article mentioning Harry Potter since the release of the fourth book. I bookmarked it and read every one of their postings within two days. When I was done I found I trusted that if the Leaky Cauldron didn't have it, it wasn't to be had. I resigned myself to the fact that there really was no publication date set for the next Potter.

Yet I had become a Leaky addict. As a journalist, I was attracted by its thoroughness. It was the only site that was treating the phenomenon as a subject to be reported doggedly, and I checked it obsessively. I also began to send them links to articles mentioning Harry Potter when I found them.

In the meantime I joined several online message boards and mailing lists to talk Potter, and even became active at Hogwarts Online, Leaky's sister site. The site sorted everyone into separate houses (I got Gryffindor), and hosted interesting and vibrant message boards. On these boards I found that some of the "students" wanted to start an online newspaper about their community. The idea of helping them do it appealed to me, so I assisted in creating the *Spellbinder*; the "reporters" wrote stories about what was happening in their online world, and I edited them. It at least felt like it wasn't wasted time, though it tied me so fast to the computer that my mother started to loudly complain that I was obsessed.

In early September of that year, Leaky posted that there was soon to be a *Vanity Fair* article featuring photos by famed photographer Annie Leibovitz, of the first in-costume shots of the child actors from the Harry Potter movies. Fans frothed in anticipation, and I was no different. I wanted, badly, to see how similar to the characters in my head the characters on celluloid were going to be.

The day before the magazine was scheduled to hit newsstands, I took a walk to my local store, hoping someone would have goofed and put it out early. The store was about a mile away but it was a nice day, and at least it satisfied my mother's whining about me never getting out of the house.

The shop was a dud—no *Vanity Fairs* whether new or old—but now I felt like I was on the hunt. I walked the mile back and borrowed the car to pursue my quarry further. The second shop I visited was dank and musty and lined with publications of all kinds—except the one I wanted. The *Vanity Fair* on the stand was not the one featuring Harry; however, the Asian man behind the counter was puttering around with several stacks of new issues, and I noticed a large brown box at his feet.

"Hello!" he said once he noticed me standing there patiently. I pried my eyes away from the box and met his gaze.

"Hi!" I said, as if he had just given me candy.

"Can I help you?"

I pointed to the box. "*Vanity Fair* is in there?"

He peered at me.

"*Vanity Fair*," I repeated, walking over to the old issue on the stand and pointing at it. "New one? New *Vanity Fair*? In there?" I pointed at the box.

Finally, he seemed to get it. "Oh, yes, yes, *Vanity Fair* tomorrow. Come back tomorrow."

"No, I'd like it now, please," I said.

The clerk looked at me as though I were a strange creature. "Tomorrow!" he insisted. "It comes out tomorrow."

"Yes," I said. "But I'd like it"—I pointed to the box, and then to myself—"now. There's a very important article inside."

This went on for a few minutes, with me insisting that it was important I get the magazine and he insisting that tomorrow was the earliest he could give it out.

"Not allowed," he said, sounding annoyed, shaking his head very fast. He turned back to the wall to arrange more magazines. "I'm sorry, no. Come back tomorrow."

Another glance at the box showed me the edge of the magazine peeking out. I grunted a bit and reached for my wallet.

"I'll pay"—I shuffled around in the billfold—"ten dollars. Ten dollars, OK?" The clerk turned to me with an eyebrow and half a lip raised in what seemed like amusement. "No, no, no bribe."

"Fine, then I'll take . . ." I cast my eyes around at the candy rack below me and grabbed an Almond Joy, a pack of Bubble Yum gum, and three packs of Tic Tacs. The junk clattered on the countertop. "I'll take all this stuff and the magazine, then." Then I grabbed a *TV Guide* and threw it on the pile for good measure, and looked at the clerk earnestly. Begging.

He started to laugh. "You really excited about magazine," he said, climbing down from his ladder and bending over to grab the issue from the box. I clapped in joy; he chortled harder, and let me buy the magazine alone. I insisted on adding the Tic Tacs.

I went right to my car and dove into the magazine, poring over the glossy prints. The first one I found arrested me: Daniel Radcliffe as Harry Potter, sitting in the space carved for him under his aunt and uncle's stairs, his big toe peeking out of his worn sock and his expression deadened, bearing the grief and banality that was Harry's pre-Hogwarts life. My pulse sped up. This was the book, this was the book, they'd gotten it right, omygod.

I kept flipping. Hermione sat at the edge of a Great Hall table, her kneesocks perfectly positioned and her expression smug; redheaded Ron wore a bemused smirk; Draco and his cronies posed as menacing thugs-to-be in schoolboy clothing. Everything looked rich and exciting, and since I had it early I felt like I was holding something privileged. I wanted to keep the prints forever, and also share them with the world. I knew immediately how.

I rushed home, scaned the photos, and posted them onto the Spellbinder—along with a scan of an *Entertainment Weekly* article that hadn't yet been posted online—then sent it all to Leaky. I'd been sending them links to articles for weeks, as soon as I found them; usually, however, they thanked someone else in the news post, which probably meant that I wasn't the first person to send each article in. This time, B. K. DeLong, who was managing the site at the time, sent me an e-mail back with effusive thanks, and posted the links to the pictures.

> *Melissa of the Spellbinder has achieved a major coup in the Harry Potter news world,* B. K. wrote. *The Leaky Cauldron salutes you!*

I sat back and watched as the online community erupted, as hordes of fans discovered the pictures the way I had. Message boards were flooded with reaction posts, as were online journals, and I beamed as I watched it happen, as something I did caused so much e-joy.

Not long after, Rames, who posted both on Hogwarts Online and on Leaky, sent me an e-mail asking me to be a Leaky Cauldron editor.

I stared at the words for a minute. Aside from B. K.'s thank-you, this was the first e-mail back I'd ever gotten from a Leaky editor, though I knew a few of its staffers and I'd been sending them articles for some time. Besides Hogwarts Online, a lot of my Potter time went onto a more adult message board, which had started as a reaction thread to a popular piece of fanfiction and become a great place for theories and discussion about the books with people my own age. I hadn't considered putting effort into actually running and updating a Potter Web site with a significant reach and growing clout. However, my interests and Leaky's seemed nicely aligned, and having just been so exhilarated to be responsible for bringing the fandom so much joy, the choice was simple. I agreed.

If my mother was concerned about how much time I was spending looking up Harry Potter stuff online before, that was absolutely nothing compared to what happened once I started working at Leaky. I didn't post much on the site in the beginning, but now it seemed all I did was hang out online looking up news articles, answering messages, and talking to Potter friends. Our arguments escalated in frequency and intensity, to the point that if we weren't arguing, we were simply ignoring each other.

Leaky was a fun hobby, but not even that could make me want to remain at my father's office forever. The summer was over and I started to itch for real responsibility. The weekend after Labor Day, I spent the night at my sister's Manhattan apartment so I could spend the following morning at her 2 Financial Center office, making liberal use of her copy machine to produce reams of résumés.

When I was done I walked across the footbridge to the World Trade Center's Borders, bought a book of Pauline Kael's film reviews, and hopped on a bus back to Staten Island for another day of Harry Potter reporting.

The next morning the particularly bright sun had just started to cook me (and my paisley pajamas) when the phone next to my head started ringing. I groped blindly for it, and was greeted by my mother's fuzzy, panicked voice.

"Turn on the TV! Turn on the TV!"

I sat up, amazed we were fighting already. "What? Ma, why?"

"A plane, it crashed! Right into the tower! It's some sort of accident! Turn on the TV! I have to go find your sister!"

The phone clicked dead. I blinked at it, then ran downstairs to our kitchen television set, which only showed me a blue screen. Cursing, I ran down to the large set, which again only gave me blue screens; the crash must have interfered with the massive antenna on top of the World Trade Center tower, which gave us TV reception. I flicked through channels until I got to Channel 2, where, finally, there was a transmission and, apparently, a replay.

A small black dot, like a wasp, slid in a straight line across the screen. It entered the World Trade Center as if it had been called there to land.

I kept waiting for the newscaster to explain why a commercial liner had just slid into the building, but it was as if my ears couldn't tune in. All I heard was fuzz. Then my eyes shifted a bit, and what I saw caused me to sink to the floor. What I had just witnessed wasn't a replay at all. It was a second crash. There were now two smoking buildings, not one. And none of it was accidental.

For a while I peered into nothingness, my awareness of the situation piling into me, weighing me to the floor as though I were a bag being slowly filled with sand. The phone rang but cut off as soon as it started. It rang again, and again. I just stared.

I started dialing. I tried my mother, who was in New Jersey at the time, supervising the building of our summer home; the call timed out without a connect. My father—nothing. My sister—

My sister. Almost invariably, at 8:50 a.m., almost precisely the moment the planes hit, she was coming up out of the World Trade Center subway on her way to her office. I had done it with her just yesterday. My fingers couldn't find the numbers fast enough, and when they finally managed to hit upon her correct cell number, I got nothing. The lines were dead.

A blink from the adjacent room caught my eye. My Internet connection's indicator light was flashing benignly at me. I was still connected. The Internet worked: I still existed in the world. I ran.

I signed on, and before I could even check my buddy list, write e-mails, or check news, scores of instant messages clotted my screen from message-board friends, Leaky coworkers, college buddies, even family. Once I let my friends and family know I was safe, I had only the Harry Potter–related messages left. Several had popped up from the various frequenters of the message boards I visited.

Melissa! Oh my god, we're all so worried about you! one wrote.

You're ALIVE THANK GOD! wrote another.

Rames and B. K. chimed in similarly, noting how Leaky's readers who knew I lived in New York were concerned for my safety. I'd only been a staff member for a few days; that people I'd never met already cared took me aback.

My little Harry Potter circle of Leaky friends, message-board friends, and members of Hogwarts Online met in a chat room. We kept each other updated on the news as the day unfolded.

I don't know where my sister is, I finally typed to the chat, my mouth dry and the rest of me numb.

Sympathy rained on me from all corners of the chat, and I gave it back to everyone else who seemed affected, and as I did so I started to regain feeling in my limbs.

Our chat became less of a news-gathering one and more of a joint therapy session. It eased, but didn't dull, the panicked thump in my chest at the thought of my sister. I had stopped redialing on my phone—I had partly given up hope it would work, but I also knew my mother would be calling me, and I didn't want to get in the way.

When the phone rang, I hit my knees on the bottom of my desk.

This time it was my mother, I noticed from the caller ID. I didn't even wait for her to talk.

"Ma! Where's Steph?"

"She's not in the buil—"

The call died, but I was heartened; if my mother knew where she was, she probably had talked to her. She was nowhere near this mess. That's what that had to mean. It was as though a fog had been lifted from my consciousness. I couldn't type fast enough to relay this to my chat, and the Potter folk responded with Internet-ized shouts of joy.

The phone rang again. I lunged for it, finding my sister's friend Jennifer on the other line.

"Meliss, I talked to your sister—they're evacuating her building."

"Evacuating?" My heart seemed to slide into my stomach. "What do you mean? I thought she wasn't in the building?"

"I don't know, that's just what—"

The phone. The damn phone. Dead again. I threw it on the desk and it bounced. I dropped my head into my hands and sat like that for several minutes, trying to block the mental images of my sister, running and coughing through the city streets.

I finally relayed this information to my chat, my fingers moving as slowly as if they were bandaged. *I thought she was safe, but now I don't know . . . again . . .* I said.

Oh, Melissa, one fellow chatter wrote. *You're both in my prayers. God is with you.*

Shortly after 10:00 a.m., the panicked voices from the other room sent me charging to the television set. The tower—one of them, I didn't care which—had started to crumble. It collapsed like a sand castle, and as it did I sank with it, to my knees. My hands pressed against the TV screen.

How could my sister have escaped this?

After a while I could no longer see the broadcast but just the multicolored rivulets of light forming the picture on the glass. The chat went on without me, line after line of black text scrolling upward into oblivion.

Finally, after an eternity, the phone rang again. I nearly twisted my ankle in my rush to get to it. With no preamble, my mother said, "I talked to your sister. She's safe."

My sister had a choice that morning: run an errand before work and go into the office later, or leave work early to do it. She had decided to go to work first, but as she stepped out of her SoHo apartment door, she thought better of it and switched her day around. She'd been safe the whole time, through luck.

I hung up the phone, shaking badly and still crying, and feeling a selfish wave of relief. I groped my way back over to the computer, and considered for a moment turning it off; it seemed a lot less necessary, now.

I relayed my good news to the growing list of Potterphiles in our chat; messages of joy and hope and prayer flooded my screen. I wrote another, more relieved message to one of my discussion lists:

My whole family is okay, thank God, I wrote. *We must have been touched by an angel.*

Feeling somewhat sated and calmer than I'd been all day, I prepared to shut down the chat program and get off-line. But before I could, one of the younger members, nicknamed Corey, sent me an instant message.

I just don't understand, he said. *I'm crying right now and I can't understand why anyone would do this.*

As I started considering an answer, a key turned in a lock upstairs.

"Meliss?"

My father's voice was booming through the house at its usual volume, yet it sounded more timid than I'd ever heard it. I abandoned the computer and screamed *"Daddy!"* like a child, shot upstairs like a bullet, and hugged him. "Did you see? Can you believe . . . ?"

He nodded wearily and loosened his tie. Every line in his face looked deeper. "I was at the Staten Island Hotel. At a meeting." His eyes looked far off. "We watched from the roof. We could see the smoke from there."

We walked down the stairs and he took his usual spot on our living room sofa, and clicked the television back up to full volume. The living room, and house, seemed full again; it no longer felt as though I were using the computer to touch the outside world. Yet from the corner of my eye again, I saw a blink, and remembered the instant message I was neglecting. As though it had me on an invisible string, the computer drew me back.

In my absence four more instant messages had popped up; they were all from Hogwarts Online members and Leaky readers who simply wanted to talk—about today, about Potter, about anything to either comfort them or keep their minds off of what was happening. I didn't want to leave them to do it without me.

In the few hours that followed, my mom came home. We had a silent, prayerful dinner together. I spoke with my sister. We discovered which of our friends and family had missing friends and family. We drove along the main arteries of our town to see kids out with jumbo-sized American flags, waving them as they ran up and down the street. We sat together without fighting or worrying about my job situation.

And through the night, I kept checking in on Leaky, on my e-mail, and on my chats and message boards. My mother wanted to know why, today of all days, I still couldn't get off-line.

I wasn't sure. But I knew I was finally doing something useful.

CHAPTER FOUR

Public Assistance

ithin hours of the release-date announcement, *Deathly Hallows* had reached the top of the Amazon.com bestseller list. Pre-orders were about six times higher on the first day for book seven than they were for book six, and book six had broken all records (which were set by book five) on its debut. It took Amazon U.K. only two days to rack up 100,000 pre-orders for book seven; for the previous book, this had taken six weeks in the United States, which has a market at least five times larger than the U.K.

About thirteen years previous, Jo Rowling was trying to get just *one* sale. The paper on which she wrote her first letter to the Christopher Little Agency is no larger than a photograph, and with age has become nearly translucent. The writer of the blue-inked note had either never read a style book on query letters or didn't hold to formulas; there was no snazzy introduction or list of credentials, hardly a sales pitch at all. She sent it to Christopher Little because she liked his name, which she found in a listing of London agents, and dated it June 1994 even though it was 1995.

Dear Mr. Little,

    I enclose a synopsis and sample chapters for a book intended for children aged 9–12. I would be very grateful if you could tell me if you would be interested in seeing the full manuscript.

        Yours sincerely,

        Joanne Rowling

The Christopher Little Agency is a London secret. It's buried at the back of a residential street in Fulham, inside a white building in one of the most exclusive parts of one of the city's most expensive neighborhoods. The building is called Eel Brook Studios, but doesn't give off any air of even being an office building; to get to the entrance you must go through to the back of the complex and up a few flights of stairs, to find yourself overlooking backyards of residential homes. Inside, the small book-lined and labyrinthine office feels more like an apartment. Harry Potter books now take up an entire wall, and some parts of adjacent walls, with all their editions and covers and translations.

At the heart of the office, working next to each other, are Christopher Little and Neil Blair, the firm's in-house lawyer who spends most of his time on Harry Potter–related issues. Christopher towers, at least to a short person, and has tufty white explosions for eyebrows, which sometimes point in opposite directions. He has a look of perpetual surprise and an always-imminent smile about him, a kindly grandfather. But he's also the possessor of an intent stare, and though he speaks in soft tones, words sometimes fly off him like flint sparks.

He wasn't the model of a modern major agent when Joanne Rowling wrote to him; he was new to the industry, having spent years in Hong Kong working in shipping. When he returned to London as a businessman, an agent friend teamed up with him and they worked out of the Fulham building, and before long Christopher had started to pick up the literary trade.

In late June 1995, Bryony Evans was in charge of reading selections from the "slush pile"—the publishing term for unsolicited submissions—at Christopher Little. Of all the people who can now say that they championed Harry Potter early, Bryony is the first. It was supposed to have been automatically rejected, but she liked the folder it came in, and read a few pages, and it made her laugh. If she hadn't brought it to Christopher Little and handed him the three chapters to read, it would have gone in the dustbin. Even after she handed it to him, Christopher only gave it a slight promotion: it was now part of a smaller pile of "slush stuff" that he brought to lunch to riffle through while waiting for a guest.

When his lunch appointment arrived an hour late, he tapped Christopher on the shoulder and said, "You've got something there, haven't you?"

Christopher said, "How do you know?"

"Because this extremely pretty girl walked straight past you and you never noticed."

The book was "four weeks" from being completed, according to Joanne Rowling, and she got to work finishing it while Christopher considered its merits. It was all wrong for the market. The boarding school, the children who mouthed off, the milk bottles on the doorstep, the intently British atmosphere of it, and its length, nearly 300 pages, were all just wrong.

At this point Jo had spent nearly five years writing the first book and creating the world around it. She had moved to Portugal to teach English in 1991, and then back to Britain around 1993, now divorced and with a young daughter. In that time she had produced at least 50 pages of rough notes on Harry, as well as the first three chapters "almost exactly as they appear in the book, plus the rest of the story, plus even more background of the seven-book story," she said. "About a year after I returned to Britain, I finished the book. I really believed in Harry. I think you've got to. Even if you've written a lousy book. Because writing is just a lonely slog and you have to believe in what you are doing, otherwise you live a dreadful existence." She had read about the book market, how anything over 45,000 words would never be published, but she "really liked" her book and decided to continue.

She trained as a teacher but couldn't find work, and she and her daughter were wearing clothes out of charity shops to get by. Benefits didn't cover her to the extent that she could pay for child care while she worked. It was either a full-time job plus day care or take care of her daughter herself and write. It was time to take the mountains of papers she had poured out of her imagination, and find the first Harry Potter book inside them. She spent her days walking around Edinburgh with her daughter Jessica in a stroller, getting her to sleep—then rushing into the nearest café to write. Still, today, guilt shades her eyes when she talks about that time, about the indulgence of writing while living on assistance.

She sent the manuscript to two publishers, unsolicited, and a few agents, including Christopher Little.

"And then I couldn't sell it," Chris said flatly, with no trace of the surprise some would show at that pronouncement today. The biggest blockbuster anywhere, that connects with people of all ages, across all race lines, even in some of the most ravaged and terrorism-laden areas of the world—and no respected children's publisher in Britain could sense its merit? Penguin, Transworld, HarperCollins, all said no. He sent it to nine publishers and got nine rejection letters, all of them very nice, but still rejections. The underlying theme was consistent: boarding school is for the rich and elite, and this book is about three times as long as children's novels should be. Too much, for a first-time author. Maybe if R. L. Stine handed in something that long, it would get published.

It wasn't until the Frankfurt Book Fair that Barry Cunningham entered the picture. Barry Cunningham was new at Bloomsbury, as was the publisher's children's book collection. He was starting their young list from scratch. Like Christopher, Barry had a business and marketing background, so he, like Christopher, didn't apply the popular conceptions to his work. He'd had success publicizing Roald Dahl and Spike Milligan, and became marketing director of Penguin, then Random House. He knew what he wanted: books children hugged, books they loved, books that made them feel like the author was their best friend. Not the books that were prevalent at the time, "books dominated by 'issues,' or 'problems,' which were very popular with teachers and adults but I felt didn't have the sense of fantasy and adventure that children really responded to," he said.

He took Harry from Christopher and read it in his house on Dean Street that night.

"You always look back on these things and think, 'Did it stop raining? 'Did the clouds part? Did all the traffic in the street stop?' None of those things of course happened. I just really liked it from the first."

It was very long, and it had a hard title. *Harry Potter and the Philosopher's Stone*, a mouthful for anyone, even if the word "philosopher" was accurate to the book's context. The magic sport was also confusing. But it had a lot of other somethings going for it. One of those somethings was another fierce advocate named Rosamund de la Hey.

In the small clot of adults in which Harry Potter found his first, and most influential, fan base, Rosamund gets the role of cheerleader. Everyone involved at the time now remembers her fervor for the book and the way she helped gear up Bloomsbury to think of

Harry as special and treat it as such. If the best thing that can happen to a book before it's published is for the publishers themselves to be excited about it, Rosamund can be thanked for running the first Harry Potter marketing campaign.

She had just gotten a job in marketing at Bloomsbury when Barry handed her the manuscript of *Philosopher's Stone*. He told her it was "a bit special." She'd soon regard that as an understatement: she read it overnight and fell head over heels, calling it the funniest thing she'd ever read and found herself pinning people to walls at dinner parties and telling them about it. She knew that it would be a better book outside the publishing house if it had fans within it, but that's not the entire reason she and Barry's assistant rolled up the book's first fifty pages like a scroll and stuffed it with Smarties candies and distributed them to everyone upon whose head the decision to purchase the book lay. Nor was it entirely because they felt like it was worthy of the much-desired Smarties Prize. The children's list at Bloomsbury was under two years old and hadn't established itself in sales terms, so each acquisition became a challenge. It was a gimmick, one that made the pages look like an academic scroll with a treat inside, and whether or not the people to whom the scroll was left had read it, they remembered that it was the manuscript that had literally been tarted up.

"We had to really fight to make ourselves heard, but that's quite characteristic of children's list publishers. You have to jump up and down and shout and scream," Rosamund explained.

Barry received Bloomsbury's blessing to proceed, and the next day, negotiations with the Christopher Little Agency took all of five minutes. Barry paid what he remembers to be £2,000 for the British rights, though the first offer was for £1,000 globally.

At the same time HarperCollins had come back to the table, and wanted to see the full manuscript, though they were hedging and hesitant. Chris called J. K. Rowling, who was still just "Joanne" then, and asked which publisher she preferred. She had to stop him to figure out what he was actually saying.

"I said to him, 'Are you saying that the book is definitely going to be published?' I had to get that really clear. I needed him to say, 'Your book will be published.' And he said, 'Yes, yes, yes!' " she said, imitating Christopher's "duh" tone of voice. "And then I screamed."

"So we took the second worst offer in history," Christopher said, joking. Though Jo would have "sold everything to Bloomsbury for 50 pence," Christopher held on to the book's world rights, advising Jo to "beg, steal, borrow," and do whatever she had to in order to survive while he played a cooler hand and secured the best international deal he could.

Soon after, Jo Rowling, Christopher, and Barry finally met at a restaurant outside Hamleys in London. They had to describe themselves to each other beforehand, as though on a blind date. It was a celebratory lunch as much as a first meeting, but both men warned the author not to get ahead of herself, not to quit a day job or think that there would be a lot of money coming. No big money ever really came from children's books, after all. Some "successful" children's authors still only made a few thousand pounds a year. Jo Rowling said that Barry was the only one who told her he thought it would do well. He was the first person to tell her so.

A few small things had to be changed about the book. It needed slimming, for a start. She had written the book out on a typewriter, because she couldn't afford a computer, so little mistakes recurred. She spelled "apothecary" wrong throughout, and still looks embarrassed mentioning it. Yet every change, or suggested change, felt like "a terrible travesty, because I had slaved so hard on it," she remembered.

"All first authors are nervous," said Barry. "You're like their first boyfriend. It's a very delicate relationship. I don't think we ever had a situation where I was trying to push her into something that was unreasonable."

There was no e-mail, because Jo Rowling still didn't have a computer; they would leave each other phone messages when they had something to say, and sometimes things got lost in translation. Once Barry left a message with some questions about Quidditch, and Jo called him, upset and "in real nervousness," worrying he wanted to cut it altogether.

Most edits were small; Jo Rowling doesn't remember shaving much but does remember fighting for two things and winning: her title, and to keep a seminal scene in which Harry, Ron, and Hermione become friends by knocking out a twelve-foot mountain troll.

"My self-esteem generally at this time in my life was rock bottom," she said. "No one could have felt they were a failure more than I, but there was one area of my life where I had—was it confidence? Yes, it was. And it felt brave to argue with Barry because he was giving me my life's ambition and I desperately—desperately—wanted to please him."

She was intent to show that something huge had to happen between Ron and Hermione to make that first connection, and had the same sure-mindedness about her plot and characters that later became so characteristic of her later public persona.

"Do you just have a boy like Ron come round to her qualities? It's just not going to happen. And unless she's an extremist she's not going to reveal her good qualities, because they're both *eleven*. And you need something like that when you're eleven. So I really argued to keep it."

The scene remained and has become one of the most treasured of the first book, especially for the line: *There are some things you can't share without ending up liking each other, and knocking out a twelve-foot mountain troll is one of them.*

Barry would leave Bloomsbury to open his own publishing house before Harry Potter saw a shelf, but things were already moving swiftly without him. Rosamund and others at Bloomsbury, including the book's new editor, Emma Matthewson, asked that the author change her published name to her first two initials instead of "Joanne," so that she didn't turn off potential boy readers with her female-ness. No middle name? No problem: she took the name Kathleen for her grandmother and the transformation to J. K. Rowling became complete. The first Harry Potter was ready.

Harry Potter may have struggled to break into the real world, but it wasn't without its blessings and portents. Maybe there was some benign force leading Jo Rowling to bring her book to the exact right people at the exact right moment. No one involved in any step of the process admits to knowing, or being able to guess, that Harry Potter wasn't exactly "just another book," yet the fact of its publication at all—this long, nonpolitically correct, weirdly titled book about magic—proves that wrong. And it certainly wasn't "just another book" to Jo Rowling, who finished it around the beginning of August 1995, lying on her stomach in her dingy apartment in Leith while her daughter slept. She wrote by hand, and had finally scrawled *The End* at the bottom of her page. Even today she reenacts the moment like it's been perfectly preserved in her mind: eyes racing back and forth over the final words of the full manuscript, hair almost a closed curtain around her face, hands frozen midair as though any movement would sweep it all away.

I've finished it. I've finished my novel, she thought.

She rose and drew back the curtains to discover night had fallen while she had been writing. And just like the opening chapter of her first book—the opening chapter of a series that would soon become a phenomenon, an opening chapter that would mirror itself in the world, in which everyone was talking about Harry Potter, the Boy Who Lived—she found a tabby cat sitting on the brick garden wall, staring back at her.

"Good night, Professor McGonagall," she said.

The "long game" that Christopher Little had asked Jo to play started to pay off in early 1997, a few months before the first Harry Potter book was slated for publication in England. Arthur A. Levine had just opened an imprint at Scholastic Corporation, a huge and growing larger publisher whose revenues had come within grabbing distance of $1 billion for the previous year. The Goosebumps products alone fueled a $21 million year of television, movie production, and merchandising licensing revenues for the company, for a total estimated $80 million to Scholastic overall. The series was beginning to plateau, however, because nontraditional book outlets like supermarkets were returning their unsold copies. Still, the franchise was pushing about a million units each month. At the time Scholastic's vice president of finance, Ray Marchuk, called the R. L. Stine series "the most successful children's book series of all time."

Arthur's new imprint, Arthur A. Levine Books, hadn't been built for blockbusters, or the ability to publish sixty-two books over five years as the Goosebumps series had done. Each book would be hand-picked and would have to meet Arthur's personal standards for young adult literature, which he admits are "ridiculously high." He was a former editor in chief for Knopf, and had deep picture-book roots. The imprint wasn't intended to publish more than seven to ten books a year, because he wanted each book to be carefully crafted, potential classics—books that children loved as much as he had loved Maurice Sendak's *Where the Wild Things Are* when he was young.

In the first ten years of his career, he learned that everyone was pessimistic about lengthy fiction for young readers. Conventional wisdom said it didn't sell.

In March 1997 he was about to publish his new imprint's first book, *When She Was Good*, by Norma Fox Mazer, a young-adult novel about two-thirds the length of the first Harry Potter. He went to the Bologna Children's Book Fair, widely considered the most important event in children's book publishing in the world. It was perfect for him, because he wanted his imprint to be about bringing the best of the world's literature to American children. Translations; international networking; and great, small finds—it was his first adventure in his new status as an eponymous publisher.

But nothing felt right; no publisher had anything that gave him a rush or held his attention or inspired the care and love he wanted to infuse into his new brand.

It was still only Bloomsbury's second year publishing for children, but with Arthur wanting children to love their books and Barry wanting children to hug them, their concepts were aligned. Arthur met with Ruth Logan, Bloomsbury's rights director, and said he had been excited about the meeting. Yet still, their offerings didn't fit. Nothing matched. Finally, Ruth crossed her arms and asked Arthur what he was looking for, and Arthur launched into his oft-repeated speech about wanting to publish books that kids "read to pieces."

Bloomsbury didn't even have the rights to sell Harry Potter abroad, but it didn't matter; if Arthur liked it he could just get in touch with the Christopher Little Agency, with whom rights had to be negotiated. So Ruth handed him the manuscript and explained that it was about to be published and that he might like it. She also told him how excited everyone at Bloomsbury was over it, and he thought her attention genuine, so he gave it a shot.

"I actually read it on the plane home, which I wouldn't have, had I not had that level of respect for her."

The book was exactly what he was looking for—funny, exciting, funny, fresh, adventurous, funny. It possessed that timelessness that he was trying to infuse into his whole imprint. Arthur wasn't making judgments based on trends, so his decision wasn't dependent on what British or American markets were doing. His self-named imprint freed him from that; all his books with his name on them should simply reflect his publishing philosophy.

Arthur wasn't alone in his love for the book: the enthusiasm of Bloomsbury's agents had been caught by a few other American publishers as well. By June 1997 there were several publishers vying for the rights to bring Harry Potter across the Atlantic.

Christopher informed the American publishers that there would be an auction, and they had a certain amount of time to make an offer, which was a risk; sometimes an agent sets up an auction with the mistaken belief that there's more interest in a book than there really is. But that wasn't so for Harry Potter, so on June 12, 1997, four publishers had to beat each other's offers until only the one with the biggest check was left standing. High-profile auctions can ratchet a book's asking price into the mid-to-high six, or even low-seven, figures, but that was usually for authors of adult books or celebrity nonfiction. Children's book advances were still considered astronomical if they hit as much as five figures.

Arthur sent out a memo the day before stating that the auction would be at 12:30 p.m., and consist of four American publishers, two of whom had already made offers.

"There are several reasons for this excitement. One, [it's] a <u>won-</u>

<u>derfully written</u> fantasy evoking Roald Dahl and Philip Pullman. First book in a series about Harry Potter and Hogwarts school of magic. First time novelist who obviously has a <u>great future</u>. . . . This book is very cinematic. The agent already has film interest."

Bidding continued throughout the day, and though it was sub-dued and consisted of a few phone calls between one agent and four publishers, by early evening the price had gone above the $100,000 mark. Arthur had been going back and forth with Barbara Marcus, who had been president of Scholastic children's book division since 1991, about how high they were prepared to go. The $100,000 offer had come from another publishing house.

Barbara asked Arthur, "Do you love it?" He said yes.

"I said, 'Then go back and bid again,' and he did, and we got it."

The final price was $105,000. It was the most Arthur had ever paid for a first novel, and certainly the highest figure heard of in recent memory for a children's book.

Scholastic justified its high bid by anticipating that the advance —which is usually repaid to a publishing house by withholding an author's royalties until the payment has been recouped—would be paid back over a few, several, or even many years. The company wanted a fantasy on its list, Arthur had a good feeling about it, and as Barbara recalls, they were going to "build a modern classic."

"It's notoriously hard to get people to pay any attention to first novels," Arthur said, "especially first children's novels. I thought surely, after some time, it would make that money back."

"We look like idiots now," Barbara said, "but that was how we were rationalizing going to six figures for this unknown property— which was a lot of money at the time."

Christopher brought Jo Rowling the news. He had called her up early in the day to tell her there was an auction going on in New York, and she said, "What are you telling me for? What, can I bid?"

"It's for your *book*." He gave her an initial figure that she can no longer remember, but that seemed remarkable. He updated her throughout the day, leaving her "walking this tightrope" between terror and elation. In the evening the final call came: Arthur A. Levine Books, $105,000.

After her phone call with Christopher, she put down the phone and walked around her apartment. Jessica, her daughter, was sleeping. She just kept walking around in silence, thinking, *I could buy a house. I could get a house.* And one with a reasonable mortgage, that she could keep up. Jessica would be able to go to a better school.

But she was also terrified. She knew there'd be press attention. She knew her story was about to undergo public scrutiny. And despite the elation that came with financial security, she felt sure that the second book, *Chamber of Secrets*, in which she was elbow-deep, was "absolute rubbish, and it can't live up to the first book, and now I've got a huge weight of expectation."

Then Arthur called and asked, "Are you scared?"

"Yes, I'm terrified," she said, but the terror lifted at the words. She loved him from that instant.

The day after the auction, having heard what happened, Bloomsbury sent Jo Rowling enough Oriental lilies to fill her apartment with a smell that she has not yet forgotten. It was more flowers than she had ever seen come at once. She stuck them in every last bit of crockery in the apartment, every last vase and pot.

"Then sure enough," she recalled, "it all kicked off big time and just went insane."

She was right about the press attention. The auction was huge news in Britain and hardly anyone failed to notice it, least of all Bloomsbury. The *Sun*, the British tabloid to whom the racy *New York Post* would be considered a modest cousin, offered Jo Rowling big bucks for her life story. She didn't sit with the tabloid, but Bloomsbury did want her to tell her story, preferably to the mainstream press in an attempt to get the Harry Potter story seen as a breakout hit that shouldn't be relegated to children's review pages and specialty magazines like *Carousel* and *Books for Keeps*.

"Partly because we loved the book as grown-ups, and partly because of the very newsworthy sales of the book, we took the view that this was a story that we could place in the news pages," said Rosamund. "We were very confident that here was something a bit special, so it gave us the brash confidence to go for the moon."

Two days before publication, the *Herald* in Glasgow published a story that began in a way that would become very familiar: "Three years ago Joanne Rowling landed in Edinburgh with a baby under one arm and a dog-eared manuscript under the other." A few days later Eddie Gibb in the *Sunday Times* ran a story called "Tales from a Single Mother." In the first week of July came Nigel Reynolds's story on page three of the *Telegraph* in London: "$100,000 Success Story for Penniless Mother."

In years to come Jo Rowling would gain the reputation of not liking the press very much, perhaps because one of her characters, Rita Skeeter, is a yellow journalist who bleeds Slytherin green ink all over the fourth estate of her world. It's also because of the joking, sometimes annoyed, way she later referred to the intense labeling she got from the press during this time; Jo has joked that she should have the word "penniless" tattooed on her forehead. Yet there were two journalists whom she remembers most fondly: one who let her take a statement off the record when she felt she had been wrong-footed into saying the wrong thing, and Nigel Reynolds, who, after their interview, switched off his tape recorder and gave her advice about dealing with the press.

Suddenly she was living in two strange worlds: one in which she was still Joanne, living in a crummy flat with a small child she now had to protect from the limelight, working off an £8,000 grant from the Scottish Arts Council so she could finish her second book, and another in which she was portrayed as the character of J. K. Rowling, a plucky woman struggling to raise her child and achieve her dreams of fame and fortune. The exaggerations played out like a Dickensian fairy tale—our heroine wrote on tea bags and scraps of napkins and shivered at night in an unheated flat until she magicked herself some riches and fame. The truth combined with assumptions and romance minted her as an icon for struggling young mothers everywhere, whether she liked it or not.

"I found the attention just overwhelming, and I had no one to talk to about it—no one. I wasn't with anyone, I wasn't in a relationship at that time. No one I knew personally had ever been through anything like this."

The American rights sale was worth about £65,625, which was still huge for a first-time author and enough to give her security— but definitely not enough to make her rich. When she got her first hardback copies of *Philosopher's Stone*, she made sure to send those to people who lived in Edinburgh, and the paperbacks to those who lived farther away, because it cost more to send heavier things out of town.

"If someone had said to me, you realize this hardback will be worth twenty thousand pounds someday, I would have fallen off my chair laughing," she said.

However, that would be one of her last acts of poverty, because by the summer of 1997 her first book had been pushed out of the nest and was proving to have a larger wingspan than anyone had anticipated. Press around the auction ensured that the first printing of 2,500 paperbacks and 450 hardbacks wasn't enough; the books went into a second printing only four days later. Bloomsbury was already getting fan mail in to J. K. Rowling, addressed *Dear Sir*.

In November Rosamund's dream and prediction for Harry came true—it won a gold medal in the Nestlé Smarties Book Prize for children, which meant credibility and a second wave of press. Using that as ammo, Bloomsbury went after the television media, "chasing the [enormously popular children's show] *Blue Peter* like crazy." Jo Rowling appeared on the show in December.

"What we were really selling was a good-luck story," Rosamund said. "It was a zeitgeist thing. A lot of different things happened at the right time."

All the elements were sliding into place: Jo's story, the press sale in America, the prize win. But something else was happening, too: in small and independent bookshops, owners were having the same reaction to the books as Rosamund had, as Barry had, as that small collection of adults who first championed Potter had, and were pressing Harry Potter into the hands of every child or parent who asked for something good to read.

By July 1998, the first book had sold more than 70,000 copies in the U.K., and, with the debut of the second, made history and created another wave of press: it was the first children's book to hit the top of a best-seller list—the *Times* in London, which had previously featured fantasy author Terry Pratchett and law thriller author John Grisham. The books had clearly crossed over into the adult market: adults were coming up to Jo Rowling at signings and admitting their love for her work, while others had been spotted reading the book behind their newspapers on trains. (This drove Bloomsbury to create "adult" editions of the books, which wrapped the same content in more dramatic, photographic covers instead of the more cartoony kids' fronts.) A crossover children's book was the kiss of life—adult books were far less likely to trickle downward in age than children's books were to creep up, but the crossover was still elusive, a bit of a publishing holy grail. Yet more and more adults were admitting that they had been entranced by the playful, and sometimes very tongue-in-cheek, slyly adult way Jo Rowling described her world.

So: children, check. Adults, check. Press, check. Booksellers, check. Harry Potter was starting to catch fire.

End-of-year reviews and recommendations for Christmas presents held a lot of happy notes for Bloomsbury and Jo Rowling. Anne Johnstone, the same journalist who published Rowling's first interview, said the book was "a gripping story told at a furious pace with lashings of imagination, wit, insight, and humour," and she had "yet to meet a child who can put it down."

Rosamund's love of Harry manifested itself in her wrapping up manuscripts with Smarties and pinning people against walls at dinner parties, demanding why they hadn't read it yet. In 1998, she got her American counterpart in Margot Adler.

As a correspondent for National Public Radio, a news and entertainment service in the United States that has about thirteen million listeners, Margot has read, reviewed, or covered hundreds of books. Thousands of them line her New York apartment; every wall in every common area is a bookshelf, leaving no room for hangings or framed pictures. She was a recipient of one of the 3,000 galleys, or bound and typeset pages, of *Harry Potter and the Sorcerer's Stone* that Scholastic sent out in the spring of 1998.

Arthur had insisted on changing the name from *Philosopher's Stone*. "If you think about marketing a book," he said, "it is possible that someone hears *Philosopher's Stone* and thinks it's a book about philosophy." He suggested changing it to *Harry Potter and the School of Magic* (which eventually became the French title); Jo came up with the compromise of *Sorcerer's Stone*.

"Truthfully, I regret it," she said. "I wish I had just kept 'philosopher's,' because there's an interesting story behind the philosopher's stone and it's a shame to lose that. It doesn't break my heart; as compromises go I think it wasn't a bad one."

The publishers had also passed the book around to friends in other publishing houses as well as other authors: Arthur sent a personal e-mail to a list of authors including Philip Pullman, Terry Brooks, Ursula K. Le Guin, Jane Yolen, and Paula Danziger, calling Harry a "real fresh voice in fantasy" that has "a lot of heart beneath it."

By June 1998, in addition to England, Harry had been published or was slated for publication in France, Germany, Italy, Holland, Greece, Finland, and Denmark. A few thousand of the softcover advanced readers' copies went out to reviewers and media, and at first were given the mild interest associated with an international story that didn't feature wacky royals or celebrities. Margot, a practicing Wiccan priestess, eyeballed it and liked the cover and the magical allusions, so she tossed it in her bag and didn't think much about it, beyond thinking she might read it with her family on vacation.

The only thing she thought was truly significant about the galley was the letter from Arthur Levine inside the cover, which she thought was "the most arrogant thing I'd ever seen in my life." The introductory note talked about the excitement of being present for the birth of a new and glorious talent, and how exciting, fresh, and wonderful the story was—vaulted language to be sure, but hardly Oedipal hubris. He promised the potential reader a struggle between skipping ahead to find out what happens next and staying on a slower pace to avoid missing "some fantastic detail." It was really the last paragraph that got Margot's attention: "I predict you'll also face another quandary: whether to share this with a friend, or to keep it for yourself, knowing how much this Reader's Edition of J. K. Rowling's first book will be worth in years to come."

"I thought, he's out of his bleeping mind. Come on. To put this?"— she said, jabbing the book, which she now keeps in a ziplock bag on one of her book-crammed shelves—with her finger. "Totally crazy."

So she went on vacation and, despite her objections to what she saw as hubris, read the book.

She loved it. So did her family. She and her kids spent a week enraptured, obsessing over it. When she returned home she trawled Amazon and found she wasn't alone, that the same opinions were being expressed online as well. She could catch a whiff of the phenomenon coming and scheduled an hour with Jo Rowling for a winter piece on NPR.

But she wasn't finished: Margot was also becoming one of Harry Potter's early wandering missionaries. She became obsessed, and expressed it in one of the only ways such early fans could: she visited every bookstore in Manhattan she could find just to make sure they were carrying the book. Independent bookstores were on the case: they had shelves and displays, and the owners were familiar with the book already and were hand-selling it as holiday gifts or just general reading suggestions. But at any chain store, at any Barnes & Noble or Borders or Waldenbooks she wandered into at the time, she was lucky to find one copy shoved between better-known titles.

"I was like a crazed loon for a while. I'd go into these bookstores and say, 'I notice you're not carrying Harry Potter. Why aren't you carrying this book?'"

The book had come out in September of that year to very few, but very favorable, reviews. *Kirkus Reviews* called it "hugely enjoyable," while *Booklist* said it was "brilliantly imagined and beautifully written." The *Columbus Dispatch* noted that a ten-year-old had read it straight through without distraction of friends, computers, or television. The praise was sparse, but where it was present, it was untempered. It was starting to rack up awards in Britain, too—the Children's Book of the Year Award at the British Book Awards, the Children's Book Award, and a second Smarties award for *Chamber of Secrets* fell into place, making Jo the first author to ever win two years in a row—and be a mainstay on the U.K. best-seller lists. Originally, Scholastic had planned to place the book on displays near the work of the veteran Philip Pullman; as a new author, this would help to give Jo Rowling a lift.

On pace with the positive publicity, Scholastic had planned to release the books a year apart, as Bloomsbury was doing in Britain. Jo Rowling came to the United States for a tour in the fall, visiting stores in ten cities, sometimes to crowds of hundreds and sometimes, as in Denver, to fifteen people ("That was a real *Spinal Tap* moment," Jo said).

The books were still all but nonexistent in the big chain stores. The hand-to-hand selling and word of mouth that had occurred in the U.K. was now mirrored in America, for a reason: independent booksellers had the luxury of choosing what they wanted to feature; they could decide what they liked and wanted to sell instead of going by incentives from corporate headquarters. So although Lloyd Alexander and Susan Cooper were the fantasy hot sells of the day, independent booksellers had the chance to have the same visceral reaction to Harry Potter as influential adults like Bryony Evans and Margot Adler and could act on it quickly—by recommending it to the first customer who came into the store or putting it on display up front—before clearing their decisions with corporate higher-ups.

At Hicklebees, a famous children's and young adult store in San Jose, California, where books seem to colorfully preen on shelves and so many visiting authors have autographed its door that it looks like a sixth-grader's notebook, members of the staff passed the book on to each other, each one liking it more than the last. Valerie Lewis, one of the store's founders, wanted to get this "great new children's author" into the store; she called Scholastic and said, "If he ever comes to the Bay area, we'll host him, even if he only has one book out."

Jo visited Hicklebees on her first tour. All Valerie remembers now was how "you probably wouldn't have noticed her in a crowd of three," at first. But when she was brought to a local school and kids started asking her questions about the series, she became "animated and responsive and caring. Her daughter was [waiting] in a hotel and I could almost feel her thinking, *An hour and a half before I get to see my daughter, an hour and fifteen minutes before I get to see my daughter.*"

Margot's piece ran on NPR on December 3, 1998, and it's remembered at Scholastic as the one that made the big difference. Something that inspired Margot's nomadic Harrying had also leaked into the piece: Maybe it was hearing Jo Rowling speak candidly about some of her quirkiest ideas (like Professor Binns, the Hogwarts ghost who hadn't noticed he'd died); maybe it was the manager of Books of Wonder, Manhattan's largest independent children's bookstore, reporting that it had sold hundreds of copies; or maybe it was the celebratory tone in Arthur Levine's voice as he introduced Jo at a publishing party. Minutes after Margot's piece ran, after it played in people's cars and on their portable radios, customers started wandering into bookstores, taking up Margot's cause, asking where Harry was and whether they could buy it.

By that time most stores had at least a copy or two on hand. The galley proclaimed the book would have 30,000 copies in its first run; by the time the first printing actually happened that number had inflated to 50,000. By mid-December the number of books in print had doubled. This was already tremendous for a children's book, and if all the in-print books sold, it would be more than enough to make back the six-figure advance that the brass at Scholastic had thought would take years to earn out. By the end of December the unthinkable happened: Harry Potter appeared at number 16 on the *New York Times* Best Seller List.

"It was brilliantly published; advertised in all the fall catalogues and magazines, Rowling toured and was interviewed. It was a lovely book to hold," said Eden Lipson, then the editor of the *New York Times Book Review* in an interview. "It was the Christmas book that children actually read over the holiday and came back to school talking about."

Whether or not it's the most true or most fair, or most reflective of actual sales, the *New York Times* Best Seller List holds redoubtable sway. It's determined by sales from a sampling of almost 4,000 bookstores and wholesalers that sell to 60,000 retailers, but that's ultimately not what matters most. Walk through any bookstore and note how many books call themselves *New York Times* Best Sellers on their front covers; probably just about as many as have ever earned the distinction. Harry Potter wasn't, technically, the only children's book of the year to make the list: also featured were actress Jamie Lee Curtis and Laura Cornell's picture book, *Today I Feel Silly: And Other Moods That Make My Day*, as well as *The Night Before Christmas*, a new version of the poem illustrated by Clement C. Moore. But not since E. B. White's *Charlotte's Web* reached the list and lingered there for three weeks in 1952 had a full-length children's novel done so well.

The books were gaining fans of such dedication that the devotees began outpacing publishers; by April they were so desperate for the second book, *Harry Potter and the Chamber of Secrets*, due for release in America in September, that they started ordering it from Amazon .co.uk for the bargain price of, including shipping, $25. By April 1999 this practice had grown so wide that Christopher Little began issuing admonitions to Amazon in the press.

Amazon claimed that this phenomenon wasn't new, just reversed. The American market is so much larger (somewhere around five to six times) than the U.K.'s that it's common practice for British customers to order American books via Amazon.com. Jeff Bezos of Amazon claimed it was the same as someone going to England, buying a book, and bringing it home. Some ordered directly from Bloomsbury. And when some posted a review of the book on Amazon .com's listing for it, they received e-mails from fans asking how they got a copy and for instructions on how to get the book themselves.

In the rules of traditional print publishing, Amazon.co.uk and other British retailers didn't have the rights to sell to the United States—but with e-commerce so new (consumers were spending a small fraction—less than a twentieth—of what they are now) the lines between the issues hadn't been finely drawn. Scholastic received phone calls from bookstore owners, complaining that they were losing sales to Amazon. At the time no one was really sure of Amazon's emerging power, but the online behemoth had, for the first time, surpassed the $250 million mark for the previous quarter. Bookstore owners worried that people would get used to shopping online.

With fans complaining that bookstores couldn't give them the book they wanted, bookstores complaining that publishers were encouraging their business to go digital, and publishers complaining that their books were being sold outside boundaries, there was a lot of general whining happening. The story appeared in the *New York Times* and elsewhere, but only fed the publicity beast by perpetuating the story of the emerging Potter juggernaut, the book that was so good that for the first time the British market was being stalked by salivating American consumers. No one sued. The issue died away quietly while the bigger story became Harry Potter's continually and meteorically growing allure.

At the same time, Harry Potter was taking its first steps toward the cineplex. The rights to the film had been secured in October 1998 by David Heyman for Warner Bros., who had moved back to London from America in 1996 to set up Heyday Films, a company specializing in family entertainment. He focused on converting books to film, because they had a higher chance of being produced than other types of projects, and because a book with his company behind it gave Los Angeles studios something more solid to work with than a new script from a young and untested writer. With books, he could actually get films made.

A girl in his office, Tanya Seghatchian, read an article in a trade journal about the as-yet-unpublished Potter, so Neil Blair, then working for Warner Bros., called Christopher Little and inquired about it. Christopher sent proofs along, almost without any result.

"I had three shelves: priority, medium priority, and low priority," David said, "and Harry Potter sat firmly on the low-priority shelf. Nobody was really reading it."

His secretary, Nisha Parti, was fed up after reading rubbish off the low priority shelf while Tania and David took things off the high-priority space. At the group's Monday morning discussion of their weekend reading, David asked, "Has anybody read anything good?" Nisha slowly put up her hand and timidly offered, "I read this book."

"What book?"

"*Harry Potter and the Philosopher's Stone.*"

"That's not a great title."

She explained the plot—young boy goes to wizard school—and

David's stance changed. He took the book home, began reading it, and couldn't stop.

"I fell in love. I'd be lying if I said I knew it was going to become the phenomenon it became, absolutely not, but I knew it was a book that I liked, that moved me, that made me laugh, that I related to it in some way. We've all been to school; I'd been to a school not dissimilar to Hogwarts, except without magic. We've all had friends who are important to us. We all want to belong in some form or another. We all have teachers that we like and teachers that we don't like and how great would it be to have magical powers? Above all, it made me laugh. It moved me, and I connected with it. It reminded me of those books I read as a child, whether they be Roald Dahl or the like, books that didn't patronize, books that treated their readers with respect, books that adults and kids could enjoy together. Such was Potter."

He sent it to Warner Bros., and to producer Lionel Wigram, another Brit at the studio whom David had known since his teens. They got involved, and "the journey began."

By now Christopher was sure that something huge was beginning. He kept asking Neil if he got it, if he understood how big of a deal this book was going to be. Neil started to understand, but few others did—there was no precedent for Potter, and while some adults could be convinced of its specialness just by reading the book, it was harder to convince the multibillion-dollar company that this wasn't the same kind of novel acquisition that they were used to and to approach it in a way that would make a writer happy, not just rich.

Jo Rowling rejected the original offer. Warner Bros. thought she had done so for monetary reasons and came back with a higher bid.

"Almost my entire reason for saying no was that I didn't feel I was far enough along with my story," she recalled. "There was nothing on the table at that point to say that there would be no non-author written sequels, which was the big deal for me," and which would assure that by buying the rights, Warner Bros. could never make a film called *Harry Potter and the Trip to Las Vegas*—that is, unless J. K. Rowling had written the book first.

Neil started arguing that the company should take a different tack with Potter than it had elsewhere. Really involve the author, involve the agent, don't just inform her of what was going on now and then. Christopher started to notice a kindred spirit in Neil, and Neil found himself at odds with his company, fighting for the integrity of a brand over global control.

"It was obvious that this was something new in terms of having a very creative person who was writing a series and had very strong views, and was enthusiastic and energetic, and I was saying, 'Let's operate as a partnership here, it would be a win-win,' " Neil recalls. "It was growing and growing exponentially, and I realized from my little office in London that Warner's was on to a fantastic thing."

It was a while before Warner Bros. came around, David admitted. "The studio always wants the most freedom they can with a piece of material," said David. "This is before the books were a success. I promised [Jo] when I met her that we would be as true and faithful to the process as possible, but the studio is always trying to protect its interest. They'd had no idea the books were going to become the phenomenon that they had, and no idea that the books would be as wonderful as they were going forward. If the second or fourth or fifth books were not as successful as the first one, or if Jo didn't write them for some reason, the studio was trying for freedom to do what it wanted with them. Which is fairly standard."

Jo wasn't yet rich, and the book hadn't yet achieved best-seller status; at the time, she was seriously considering going back to teaching and was still overcautious about her finances. The money the movie studio was offering would have solved all that. But she still said no, until her agent and the movie studio agreed that any sequels Warner Bros. wanted to make would have to come from her books.

After what David describes as a "lengthy" process, Warner Bros. secured an eighteen-month option on the book series, which could be renewed later, for a seven-figure sum.

"The zeitgeist was on my side," Rowling said. "If I had signed the moment they came to me . . ."

She trailed off but the implication was clear: her wishes as an unknown author with mild success in the United States stood a much paler chance of being respected at that time than they did in October 1998, when she was about to become a worldwide best-selling author and fans had started to become so desperate for the next volume they were quietly swiping them from the U.K. market. There would be no alienating of this massive, and increasingly detailed and fanatic, reader base. At least for a while.

Meanwhile, Scholastic was bending its schedule to accommodate the growing fanaticism. *Chamber of Secrets* was pushed from fall to early June, and *Prisoner of Azkaban* was published two days right after Labor Day, two months after it was published in Britain.

Two Harry Potter books in just over three months brought the publishing houses' schedules in line, but that kind of rush would never happen again. When *Prisoner of Azkaban* debuted in Britain in July 1999, so did the biggest and best change to the publication style of Harry Potter—and perhaps the biggest and best marketing tool the series has ever had. The set pub date.

Pub(lication) dates aren't new, they're just largely ignored. Most books tend to trickle from distributor to bookstore without fanfare, despite whatever on-sale date has been predetermined. Publishers encourage booksellers to read their books and pass them around, give them to an uncle's friend's brother's hairdresser if they want, because you never know whose uncle's friend's brother's hairdresser knows someone at CNN or an influential critic, and if the book is good enough and the press is steady enough and enough people are whispering about it, then enough people will buy it and you have a hit. Rosamund and Barry sold Harry Potter in-house by stuffing the books with Smarties and leaving them on people's chairs; marketers at Scholastic sent it around to industry professionals and wore Meet Harry Potter buttons at book fairs; Ruth handed Arthur the manuscript that she didn't have the rights to sell—who else could kickstart a domino chain? There was no formula for it. Books reach best-seller status by sales rate—if they only sell 3,000 copies but sell all of those copies in one week, they can attain a coveted spot on the best-seller lists and then sell infinitely more. Why suppress whatever publicity helps them reach that goal?

It wasn't as though Potter wasn't selling well: the first book had done three quarters of a million sales in Britain, and in America the first print run alone for *Chamber of Secrets* was 250,000 copies. When *Chamber* debuted in America it was greeted with a number-one spot on the *New York Times* list, a first for any children's book of its kind. The readers weren't going anywhere—except to the bookstore at the very first minute they could.

And someone thought that minute should be 3:45 p.m., July 8, 1999. Today, Scholastic says the idea of having such a specific release time was Jo Rowling's idea, and Rowling says the timing was Scholastic's idea, but when it first happened, Scholastic had nothing to do with it, and Jo's contribution was mostly her absence. It was all Bloomsbury. The harbinger of what would become the most physical manifestation of the hugeness of Harry Potter was originally a bit of a gimmick thought up by Bloomsbury marketing teams to make up for the lack of Jo Rowling's presence at launch. The author had been doing massive publicity, with three large-scale launches in two countries, and her time was spread thin.

"We had to think of a way of having a photo op for the book itself," said Rosamund. An embargo would generate interest, "the rationale being that kids would be out of school by [3:45] and would have time to get to a bookshop. So that was a bit of a gimmick, no question, but it also meant that they wouldn't skive school to get a copy. It kinda worked and the press really took to it."

It also presented the idea—mainly in the *Herald* a few weeks before publication—that they *would* skip school to get a copy, which to that point had been only an inference. But this gimmick played out with an implied headline—Children May Skip School to Get Book, Publishers Work to Avoid National Skiving Epidemic, News at 11!

Sky News and other media broadcast the launch from an independent bookstore called The Lion & Unicorn Bookshop. The print run had been upped to 157,000 in Britain, and overall sales were approaching a million worldwide, yet no sales figure could compete with the visual—a line of children around one independent bookstore, waiting for the exact moment they could crack the covers. Their excited faces made the story about more than astronomical sales figures: it made it about children enjoying a book.

"The sales really took off at that point," said Rosamund with a flatness that hints at the massive understatement she just made. "In a kind of exponential way."

1999: the year of three Potter book releases, the year that the series became a chronic best seller, and the year people started using the word *phenomenon* liberally next to the words *Harry Potter*. Signings were becoming spectacles. In October Jo Rowling embarked on an eight-city U.S. tour that featured the kind of receptions usually reserved for rock stars or self-help gurus. The first memory that both Jo Rowling and Kris Moran, the Scholastic publicist who quickly absorbed the Harry Potter work until it became almost her entire job, have concerns one supposedly "small" event at Tatnuck Bookseller & Sons in Worcester, Massachusetts, which had to employ seventy staffers and a local police detail to corral the 2,000 people who showed up for the event.

Jo and Kris Moran pulled up to the loading dock and saw the crowd spilling out the back of the store. Jo asked if there was a sale going on. Kris, who's small and blond like Jo and is something of her sharper-mouthed sister, gave Jo a look of amused disbelief and said that the crowd was for Jo's event. The crowd was chanting "J. K. Rowling" and "Harry Potter" with abandon. Jo became quiet, an overwhelmed look settling on her face.

They had to navigate a tight pathway to get to the signing table, amid outstretched hands and cameras flashing, and by the time they got there the chanting had turned to all-out screaming. The next day a reporter from the *Boston Globe* would say that it was as if the Beatles had come to town, and to this day Jo describes the event as making her feel like a "proper pop star." Still, somewhere between the car and the table a calm realization that this was how the tours were going to be from now on—that the *Spinal Tap* moments of the previous tour were gone—had arrived. Jo sat down at the table, looked up at Kris, and said, "Right, then," in that steadfast British way that suggests she could be settling down to do taxes as easily as a massive signing of her book for thousands of adoring fans, and started signing.

Worcester wasn't the only mob scene on that tour; it had been preceded by intense publicity, including appearances on the *Rosie O'Donnell Show* and *Today* and a press conference at the National Press Club. The tour was averaging 750 to 1,000 people at over 30 appearances. A hundred people is a lot for any small- to midsize bookstore, and Jo Rowling's crowds were downright unmanageable. The Children's Bookshop in Brookline, Massachusetts, had to keep the date and location of the event exclusive to ticket holders. At one store in Massachusetts, the signing had to be called off; the event had been badly managed, with 2,000 people turning up for what was supposed to be a 200-person event. Once the first two hundred entered the store, there was a scrum for tickets outside the door. Kids got separated from their parents, and Jo had to be sped away in a car.

So the Potter publishers instituted protocols: Thousands of people would wait in line; they were allowed one book, which had to be a hardcover American edition, and no personalization or photographs would be permitted.

Buoyed by the success of having a set pub date, the British and American publishers of Harry Potter decided on a simultaneous release for the fourth book, *Harry Potter and the Goblet of Fire*. Again, no one really remembers whose idea it was, though Jo Rowling says it may have been her idea to time the release to the minute, because if you're going to have a simultaneous publication you might as well go all the way, and crack the books right after midnight.

"It became more of a celebration," she said. "I didn't realize how big of a deal that would become."

And it became quite a photo op, even more than the post-school bonanza that had occurred with the release of book three. No more kids in school clothes, queuing in bright daylight; now they were up past bedtime. They came wearing robes and glasses and with little scars painted on their foreheads, often with parents who also had robes and glasses and little scars painted on their foreheads.

The day *Goblet of Fire* was released, the Harry Potter books had been on the *New York Times* Best Seller List for eighty weeks. *Sorcer-*

er's Stone had been on the list for six months and had peaked at number four; when *Chamber* came out it hit number one, and kept its predecessor hovering at six or higher. When *Prisoner* debuted, the three books rotated positions in the top three spots for weeks. Eventually *Sorcerer's Stone* would drop below the tenth spot, and by spring of 2000 books by John Grisham, Nora Roberts, and Isabel Allende would mingle again beside the latter two Potters in the highest ranks, but with four more books still to come it was beginning to look like Harry Potter could monopolize the list for years.

The practical reality of the *New York Times* Best Seller List cannot be underestimated; not only do *New York Times* Best Sellers usually proclaim their status on their front covers, but bookstores are in the habit of snipping the list from that week's paper and setting up a display featuring all the books on it. Being on the best-seller list earned authors bonuses from their publishers, earned publishers the most sought-after placement in bookstores, and exponentially increased any book's sales. Books that get onto the list usually stay there for at least a short while, fueled simply by the fact that they are *on* the list.

And Harry Potter was hogging it. If the past was any indication, the publicity around the release of the fourth book, the first one to be released since Harry Potter became a real phenomenon, would mean that the books wouldn't just pitch camp in the top four slots, they might be having bonfires and singing "Kumbaya" there forever. (To celebrate the accomplishment of ranking all currently published books at the top of the list, Arthur Levine's father had a printout of the list stamped onto a T-shirt, which he wore proudly.)

"Adult publishers looked at the future and saw their hopes and dreams and titles being blocked," said Eden Ross Lipson, the editor of the *New York Times Book Review* at the time. "It was clear it would dominate against all comers. Yet the *Book Review* is for adults [although it also has] regular children's features. Most of the advertising is for adult books and there was nothing comparable to Harry Potter coming along. So the idea was to break it out [of the list] before the fourth book was published."

The idea of splitting the list had never been seriously considered before by the editing or advertising departments, though other children's publishers had been asking for the change for a while so they could showcase a market that previously had no chance at attaining *New York Times* Best Seller fame.

But even that was changing: Harry Potter had not only opened a children's doorway to the List, but helped other books find it, too. In June 2000, the *Times* list also featured the 256-page *Bud, Not Buddy*, a Newbery Honor–winning novel by Christopher Paul Curtis, and *The Legend of Luke*, a hefty 412-page novel that was the twelfth in Brian Jacques's popular Redwall series—both are children's books.

In late June 2000, the *New York Times* announced it would be splitting its list into Best Sellers and Children's Best Sellers. Along with a children's best-seller list, there would now be separate paperback and hardcover lists for fiction, nonfiction, and "advice, how-to, and miscellaneous." The main adult and children's lists would have fifteen slots, and mix fiction and nonfiction together. Harry Potter cracked the *Times* list into eight pieces.

There was "relief from everyone, except, perhaps, Scholastic," said Lipson. "As I recall, they boycotted for a year or so and took no ads in the daily or the *Book Review*."

Nearly everyone involved in Harry Potter today, when discussing the splitting of the list, still gets a puckered look on their face, including Jo Rowling. Even in late 2007, sitting with coffee and sandwiches in front of a fireplace in her warmly decorated Edinburgh home, she gets pinched up thinking about it. She believed the *New York Times* was "wrong. I think the decision was taken not because they felt there should be a children's list, or an adult list, but they felt that Harry shouldn't top the overall fiction list."

Still, she sighed, and remembered, "We'd had our day. I'd had my day of being one, two, three, four at the top of the *New York [Times]* Best Seller List." And if the splitting of the list helped children's fiction overall? "If that's true, that's great. If that's true, I'm happy, and I would like to retract my former statement!" She laughs.

"But if it's not true I'm hacked off."

As years in Harry Potter terms go, 1999 was a red-letter one: the introduction of the pub date, the insane publishing schedule, the change in Jo Rowling's status in the world, the mobbed bookstores, the whirlwind tours, the slow burn toward a fractured best-seller list, and all the attendant publicity that comes with each of those elements turned a curiosity into a phenomenon. But when Jo Rowling comes to town, she's gone the next day; television viewers can watch a news segment over breakfast and forget it by lunch; interviews fresh in newspapers one morning are used to line birdcages and wrap fish the next. Publicity like that couldn't be maintained.

Word of mouth was enough to carry the phenomenon far, to nudge it right to the edge of the tipping point, but something was about to push it way over: another phenomenon was evolving next to the Harry Potter books, coming into its own as the thing that changed *everything* we knew about everything. They would both rise together and meet, and one's impact on the other is beyond measurement. For all the hullaballoo about Harry Potter taking kids away from video games and trash culture and back to good old prosaic, musty book pages, the thing that snagged Harry's ever lengthening coattails and turned them into a suit of bulletproof armor was the very opposite, made up of bits and bytes instead of words and letters, and if brought to Hogwarts would be rendered completely useless. Harry Potter was about to become good friends with the Internet.

CHAPTER FIVE

Spinning the Web

I couldn't work up the nerve to mock Cheryl Klein for lying to me about the Harry Potter manuscript. She'd committed the deed at dinner during the third week in January 2007; it had been a long workday and whoever was standing next to me at the time would have been the recipient of my rant on family squabbles, the stubbornness of technology, and my rapidly fraying patience regarding not knowing when the announcement for the release date of the seventh Potter book would come. Cheryl happened to be that person. As we walked to the restaurant and I carried on, I waved my arms around wildly.

"And, and, *and*," I said, pointing in front of me at nothing, "as I say all this, I know that manuscript is probably just sitting in your office right now!"

Cheryl was like my taller, skinnier, blonder, more logically assembled sister. Instead of feeding off my arm-flailing, coat-unbuttoned, wind-whipped-hair act, she walked primly and carefully and had dressed in warm layers that included objects foreign to me, like a hat, scarf, and pair of gloves. She always had two bags and I knew exactly what was in each: One was her normal purse, with all the lady things. The other was homework from her job as an editor at

Arthur A. Levine Books; it would contain at least one manuscript (sometimes two) and a smattering of unanswered query letters that she would try to get to at home.

For a long time I'd thought of Cheryl as "Ms. Klein." Starting in or around 2002, she would e-mail Leaky every time she found a worthwhile news tip, and it didn't take long for us to recognize that her e-mail address said "scholastic.com" at the end, google her, and discover she was part of the team editing the Potter books. As she was so unknown to us, we just regarded her as a "Ms."—she did, after all, have a hand in producing our favorite books, so was owed at least that much. But then I met her, and the prefix just seemed ridiculous. We were at a screening of *Prisoner of Azkaban* in 2004; we'd exchanged some polite e-mails and all I knew was that she'd be there. When she tapped me on the shoulder and I turned to face a skinny blonde my age, wearing a wide smile, glasses, and a blue *Order of the Phoenix* baby-doll tee, I knew this was not an intimidating woman. A few days later we went for coffee and soon were bonding over shared thoughts about the Harry Potter series and others. We saw movies, laughed hard, and eventually played Scrabble together (something Cheryl doesn't do with friends until she's sure they can take the walloping). We explored bars and restaurants in Brooklyn and whined to each other about family and men. Before I knew what had happened she had become one of my closest friends, but we kept our friendship a secret for a while, scared that the powers that be would demand that we not speak because I was a Harry Potter reporter and she might accidentally slip me some major spoilage. Had she violated some invisible work clause by befriending me?

We kept that up for about a year, before we started slowly hinting to people, publicly, that we were friends. We were met with a stunning lack of concern.

That night in January, like many nights that followed long and frustrating days, Cheryl just listened to me go on and laughed in a way I would only later recognize as knowing. She leaned in and said, so seriously I believed her, "Melissa, that manuscript is not in my office right now."

Technically she probably hadn't lied. It was probably buried in Arthur's office at the time. I'd brushed the matter off quickly, because I always felt bad whenever I pressured her about knowing the contents of future Harry Potter books before I did. Well, almost always. Over Independence Day weekend with my family in 2005, less than two weeks before the release of the sixth book, my Sicilian relatives had made sport of trying to get her to reveal the identity of the Half-Blood Prince. They casually encouraged the mafia stereotype ("I know a guy, his name is Vinny. . . .") to bully her into spilling. LauryAnn, a buyer at Macy's, offered designer handbags. We coached six-year-old Nicky to look up at her with his beseeching hazel eyes and stutter, "Who's the Habbloodprins?" My eleven-year-old cousin Joseph kept asking unrelated, short questions ("What's your favorite book?" "What's your zodiac sign?") and then slipping in, "Who's the Half-Blood Prince?" in hopes she'd flub. I only saw her flinch once, when Joseph bet her the name against a game of Scrabble. Her face tightened. Later that weekend, when I performed the unheard-of feat of beating Cheryl at said game (which was only because she had helped me a few times) she assuaged her bruised wordplay ego by leaning over and crowing, "I know something you don't know!" Then she laughed so maniacally everyone at the table joined in.

But it was now the last week in February 2007, and since this was officially the last five months ever during which Cheryl could torture me with her inside Potterology, I was feeling charitable. My friend Meg Morrison and I were visiting her Park Slope, Brooklyn, apartment for one of our "writing weekends" (really an occasional weekend day in which we ate a large home-cooked meal, indulged in kvetching/kvelling/gossiping, then worked on our individual projects), and Cheryl was already smirking as she served us portions of pancakes. Meg and I were almost completely ignoring her, as we had to if we were going to continue our current conversation, one of our canon-thump rolls, in which we went down the list of unanswered Potter mysteries and tried to untangle them by treating seemingly minuscule plot points like groundbreaking evidence. Today it was all about the character of Bellatrix Lestrange, the Death Eater who made Lady Macbeth look like June Cleaver.

"That ____"—Meg called her something unmentionable—"knows something. She knows about the Horcuxes. She said Voldemort trusted her with his most *precious* something and then she got cut off." Getting cut off is any Rowling-studying fan's signal that important information has been revealed or disguised. "She probably wears it around one of her legs, the hairy beast."

This wasn't the first time we'd talked about this clue, but it was the first time since the announcement of the release date. Every conversation since had this kind of urgency to it, as though we were trying to disengage a bomb before the clock ticked down to zero.

When I first met Meg, I had only been acquainted with the Harry Potter fandom for a few months. My Leaky work was mostly sparse; it had been a year and a half since the release of the fourth book and there was no clue that another was forthcoming any time soon. The first movie had been released in November; I'd traveled to my college town of Washington, D.C., to see it at the Uptown Theater, which housed a screen roughly the size of a building. I lined up three hours early to get a prime seat, and as I did, costumed people seemed to appear all around me. I waited between a Hagrid and a Rita Skeeter, sat with them as the old-style theater filled up with fans of all ages, and twittered in excitement, as did everyone else. When the lights went down and the WB logo flashed across the screen, the cheers and whoops sent a sentimental thrill through my body. No Harry Potter film moment, ever, for me, would match the time I first saw the words Privet Drive emerge from the darkness on screen.

Otherwise I was spending my Potter time talking with the same group of adults I always had; I'd spend hours e-mailing with them each night, discussing plot points and characterizations. In my thirst for everything Potter I'd also become more closely acquainted with fanfiction, which had previously been a new phenomenon to me. The first time I'd ever looked for fanfiction I'd been slightly traumatized by the experience. I went to the default fanfiction site for alternate fiction about characters from copyrighted properties, FanFiction .net, which housed more Harry Potter fanfiction than anything else (I noticed as I skimmed the directories that *The X-Files* had a lot as well, but nothing close to the amount of stories which were Harry related).

I clicked on my first story hesitantly, caught between wanting to keep my Potter experience pure to Jo Rowling's telling of it and being so desperate for new stories about my favorite characters that I'd settle for those from another's pen.

Curiosity naturally beat purity, so I clicked on the first story on the list and found myself staring in horror at a one-page story that was so full of sentence fragments, grammatical errors, and narrative interruptions that it looked more like a toddler had been at the page with magnetic letters than someone had actually tried to craft prose. It took a half hour before I ran across a piece of fanfiction by an author who respected commas, but after that, by clicking links to each author's favorite stories and searching through the highest rated lists, I finally started to uncover readable work. I didn't understand a lot of the notation—AU, MWPP, pre-GOF, H/H, H/G, slash, and so on—and even when I found a fic that wasn't stupefyingly bad, it felt wrong, like literary karaoke. The community seemed to judge most work by how close the author came to mimicking Jo Rowling's style; any author who came close—and many who didn't—bore reviews that read, *Are you sure you're not J. K. Rowling?* Only the more advanced, or prolific, writers could shed that mantle and receive reviews based around their markedly different styles.

It took about a week for me to get used to seeing Harry, Ron, and Hermione's names or the setting of Hogwarts used in other people's stories, but once I did and found a few authors I liked and followed their recommendations, I quickly learned about several non-Fan Fiction.net sites that housed reams of well-written Harry Potter fiction. Several people pointed me toward some of the more popular sagas, one of which, *The Draco Trilogy* by Cassandra Claire (who now publishes best-selling novels under "Cassandra Clare"), seemed to be considered required fandom reading. In it, Draco plays the lead role, wears leather pants, and mouths off in a much more sardonic and ultimately likable fashion than in the books. I found the story well written and funny but the softening of his character ultimately turned me off; I didn't want to read about him if he was characterized differently than in the books.

I read fanfiction because I wanted to spend more time with the characters I knew from Jo Rowling's mind, and the only site that I personally felt came close to doing that regularly was the Sugar Quill. The site's chief goal was to encourage fanfiction that didn't contradict anything about the canon, and it had a Professors' Bookshelf of preferred stories, which made the whole overwhelming world of Harry Potter fanfic so much smaller and more manageable that I got hooked. I'd spend hours on the site's message boards, not only discussing fanfic but also trying to work through the clues of the series. What happened *right* before Dumbledore left Harry with the Dursleys? What did James and Lily do for a living when they were alive? I also relished some of the more serious discussions on more philosophical topics, like whether Sirius or Remus were worse off after the first downfall of Voldemort, or whether it had been an antifeminist cop-out for Hermione to straighten her hair for the Yule Ball in *Goblet of Fire*.

Meg was one of two people who ran the Sugar Quill, so when Heidi Tandy, then an editor on Leaky, said that Meg and I worked near each other and we should meet, I was genuinely excited. It was early 2002, and we were halfway through the wait for book five. I had also managed to get a job at MTV Networks as an editorial assistant on the company's internal magazine, *The Pages Online*. It started out, as promised, with some administrative work but just as much reporting and writing; two weeks later, after a company-wide 500-person layoff that I'm sure I only survived because my pay was low, I became mostly the second personal assistant to a woman named Denise who, it seemed, intensely disliked me and saddled me with a never-ending list of personal tasks thinly veiled as professional responsibilities. I pegged it as the "hell job" I hoped to avoid out of college. I wouldn't have minded if that had been the description for the job for which I'd applied, but after three months and many whispered commiserations with coworkers, I was able to refocus on my dumb luck at being able to get a job after September 11 at all. Although the late nights, fetched lunches, and ninety-minute commutes left me tired and irritable, I was managing. The long rides to and from Staten Island, however, made it hard to socialize with anyone on a weeknight, so I jumped at the idea of meeting a fellow Potterhead nearby.

Soon I was waiting for Meg at a nearby Scottish pub. She was an assistant, too, at a Broadway producer's office, and was even later to our appointment than I had been. She'd assured me she would be the one who looked like Lily Potter, and she wasn't kidding; she was easily the tallest female my age I'd ever met, with the reddest hair, which fell all the way to her waist in heavy locks. I waved and she sat across from me, and within minutes we were sipping wine and discussing our separate fandom experiences. We swapped September 11 stories, as it seemed everyone in New York was doing at the time, and I explained how the Potter community had gotten me through the day; I also told her how much I appreciated the Sugar Quill, both for teaching me about fanfiction—I was even acting as a "beta" reader for my online friend Rebecca, editing and fact-checking her three-part series about Severus Snape—as well as providing me with a small knot of adult, similarly passionate fans who didn't want to reimagine Jo Rowling's work, just celebrate it and mine it for clues. Sometimes the act of participating in fandom felt like being part of a long, global, real-life version of the movie *Clue*, in which Jo was the madcap butler, performing a complicated and dizzying act of explanation, and the Sugar Quill community was helping me track, record, revisit, and discuss each crucial plot detail so I could try and figure out whodunit before the plot resolved itself. Even though we knew we had as much chance at guessing the ending as Harry did at getting through a school year without a death match, it was nonetheless maddening and exciting to try.

I was also immensely grateful to the "SQ," as fans called it, for explaining and making accessible to me a rational forum for "shipping" discussion. The whole concept of "shipping" was new and confusing to me, though it started to explain some of the fanfic notation I'd come across—H/H meant that the story was Harry/Hermione, or a story whose romantic persuasion favored Harry and Hermione. Not all the abbreviations were obvious: R/H was Ron and Hermione, but H/R was usually Harry/Ron. Sometimes Hermione was abbreviated as "Hr" to avoid confusion with Harry (H/H was often rewritten as H/Hr), and putting Snape and Harry together (I confess my mind screamed "yuck!" at the idea of the foul, greasy Potions master ever enjoying a romantic relationship with *anyone*, never mind my favorite wizard) resulted in "Snarry."

On some forums there was no taboo on portraying adult/minor, teacher/student, or even incestuous relationships. While part of me could understand why fanfic authors would want to explore those relationships fictionally inside the construct of the world Jo had created, and I could even see it as a healthy outlet for creative expression, I just couldn't read it. Harry felt too dear to me to exclude him, mentally, from the same societal protections I encouraged in real life. Thankfully, at the Sugar Quill, I found a community full of people who felt the same way; they only wanted to explore relationships (the word which is at the root of the term "shipping") that were consistent with the character relationships represented in the books. They still flirted with unproven pairings, like that of Sirius Black and Remus Lupin, or mildly impossible but nonetheless immensely writeable ones, like Draco Malfoy and Ginny Weasley, and those were welcome dabblings. Above all things, however, above all else, they were steadfastly, resolutely, in the camp that said that Jo Rowling was purposefully writing the Harry Potter books in such a way that Ron and Hermione were destined to be paired, and it was this, more than anything, that made me want to hug Meg on sight.

"I don't get it," I told her, leaning forward in my seat. "I don't under*stand* how anyone could think that Harry and Hermione are going to get together!"

I'd spent weeks online, agog, watching as fans passionately, militantly, argued that Harry and Hermione were destined for a relationship in the real Harry Potter books and not just to continue to enjoy their rampant alternate-universe (AU! another acronym learned) fanfic pairings. I had absolutely no problem with people who *preferred* that Harry and Hermione ended up together, but thoroughly failed to understand how anyone could read the books and not only think Harry and Hermione were a good match (which I understood if I didn't agree with) but dismiss the idea of Ron/ Hermione out of hand. It had gotten frustrating; as a newbie on one message board, I'd timidly voiced my opinion without realizing I was on a site heavily slanted toward H/H shippers, and I was quickly shouted down by so many members I didn't bother going back. So, to find Meg and the entire Sugar Quill community was like being given my discharge papers from the nuthouse.

Meg peered at me for a moment after my H/H exclamation; then her face opened into a grin and she laughed. "Oh, I knew I'd like you," she said and we both cracked up.

We started e-mailing furiously, and the elation of having a real-life, nearby friend who got it, who understood my obsession, was like a drug. Soon we had started our writing weekend tradition, in which we'd laugh over coffee, talk about life and men, and use the time to shake off our crap jobs by hanging out with Harry Potter. Our meetings were like a much-needed antidote to the dour-faced life under my boss. At work, my supervisor and I could huddle in the kitchen area and whisper our gripes; with Meg, I could complain with loud abandon. Later, after another downsizing, when the "editorial" part of my job was completely stripped away and I was spending most of my time filing Denise's credit-card receipts, hanging with Meg and talking Harry Potter made it more bearable.

Our friendship, like so many others at the time, transcended the book series we both loved, but had only been made possible by a collision between Harry Potter and the Internet. We had the general sense that we weren't the only ones whose lives had been similarly affected by Harry Potter, and that feeling of community was starting to bind our Potter-related activities like the tendrils of a slowly snaking plant. It was happening all over the world; the rapid spread of fanfiction, message boards, online chat rooms, and fan sites kept fans occupied and entertained between book releases and allowed new fans to celebrate with those who were like them. Meg and I hadn't fully "hung out" unless we had read message boards together or posted on them, or shown each other fanfiction our other online friends enjoyed. Our community, which I had only recently learned was called a fandom, started to rise off the computer screen and take on a form other than that of handles and screen names.

At that point, the online fandom had just hit its flash point, which had been a few years coming; though the seventh Harry Potter book would have a record-breaking first print run of 12 million copies in the United States, before *Prisoner of Azkaban* was published, global sales of Harry Potter were just approaching one million. Soon that number would balloon to 7.5 million total copies sold. If every one of those 7.5 million copies represented just one reader, and all those readers bought one copy of the future books, that figure would represent about 30 million copies sold. Yet the books' popularity wouldn't just grow by a factor of four, or five, or six, or ten over the coming years. After *Azkaban* but before *Deathly Hallows*, that number would inflate to 325 million—or almost forty-five times its business since the sale of the third book. The books were blazing precedents on their own, and would have burnt up existing publishing records whether they had a constant digital supply of gasoline or not, but the Internet, a limitless repository of discussion and enabler of obsessive personalities everywhere, gave Harry Potter an additional star turn as the first property to enjoy a ravaging, insatiable fan base online.

In 2000, the UCLA World Internet Project estimated that the Internet had become the "fastest growing electronic technology in world history." It took the Internet a fraction of the time—five to seven years—that it had taken electricity, telephones, and television to become part of a significant number of American homes. The first popular Internet browser, Mosaic, was making Net surfing popular from 1993. About three years later, the Internet was in use by about 19 million people in America; by 1998 that number tripled, to 57 million—or 104,000 per day, 72 per minute. And in 1999, that rate accelerated by close to three times, to about 274,000 new users per day or 190 per minute. By the time 1999 flipped over into 2000, more than 100 million people in just America were connected, and it was flourishing similarly in Sweden, Britain, Japan, Singapore, Korea, and Spain.

The Internet's user base tripled between 1998 and 1999. Between January and April 1999, during which time no Harry books were published, the series' global absorption rate had been quintupled, from 150,000 to 750,000 copies. About a year later, that number became 19.8 million in the United States alone—more than 26 times what it had been. Print runs for *Harry Potter and the Goblet of Fire* were planned at a million and a half in the U.K. and 3.8 million in the States, and incrementally increased elsewhere in the world as well.

In that crucial period, between 1999 and 2000, the Internet changed Harry Potter about as much as the Internet was changing everything else. The Internet at the time was a shadow of what it is today: the pages were called "dynamic," but the information was really static: information lay flat on the page, perhaps sometimes linking to another article. Leaving comments or otherwise allowing a page to interact with users was a severely limited practice, except in the form of rudimentary message boards, which were the user-friendly answer to Usenet newsgroups and other bulletin-board- or e-mail-based systems of earlier years. Communities easily formed on message boards, which required an identity and sometimes, at that point, a profile, in which you listed details about yourself that may or may not have been honest, and allowed others to see this true-or-not personality.

By the first quarter of 2000, more than three quarters of people were checking their e-mail at least once a day; more than half had achieved a high-enough trust threshold to buy things online; less than 10 percent felt the Internet was too expensive. Most used it at home, and for Web browsing, e-mail, hobbies, news, and entertainment info—it was least frequently used for jobs or homework. The UCLA study showed that Internet use corresponded to education: the more education, the higher the chance they were comfortable with the Internet. Similar things happened regarding income; more than 80 percent of people who made $50,000 or more per year used the Internet. Use declined sharply after the 46–55 age bracket.

People still shied away from meeting people online—except when they were under eighteen years old. Most did not reveal personal details online—except when they were under eighteen.

At the same time, the first Harry Potter Web sites were becoming known. The first fan sites, period, were becoming known, and because Harry Potter was the story of the day, and Harry Potter fans have never been known to let a good obsessive detail go untouched, Harry sites were becoming the most articulate and detailed fan sites out there. The nature of the plot of Harry Potter, like any good mystery, was to leave fans desperate to figure out the next step. As it became easier to navigate and communicate via the Internet, through rudimentary pages, precocious teens learned how to create those rudimentary pages and put them online.

In 1997, Jenna Robertson, a teen from Nevada, started what quickly became the most comprehensive Harry site of the day: it was called the Unofficial Harry Potter Fan Club and it was the first site I stumbled across in my early attempts to find a related community. It created an early standard: be obsessive, and give fans something to do while they waited for a new book. The site featured origins of Harry Potter words and names, puzzles, fonts, excerpts, fan art, fun quotes, fanfiction, and other distractions. Other sites were coming up, too: one of the first fanfiction sites, Harry Potter's Realm of Wizardry, started up in 1999; MuggleNet.com started in 1999 as well, drawn from the head of another bored teen, Emerson Spartz, and followed a similar model to the UHPFC. A lot of fan pages were hosted on Geocities.com or Tripod.com, early and popular distributors of free Web space in exchange for ad displays; one of them was the Leaky Cauldron, which went live in July 2000. Then fans became comfortable with the Internet domain registries, snatching up lots of smaller domains such as HarryPotterFans.net (the home of the Unofficial Harry Potter Fan Club), HarryPotterGuide.co.uk, and DProphet.com. The common rule for a fan site was simple: it must be run by fans, and it must incorporate some word or aspect of the series into its title. Beyond that, just have fun.

Social networks were becoming popular as well. Though they would peak to the point of insanity by 2007, where almost everyone who went online regularly had some sort of connected journal, Facebook account, or MySpace page, social networks began just as the Internet was hitting its stride. LiveJournal.com, founded in 1999, soon emerged as one of the strongest brands of glue between online friends. Previously, to get updates on your friends you had to go through the somewhat clunky process of seeking out their latest posts on message boards, or sending/receiving individual e-mails, or becoming part of a private e-mail group in which one message is distributed for everyone to read. LiveJournal was about making it personal. You got a user name, and "friended," or added, names of people you liked. Everyone on your list was added to a "friends" page so that all you had to do to keep up with your online network was click a link and scroll through the day's updates. Comments were integrated, so you could quickly leave a note of support, or laughter, or even a nasty comment, on someone's journal—in other words, you could build your friendships digitally. And then communities cropped up inside LiveJournal, so if you were someone who really loved Harry, you could simply join the Harry Potter community. If that was too large or too bland, you could then join the Draco Malfoy community. Or the Draco Malfoy Luvs Pansy Parkinson 4EVA community.

LiveJournal, along with the small networks like it, was like a spiderweb growing underneath a community, catching the members and connecting them to one another without requiring effort on their part. Since your friends on LiveJournal tended to share your interests, your friends' posts tended to be interesting to you, and it was easy to become addicted to reading and responding to other posts. The more friends one had, the easier it was to gain new ones; if someone looked at a user's friends' list and saw your name, which was more likely the more friends you had, you had just opened yourself up to a much larger audience than if your content sat on an isolated blog that someone had to actively seek out each day.

And so LiveJournal bloggers who shared an interest in Harry Potter were growing and grouping, and had been for years; they played role-playing games, wrote fanfic that interested one another, posted icons, and shared theories and essays. At the time, about 40 percent of users were under eighteen.

If the first three Harry Potter books were aimed at ages nine to eleven—and the judges of the Smarties Prize seemed to think so since in December 1999 it made Jo Rowling the only author to ever win the award three times, also in a row—then by 1999, those who had picked up the books as nine-year-olds were now eleven and twelve. Those who started at ten, or eleven, or twelve, were now preteens or full-fledged teens. In America alone Harry Potter absorption was bounding, multiplying, mushrooming outward, and feeding on only itself to do so, and children of that age were the same ones who were most likely to give out information on the Internet or form social connections online. The exact right people, the exact right fans, at the exact right time.

It was a lot easier, as a young adult, to be a fan with the Internet than without it; nondigital fan cultures used to connect via magazines and newsletters mailed to their homes, and since it usually took an adult to seek out a fanzine, children were largely left out of the picture, or at least left to be fans in the isolation of their neighborhoods and schools. Now they weren't only forming social connections but using Harry Potter to explore literary concepts by writing fanfiction. They were developing their artistic skills by drawing their favorite Harry Potter characters and scenes. Since socializing online had developed to the point where any piece of fanfiction or fan art was likely to receive responses and reviews, they were also becoming used to receiving and implementing constructive criticism.

This public use of Harry Potter for creative, if not wholly original, endeavors eventually attracted the attention of the flowering franchise's lawyers, who asked Jo Rowling whether she wanted to do anything about it. If she had started applying rules and regulations to her fandom the way popular author Anne Rice did in 2000 when she banned fanfic of her work ("It is absolutely essential that you respect my wishes," the author said on her Web site), it would have had an incalculable effect on the progression of her fanbase and probably driven most activity to password-protected or off-line communities. Instead, she chose not to do anything about it, and I asked what had led her to that stance.

"It was largely kids writing for kids—initially. I felt that we needed to be hands off, accept it as flattering," she said. She shifted a little as though something has tickled her back. "I've never read any fanfiction online. I know about some of it. I just don't want to go there. It *is* uncomfortable for the writer of the original work, I can say that freely. You appreciate what's flattering about it and yet, it's not a comfortable feeling to see a kind of cardboard version of that world erected and stuff moved around and the laws contravened. But if the Internet had been around in the time of Agatha Christie, this would have happened to Christie. Or Dickens! It would have happened to Dickens. Because there were writers who had very, very, very popular characters who created a world that people found immensely attractive. They wanted to go into that world and a great way of inhabiting that world was to write that world themselves. But of course it didn't [happen to them]. It happened to me, and I was the one who had to deal with [the repercussions]."

It soon became necessary to distill her stance; if she was okay with all fanfiction, was she okay with pornographic fanfiction? Or slash fanfiction, which were stories usually associated with male homosexual characters and the explicit details of their sexual relationships? Does encouraging (or at least not discouraging) fanfiction mean that writers of such stories can sell their work? The boundaries weren't defined, and though there were already vocal online fandoms for other works, none were so big or had so many members testing the outer limits of an author's permissiveness.

There's also a sense of entitlement that comes with creation, whether or not it's justified; while the community mostly displays a willingness to overcredit and overdisclaim (it's not uncommon to see a note atop a story that reads something like, "All these characters are J. K. Rowling's, I own nothing, I do this for fun, it's not my copyright, please don't sue me!") in the spirit of celebration of the series, there have been times when others have taken a less gracious stance. As she remembered one of these times, Jo looked down at her table and adopted the slight smirk that usually preceded a humorous anecdote.

"There was a fanfic writer," she said, "who wrote to my agent to say, 'How do I stop people copying my [Harry Potter] work online? How do I prevent them, legally?'" She paused for emphasis, but there was no need; I was laughing already. "There you are. It's all smoke and mirrors and you think, does anyone know what's real here and what's not?"

When Warner Bros., having just acquired the rights to Harry Potter, told Jo they were going to try and "corral, loosely, the fan sites," she thought of it as a relief.

"There's always the worry that things get hijacked, and this has got nothing to do with money, for really nefarious purposes. How am I going to control it? So, to me, it was a relief to know that someone was making sure that what was going on was okay. I was involved so much that they said, 'Are you okay with us doing this?' and I couldn't see a problem with it."

But again, Harry Potter fandom on the Internet was new, largely untested, and not yet understood by those inside or outside it; when Warner Bros. instructed its legal department to send letters to owners of sites that used the terms and images from the Harry Potter books they forgot to add, "but perhaps phrase it differently than a standard cease-and-desist letter, because some of these sites are run by children."

The blanket cease-and-desist letters that went out to owners of fan sites were, instead, on Warner Bros. letterhead, in a sober and polysyllabic legal cadence that would be enough to make a thirteen-year-old tremble—which is exactly what happened.

Claire Field, a British teen who ran HarryPotterGuide.co.uk, received a letter in early 2001 stating that her domain name was "likely to cause consumer confusion or dilution of the intellectual property rights" of Harry Potter, and that the domain name was "in our opinion . . . likely to infringe the rights described above," and that they would "put this matter into the hands of our solicitors" if she did not transfer the domain to the company.

Before she did anything else, she went to her father, who went to the press. The Brit tabloid the *Mirror* ran a feature story on Field, portraying her as a hapless victim of corporate avarice.

"Outrage. Absolute outrage," remembers Jo, and she was right: within weeks the resistance, PotterWar, was born.

At the time, Heather Lawver was a sixteen-year-old living in Virginia who ran a small site called The Daily Prophet, after the wizarding newspaper of the same name. The site was written a bit like fanfiction with a twist; the writers would take on Hogwarts identities like Cho Chang (who is from the books) or Larissa Potter, Harry's long-lost sister (who is definitely not in the books), and write in character, as though they were columnists in a newspaper. Like so many others, Heather had started the site when she was bored, but not just because she was out of homework or chores: Heather had been diagnosed with a bone infection in her left foot, and was confined to her bed.

Quickly she had a staff of volunteer children writing stories; she held them to Friday deadlines, relying on her love of writing and commitment to give one girl the credentials to be their editor at thirteen years old. One of her staff members, Lindsay, about twelve years old at the time, contacted her, crying, saying she had gotten a nasty letter from Warner Bros. and thought J. K. Rowling was personally upset with her and her site, besthogwarts.com.

"It was a really small kid Web site," Heather remembered. "It was nothing more than 'We love Harry Potter,' and that's it, and I was really infuriated by it because the timing couldn't have been worse. This poor girl, her father had just died the week before, she was already really vulnerable and upset and hearing her thoughts after this really scary legal-speak letter . . . she thought she was going to be taken to court and her family would lose all of their money and it would all be her fault. She was ready to turn everything over, and I said, 'Hey, wait a minute, no, they don't have the right to do that.' "

Heather's family, big fans of "Weird Al" Yankovic, had some familiarity with parody law and copyright infringement, and felt the free publicity Lindsay was giving the series was worth whatever overlap between parody and her Web site occurred. So Heather, stuck in bed, started doing Internet searches. She found out that the letters had been traveling all over the world, to Singapore and Poland and kids all over the United States and the U.K.—like Claire Field, whose lawyers she contacted.

Meanwhile, Alastair Alexander, an activist from London, was also fighting against the cease-and-desist letters; he had set up Potterwar .org.uk just to try to bring attention to Claire's plight. He had successfully led a similar campaign against eToys.com and was starting to gather the troops again. By February 2001 he was organizing a worldwide action campaign; he posted portions of Claire's letter on the site, started collecting news about the case, and suggested that everyone stick it to Warner Bros. by buying any Harry Potter–related domain name they could think of, a team action he called "S-Potter-cus." Sites supporting the PotterWar effort included HarryPotterWarnercan suemyarse.co.uk, and HarryPotterSucks.com.

Heather told Alastair she wanted to do something "very big, on a very global scale, to take them down." She had a plan: she wanted to hit Warner Bros. in the wallet.

But Warner Bros. was already backpedaling. After the first press reports about Field, Diane Nelson, then the senior vice president of Warner Bros. Family Entertainment, told *Entertainment Rewired* magazine, "we've been naïve . . . the studio's letter is an act of miscommunication. We never intended to shut down any Web sites."

Later, I'd hear the same; a Warner Bros. executive, with whom I was speaking on an entirely unrelated matter, was reminded of the old PotterWar and started shaking his head regretfully at the memory. He looked even embarrassed to mention it; he said the letter campaign was a big mistake, a matter of the law office doing what was technically its job but also not the right thing to do by fans, and had only happened because person A hadn't told person B what they intended on doing.

Diane Nelson still talks about it that way, too. "We made a mistake," she said. "We spoke with the girl's father and apologized. We recognized we were wrong and were fully prepared to change how we handled it."

The company had also just come out of a bit of an awkward phase with the property. Warner Bros. seemed to be struggling to fully grasp what it meant to have such an ardent, young, preexisting fan base, as well as involvement from the author—an author who had specific wishes about keeping the series free from overcommercialization. Studios weren't used to working or engaging with writers to shape a brand; it wasn't in their DNA. Nelson admits there was a learning curve—especially when substandard merchandise like Harry Potter paper towels and toilet paper, or prototypes of boys' underwear bearing the phrases Wingardium Leviosa and Never Tickle a Sleeping Dragon, made it to production. Or when a vibrating Harry Potter broom appeared on Amazon, and gathered some reviews that could be taken in naughty ways, like, "I was surprised at how long [my daughter] can just sit in her room and play with this!"

"The reality is, we had an opportunity," Nelson recalled. She and others at the company repackaged their entire marketing plan, instituting closer guidelines and controls, to try and approach Harry like an "evergreen" brand—one that they had to nurture now, because it wasn't going to fade. "I'd stand in front of hundreds of licensees and do speeches about how we were treating the brand."

There would be no product placement, and they would never use images from the films on the products. They ditched the typical global marketing partner scheme, in which about twelve big-name companies or manufacturers tied themselves to a property to help increase saturation worldwide. They only partnered with Coca-Cola, and then only allowed the Potter name to be associated with them for philanthropic purposes; there was no chance Harry was going to appear on a Coke can or slurp some fizzy drinks at the Great Hall's Gryffindor table. Only a Harry Potter logo ever appeared on a bottle, and even that campaign was short-lived.

While Warner Bros. and the Field family worked out their differences (Claire's Web site chronicling the incident says that Warner Bros. kept demanding the domain name) the PotterWar continued. Heather organized a worldwide boycott of Potter-related merchandise (except the books, because there was no grievance with Jo Rowling herself) and acted as the organization's spokesperson, a deliberate choice to remind their audience of the young, sweet face of Potter fans. She appeared in newspapers and on morning talk shows; and her youth, her eloquence, and her passion for bringing Warner Bros. to its knees made great media and garnered a lot of attention. I even took my best shot at writing a scathing piece against Warner Bros. for my entertainment column at *The Hoya*.

By June Heather's bone infection, osteomyelitis, which can migrate to one part of the body without leaving traces, had spread to her brain, giving her little to no motor or speech function. The letters to Potter sites were thinning, disappearing as though doused with acid. The Field case was dropped. Heather, meanwhile, was told she was going to die within six months.

"We knew we had won when the letters had stopped going out en masse; we knew we had won when Lindsay had her site, and she was taken off the radar, and she was no longer being threatened. [Alastair] had hoped to get at least a few more of our demands, but I needed to take care of myself. So it ended before its time. I was afraid that I was going to die completely senile at the age of sixteen, but PotterWar did a lot to kind of close things. If I had died, I would have been happy with the life I had led. I'd done something that wouldn't be forgotten, and I'd left my mark, and could leave happily."

Heather still doesn't know why she didn't die. Around August, her memory started coming back. So did her speech function. "Within a couple of weeks, I got better, and there's no explanation for it. I went to see every specialist I could—there is no medical explanation of why it went away."

To get rid of the bacteria altogether, doctors amputated half of her left foot; by the time Heather was seventeen, she was back to normal, but by age twenty she was diagnosed with Dercum's disease, which causes inexplicable pain and weight gain. Since there was so little known about the disease, she did what came naturally: she founded the Dercum Society, an organization meant to inform the public, comfort victims, and help support research for the illness.

Today PotterWar is an old reminder of the preenlightened Potter fandom; Warner Bros.' new attitude would soon branch even wider, in ways that directly changed the way studios treat all fandoms. The only concrete action Jo Rowling and her representatives generally take against sites now is toward those that are selling unauthorized merchandise or associating the series with pornography. Usually a representative will contact the webmaster and request that, if nothing else, they put their content behind a password or other age restriction, though sometimes they're requested to cease operation altogether.

Claire's site, HarryPotterGuide.co.uk, is still up, though it runs a disclaimer on top of its home page.

"This site is an unofficial Harry Potter site, and therefore should only be entered by people who fully understand that the site holds no connection to J. K. Rowling, Bloomsbury, Scholastics [sic] or Warner Bros. It is however meant as an educational experience for all ages, and is non-profit. If you fully understand this criteria, then please feel free to click on the banner below and enter."

CHAPTER SIX

Rocking at Hogwarts

t the utility entrance to Webster University in St. Louis, Missouri, Paul DeGeorge emptied half the contents of his van onto the street and buried his head in a soiled, white button-down shirt. He emerged with his face crumpled.

"You see this?" he said, shaking the shirt near my face. It was as smelly as fermented socks and still wet from the night before, which I could tell because Paul had just brushed some of the foul material across my nose. I crinkled and jumped back.

"Done!" He tossed it hard to the back of the van, where it fell into a crevice unoccupied by duffel bags, guitar strings, and the detritus of four years of touring. He bent over the bag of shirts again, like a Dumpster diver. "Those are the unused ones," he said, indicating a bag he wasn't even touching. "I'm trying to max them out."

It took three more smells, and then—"We have a winner!" The semiclean, least-smelly-but-still-pretty-rank shirt, the one that wasn't yet translucent, limp with sweat, or growing mold, was on him and buttoned up in a flash, straight up to a grinning face that might have belonged to a kid who had just romped happily through a sewer.

Inside, the college's Potterholics Anonymous club was busy turning their college group room into a mini-Hogwarts. Four girls, each with a corn-fed, happily midwestern quality, hung twinkly lights and banners representing the four Hogwarts houses.

"We tapped a keg!" one shouted.

"It's root beer," said another, rolling her eyes. "You can't say it like that when it's root beer."

Members of the band slowly rolled and hauled equipment in from the beat-up old van in which Paul had been shirt diving. A set of speakers that looked like it had once toured with Spinal Tap was propped up at the front, while Brad and Joe, their opposing statures like a string bean next to a baby carrot, weighed the merits of several wobbly platforms to see just how hard they could jump on them before they broke. This was arguably more important than a sound check.

The pixie-haired Emily, wearing her ever-present mini-backpack shaped like an owl, arranged T-shirts of several variations, CDs, posters, and toothbrushes out on a rickety folding table, then untangled a set of white fairy lights and draped them around her designated area as though she were a fairy herself.

Their setup done, the boys lingered around the space, waiting; Paul lay on his stomach on the air-conditioning unit, fiddling on his white laptop despite the large crack that had created a huge purple bruise on his screen. Brad sat behind the drums, his long arms and legs folding into position, and tapped out practice rhythms; the drumsticks moved lightly, as though of their own accord, but in time with his long, swinging hair. Joe's explosion of brown curls could be seen above the tilted plank of the baby grand piano, as he happily improvised ditties that tinkled throughout the room.

"Listen to this." Paul threw his legs under him and was sitting up in a flash, and the others crowded around to hear. "We recorded it just before we picked you up," he told me. "In the van."

A one-line wisp of computer-generated piano melody, topped with a rough and warbly vocal, came from the computer.

"Whenever I cut my hair / It always grows back fast / Whenever I cut my hair / It always grows back fast."

It was less than a minute long. Paul and Joe were grinning like Cheshire cats, and I privately wondered whether the rest of the song—the length, the content, the instruments, the arrangement—had gotten stuck in a wormhole.

"It's, um, it's good," I said warily, but the boys were busy chuckling in a self-satisfied way, repeating the track, and singing along.

A loud peal of laughter drew my attention to the small vestibule outside the room, where a knot of people were already waiting. Any other day they might have passed for students, but today there was no question why they were there, even if I didn't already know the answer. One look told it all: the small and geeky, in their robes and striped scarves; the parents carrying eight-year-olds on their hips; the Goth girls in dark lipstick and black Slytherins Do It Better shirts, the preppy collegiates in neat sweaters and Dockers, and the eighteen-year-old boys with gelled hair and hard faces, holed sweat jackets hanging over their Save Ginny shirts, were all there to take part in the adrenaline shot that was a Harry and the Potters concert.

By the time the doors were ready to open, the Potterholics had managed to transform the bland room, with its gray-knotted carpet and vaulted ceiling, into a dark and chapelesque space, hung with streamers and Hogwarts house banners, and a looped clip of floating candles from the Harry Potter movies playing on the wall.

The doors opened, and the band hardly looked up as the motley crowd streamed inside. Some of the girls giggled and eyed the guys, but for the most part the crowd didn't pay the band much mind; the band paid them the same courtesy. Paul and Joe in their civilian clothes weren't nearly as interesting to this bunch as the alter egos they were about to become. The brothers and their drummer casually strolled the room, while Emily presided over an already storming trade in T-shirts. A local band friendly to the guys named Someone Still Loves You, Boris Yeltsin—who once had a song of theirs featured on the popular teen drama *The O.C.*—opened for them, and the crowd acted respectfully at first, but were screaming, jumping fans by the end, completely devoid of the conventional attitude of ignoring the opening band.

When it was time, costume change took about ten seconds: two red-and-gold ties laced around each brother's smelly white collar, gray cashmere sweaters fell from mops of brown curly hair down to studded silver belts. In a complete inversion of the lazy calm of half an hour ago, the two DeGeorge brothers, transformed into slightly altered mirror images of themselves, ran onto the stage in their Saucony sneakers and waited for the crowd to stop screaming. Paul shouted, "I am Harry Potter!"

"And I am Harry Potter!" Joe replied.

"And we are Harry and the Potters!"

That is the integral start to every Harry and the Potters concert, and by now there have been hundreds. That goofy supplication, a request for the audience to accept their premise and take the comedic leap with them, is as essential a part of the show as the music itself. And that premise is that the DeGeorge brothers aren't just two science nerds from Norwood, Massachusetts, with a passing resemblance to Harry Potter, who sing songs about Hogwarts and magic, but that they are two separate versions of the boy wizard himself, the elder of which traveled back from the future to start a band with his fourteen-year-old counterpart.

It's a premise that could have only started as a joke, and that's exactly what happened. Sort of. The story of their origins has been told and retold until worn thin, a smaller-scale model of the story of Jo

Rowling's famous train ride. The two DeGeorge brothers, for a laugh and because they looked like the boy wizard, started a band about Harry Potter, and five years later were a sensation. But it was a joke. They always say it started as a joke.

That's actually a half-truth; the boys' original aim was certainly to make their friends laugh, and the whole time-traveling-wizard/ rocker concept—worked around the boys' physical appearances, a fleeting whim of Paul's, and a gumbo of ideas from their favorite geek-out movies *(Bill and Ted's Excellent Adventure, Back to the Future, Ghostbusters, The Goonies)*—was a kind of silly stunt worthy of "Weird Al" Yankovic. But there was nothing terribly flippant about the band's birth, about Paul and Joe hastily but earnestly writing songs at their parents' kitchen table while their father served up a barbecue for their friends outside. There was nothing disingenuous about their insistence, from day one, on carrying Harry's idealism and morality into their songs. Paul's idea for the band had come more than a year previous, and he had tried (sometimes by rambling in drunken urgency at friends' parties) to convince his musical friends to get involved in it. Some of the songs they wrote at that first session later went unchanged onto their first album and still comprise their most popular show fare. Later, hundreds of spin-off bands would give themselves names like The Butterbeer Experience and Justin Finch-Fletchley & the Sugar Quills, claim the DeGeorges as inspiration, and incorporate their do-it-yourself spirit and Harry-centric creativity into a blossoming new music genre that Paul and Joe called "wizard rock." Harry and the Potters had always been funny, but were always more than just a joke.

Technically, they did not write the first wizard rock song. That honor goes to the Switchblade Kittens, a punk band who had minor success when three hundred college radio stations picked up their version of the Celine Dion dram-o-rama "My Heart Will Go On." The Kittens wrote a short song that caught the Potter fans' zeitgeist between the release of the fourth and fifth Potter novels: "Ode to Harry Potter," a song apparently sung by Ginny Weasley about her unending crush on the Boy Who Lived:

> *I can't help but blush when you're near me*
> *But you just exclude me from your circle of three*
> *I'm right in front of you*
> *But you don't see*
> *You treat me like I'm a Colin Creevey*

Set to electric guitar and keyboard melodies that wouldn't have been out of place in an eighties video, the fun, danceable tune was released at the end of 2000 and by the end of 2001 had been downloaded more than three million times. It was passed around between Potter friends the way must-watch YouTube videos are shared today, partly because at that time the fandom was still new enough that we were all agog that Harry Potter–themed music even existed. I was handed my copy on an audio cassette at one of my first gatherings and urged that I *had to listen to this*. I did, incessantly.

By 2003 the Kittens had performed at the first-ever Harry Potter conference. Paul and Joe had no idea what had started: they hardly knew there were Harry Potter Web sites, never mind gatherings.

Norwood, Massachusetts, the suburb that produced Harry and the Potters, looks like anything but a breeding ground for future standard-bearers of time-traveling rockers/wizards who advance anticorporate agendas. The town looks more like it walked out of a pastoral painting: the clean town square; the neat hedges that curve around driveways; the old, ornate, and architecturally distinct houses exude a massive dose of New England charm without being too affluent, touristy, or snobby about it.

Music had always been a large part of the boys' lives and was never an excuse for them to be overly serious. The elder DeGeorge was just reaching puberty as the early 1990s saw the surge of the supergroup New Kids on the Block, and though a fan of the sugar-pop music, Paul had created a parody band by the time he was in fifth grade. The New Kids' hit "Cover Girl" became, to Paul, "Shaving Girl," and "Didn't I (Blow Your Mind)" became "Didn't I (Blow Up Your Garage)?"

"Weird Al" Yankovic surely had a hand in these farcical leanings, but almost more to blame than anyone else for the Harry and the Potters revolution is They Might Be Giants, the band known for its superfluously catchy, short songs about unusual subjects like math. Through TMBG, it seemed cool to be weird, cool to like traditionally dweeby things like math and science, and cool to use music to tell short, funny stories instead of bemoan your love life. Paul passed the music on to his barely school-aged brother, and by the time Joe cleared sixth grade he was playing in Ed in the Refridgerators, a band with a misspelled name that clearly had TMBG to thank for its inspiration. The songs were about random subjects like having cooties or taking care of Sea-Monkeys (as literally derived from the instruction manual), and typically lasted no longer than a minute or two (which might have been because Joe was playing on Paul's old 1963 Gibson Melody Maker, which was so battered it fell out of tune after about that length of time).

But as Joe grew up trying to express his adolescent self through light and catchy music, Paul's tastes started running darker, and truer to the age. The New Kids' sugar high was over, and teens were swinging the other way musically, with a new genre of music that plugged into their disenfranchised feelings. Grunge music had arrived from Seattle, and as Paul was turning to music the way some other boys turned to sports, he found that the movement's forefront band, Nirvana, had songs to offer that thrummed with anger, confusion, and the familiar teen disillusionment. In particular, "Smells Like Teen Spirit" spoke to Paul's feelings of frustration and helplessness during his most awkward growing phase. Through Nirvana he found the Pixies, the already defunct alternative group from Boston who had had a lot of success overseas. The idea of listening to music that wasn't massively popular presented Paul with a secret allure, like he'd be part of an exclusive club that didn't include inaccessible high school girls or other trappings of typical teenage life.

He wandered to the record store to pick up *Surfer Rosa*, the Pixies album that Kurt Cobain spoke of most often. The famous cover of the album arrested him when he saw it: on it, a flamenco dancer, topless, chest thrust outward as though performing a dance move, stands in the center of a ruined room. There's a poster on the far wall that's been ripped to shreds, and a crucifix on the other side. Religion, freedom, brashness, and sex in one picture—it seemed to dare Paul to enter.

"I was, like, am I even allowed to buy this record?" he remembered. He talked himself into it, nervously approaching the counter with his money and scurrying home with it in his hands lest the Music Chaperones came to nab him. He remembered putting the album in his "crappy little boom box, and the world changing instantly. It's just an assault. It totally changed the way I look at music."

Instantly he knew why Nirvana said "Smells Like Teen Spirit" was their attempt at ripping off a Pixies song. It was just blaring, direct, unvarnished sound—no comfort, no conformity. He thought it was the best thing he'd ever heard in his life, and began wearing an old Pixies shirt like a second skin.

He bought a guitar, became a DJ, and started frequenting the famous Lansdowne Street, a strip of nightclubs and music venues in the area. But he still thought music would only be a hobby.

I joined the guys in St. Louis in the first week of March. They were halfway through their spring-break tour, which had been scheduled around Joe's break from school. By 6:30 a.m. the morning after the Webster University show, we were awake and on our way to Troy, Michigan, a nine-hour drive. We were running late by 8:00 a.m. because during breakfast, someone made the mistake of mentioning to Paul that the motel had a Ms. Pac-Man machine. We almost had to pull him out of the place with bagel tongs from the continental breakfast tray.

The van sometimes looked tan, and sometimes gray, and was always dusty; the finger-written "I love you Harry Potter!" may have been there since 2003. They bought the van for $14,000 a few years ago, and it holds the secret to their success: the traveling public-announcement system. They bring the show with them, so that they can play a full set anywhere there's electricity.

Large as the van is, on the inside you have to pour yourself into a seat; after everyone piled in and we hit a few road bumps, the excess merchandise, clothes bags, food, water, pillows, mix tapes, CDs, and other junk accumulated over the years shook down around us and held us in place. It was not worth the energy to shift position; the front seat, with your knees smacking the dashboard with each bump, was luxury.

Everyone had a job. Emily, who ran merchandise and often acted as a den mother, made sure everyone had water, then took out a laptop and started updating the band's e-mail list, copying the new addresses out of the notebook they keep on the merchandise table and into their Excel spreadsheet. Paul's proud of his spreadsheets: as the de facto band manager, he created spreadsheets that tracked merchandise sales, attendance numbers, and costs of touring, so that he could accurately predict how many people they could expect at each venue, how much they could expect to spend, and how many T-shirts they'd need of which sizes on which part of the tour. When she was done updating the lists, Emily started counting the money from the night before, which was kept on her person at all times, in a little backpack. One person had to keep track of directions, which were usually loaded onto a computer from the last time the group had Internet access; the computer stayed live via an adapter stuck into the cigarette outlet. Someone was always in charge of the music. And usually one person at any time could sleep.

It was snowing by the time we arrived in Troy and navigated to the church. The guys had played in churches before, usually in a workroom with fluorescent lighting and blue carpets. This church seemed to grow out of the hill it was on, like a hut on a sand dune. We were already late, so there were at least ten kids spilling out of the entrance. By now I was de facto crew, so like everyone else I shouldered some gear and prepared to help make setup quick and painless; we followed our guide who was leading us to the setup spot, until we got to—

"The sanctuary?" I said in disbelief.

Paul and Joe looked beside themselves with delight. No bland activities room this time; the altar had been moved back to leave room for the musical equipment, and the concertgoers were all sitting in the pews as if mass was about to start. Something about the sheer blasphemy of it all instantly keyed the Potters up, and the prospect shook off the cobwebs after our long, cramped, quiet drive. They skipped up and down the steps to haul equipment, exhorting about how cool it was going to be to play "The Weapon" or "Save Ginny" under the huge metallic crucifix on the far wall.

Unconventional performance spaces was a specialty of the De-George brothers. Paul went to college at Tufts, where he quickly took over as booker for the university's concerts, and immediately started thinking about ways to parcel out their budget more effectively. Instead of renting out a PA system for each show, he convinced the organization to buy one, which paid for itself quickly in saved rental fees. He shaved costs further by hosting shows in campus living rooms and classrooms instead of renting halls. By the end of the year he left the group with a rare budget surplus, and used it to book better bands, buy better sound equipment, and do other things that he had no idea would inform his later career.

He graduated in 2001 and went to work in Boston as a chemical engineer, helping to develop vaccines. He was starting to feel frustrated with the whole Boston music scene, and the continuous booking up of his beloved Lansdowne Street for concerts produced by Clear Channel. All his old haunts, and the places in which he'd found his musical identity, were becoming sanitized and corporate. As a small act of protest, he started a record label named Eskimo Labs and used it to support and produce albums for bands he liked.

That summer he and his brother read the Harry Potter books. All Paul's—and by extension, Joe's—ideas about the corporatization of rock, and the way the feeling, the connection he remembered from music was being supplanted with efforts by companies who were only concerned with profit margins—were being mirrored in Harry's fight against the establishment, his underdog status, and his ability to overtake power figures. One day, offhandedly, Paul wrote in his journal, *If you want real rock, you have to go to Hogwarts.*

The thought nagged at him. *Wouldn't it be cool if Harry had his own band?*

Joe was happily strumming along in Ed in the Refridgerators, playing in shows and on radio stations that liked his barely-old-enough-to-rock-out vibe. As he grew, he, just like Paul, started to resemble the now-famous boy wizard, and during an Ed show, someone actually shouted at him, "I love you, Harry Potter!"

That was it for Paul. After the show he pulled Joe aside and told him about his idea. Harry and the Potters—it would be Harry and his friends, such as Hermione on bass and Hagrid on drums—and Joe should just take the idea and go.

Joe's friends weren't into it, so the idea went nowhere until summer 2002, when a potentially good rock show went bad. Two of three bands canceled on the DeGeorge brothers, leaving the concert they'd planned for their backyard little more than a garden party. Six people showed up.

Paul, half joking, half happy for the risk-free environment in which to try out his idea, grabbed Joe and blurted out, "Let's do Harry and the Potters."

They sat in their cramped kitchen at a wooden table that overlooks the backyard, and wrote three songs that would do the work of explaining the concept of the band to them and to their showgoers. They didn't want to fight over who would be Harry, so they took a page from *Back to the Future* and implemented a time-traveling story in which Harry in his seventh year, as played by Paul, had gone back in time to start a band with his former self.

Harry Potter Year 7 and Harry Potter Year 4 became Harry and the Potters, and their first songs were dabblings in what would eventually become their signature simplistic, narrative style. "Problem Solving Skills" tells the tale of saving the Sorcerer's Stone, while "I Am a Wizard" is the musical interpretation of the first few chapters of the first book. They wrote a song about Quidditch that was never played again and the mention of which still makes Paul wince. They tried to write songs about things that were unique to wizards: You can't take a bus to school like everyone else? You have to take the train? All right, here's a song:

> *The bus don't go to Hogwarts*
> *You have to take the train.*

They decided, almost instantly, to write all the songs from Harry's perspective, partly because "writing songs about yourself is really funny," Joe said.

"It just made things really interesting, because you could work with the character instead of working from the outside," said Paul. "You can craft a personality. It's not only easier but I think it presents a more interesting listen. Because the listener is getting a character's perspective, and we put so much of our own selves into that character, too. Our Harry is a lot more outgoing, obviously."

"And not as much of a jock," said Joe. "More of a punk rocker."

"We tell people our band is what it would be like if Harry quit the Quidditch team and started hanging out with the band geeks."

They rustled together graduation robes, a sweater vest Paul dug out of his closet, and whatever ties they found that looked close to the Gryffindor colors. They wore their own glasses.

They didn't care how good they or their just-created songs were: they went out to their backyard thinking, *We wrote all these songs this morning! Look!*

They played, opening for Joe's band, and their friends had a non-reaction, as though the brothers had gotten a funny new pet or showed them an interesting Internet link. It was a similar non-event to their parents, who had seen enough of their goofy band ideas to view this as an equally passing notion. Dad DeGeorge made burgers for everyone, and the idea could have died right there. Joe continued his Ed gigs. Paul went back to playing in his band, The Secrets, which broke up shortly thereafter over creative differences.

But when, only six months later, they learned that the fifth Harry Potter book was coming out, they thought it might be time to try again. This time they'd try to book some shows. They sent a demo CD to a manager at Borders, and soon had their first gig as the Harrys.

"We booked these shows at Borders [for the release of the fifth book] and thought, oh, man, we've got to write some songs," said Paul.

They wrote a CD's worth of material in April, intending on having their first album ready for sale at their shows. They divvied up the work: Joe took *Harry Potter and the Prisoner of Azkaban*, Paul took *Harry Potter and the Chamber of Secrets*, and the brothers made notes about which parts might be good for a song. Paul would pick out a melody on his Casio keyboard, and bring the recording from his Jamaica Plain apartment back to Norwood for Joe to add a vocal or keyboard track. It was musical short-order cooking: one added salt, the other pepper, and they put the product on the counter. Another song done!

They released the self-titled album at the same time as book five and with about opposite the amount of fanfare. Despite the many mistakes, rough performances, and thin sound quality, it boasted undeniably catchy melodies and set up their entire ideology as a Harry band. The songs were short, fun, about the books, and very repetitive. They only worked particularly hard on one song: "These Days are Dark," a light pop track about the fight against Voldemort, that insists:

> *These days are dark*
> *But we won't fall*
> *We'll stick together*
> *Through it all*
> *These days are dark*
> *But we won't fall-all-all.*

The mood is lighter, even cheery, compared to the end of book four, the narrative ending point to their album, which sees Harry leave Hogwarts under the gloomy shadow of Voldemort's return.

"That's what everyone was left with for three years until the next book," said Joe. "And everybody's hanging on that, and we didn't want the album to end on a negative note."

For their logo, they wanted something iconic, something that said rock and Harry Potter, but had the minimalism they already recognized was evident in their songs and style, so a friend designed a logo in which he wrote *Harry and the Potters* in the same font that's used on the covers of the American editions of the books; on that cover, the *P* in *Potter* extends down as a lightning bolt; for the Potters' version, the first *H* does that, and so does the last *S*, scissoring out in a long lightning bolt until it intersects a guitar.

Paul used $1,200 of his own money to pay for the pressing. They silk-screened T-shirts in their backyard, using photo emulsion chemicals, and had several of Joe's friends stamp out about two hundred. One design, their Save Ginny! tee, is their most popular seller and still sports the same rough-hewn image: a silhouette of a basilisk that looks more like a construction crane than a snake, and a paper-doll-like girl, with the Save Ginny! motto printed in black and white on a grass-green shirt. Their one other design was a T-shirt print of their album cover.

Since their first show the previous June, they'd found real Gryffindor ties on eBay, gray cashmere sweaters (the fabric was vital, since cashmere repels the stink of sweat) from a vintage clothing store, white-collared button-down shirts (also from eBay), Converse sneakers, dark jeans, and black leather belts with several rows of studs on each side. Paul thought the latter would be a nice punk-rock touch, as if Kiss had given it to Harry for Christmas. They ditched the robes—too hot, too constricting.

Just before their show at Borders, a woman called asking if they wouldn't mind doing a photo shoot to promote a local bar. It would be at The Rack, a now-closed pool hall/bar/meat market in Boston, next to a pizza restaurant and as flashy as the red neon sign above its doors. The photo shoot would be racy, advertising the boys as sex icons in Gryffindor ties.

"*Ew*, no way," Paul said, face crumpling at the memory. "Why would Harry Potter appear in an ad for a bar for some stupid publicity photo?"

They hadn't even played for a real crowd yet and already had an offer to use Harry Potter's icon status to do what they considered to be selling out. An ethos emerged. Their strong adverse reaction was fueled by their identity with Harry Potter. Harry Potter would never pose with sexy girls for publicity. Harry Potter would never play a show that kids couldn't get into, to help sell alcohol. Harry Potter would never sign with Live Nation. Harry Potter would never milk their listeners and fans for overpriced merchandise or albums. Harry Potter would fight the dark forces of evil and the record industry establishment as if they were one. Harry Potter became an invisible partner to Harry and the Potters, whose moral choices would abet and guide their own as they tried to carve a niche just left of the music industry.

On the way to Toronto, the next stop on the tour, we started talking about Joe's glasses, which were causing Paul a slight anxiety attack.

"These are my glasses from junior high. One of the ear things broke so I held it together with duct tape. And one of the screws fell out, so I flossed it together."

"Flossed it together?"

"Yeah, there's floss where there should be a screw." I checked—the floss was curling out the side.

"Just like Harry's," I said.

"I'm trying to buy him new ones," said Paul, in an undertone.

"Forget it. No way. These glasses are mine."

"Can you at at least get some as backup for the summer tour?"

"Why?"

"What if you lose the lens?"

"I won't lose the lens."

"You'll lose the lens."

"No way."

"You almost lost the lens twice."

"That's only because the floss was loose."

"But what if the floss comes out, you lose the lens, and you don't know it?"

"That won't happen."

Paul threw up his hands. The brothers were similar in many ways, but much more different than they were alike. Paul was the logical, sometimes uptight one, who worried about the status of instruments, the merchandise, and how much time they'd need to get to each location; Joe seemed to live on a different plane than most people and was as likely to lurch into an improvised song or start talking near-nonsense in a strained, alien-type voice, as he was to partake in a rational discussion. Other times, he was just quiet, and I found myself curious about what was going on in his head more often than I was about most people.

The show in Toronto was at the Tranzac club, a nightclub that sometimes served as a theater or community space, but had a proper stage setup and sound system. A folky band with at least six members, with some on triangle, glockenspiel, and instruments I couldn't recognize, opened for the guys. Their music was pretty enough, but I could barely hear the words, and when the set was finished I realized that the main singer had spent so much time looking at his keyboard that I had no idea what his face looked like. About fifty people offered them polite applause, and when they were done, the band got beers and stood by the bar, watching the three hundred or so fans waiting for the Potters. "You can tell their fans by the scarves," one said to the other, with a hint of derision. But by the middle of the set—the Potters' loud, thumping set, full of a kind of energy I couldn't even imagine having, and with the boys emanating a volume of sweat I couldn't imagine possessing—their stance had changed. As Paul and Joe urged everyone to believe in the power of love and use their imaginary magical guitars to fight the forces of evil in the universe—as they insisted that music and, somehow, the plot of *Ghostbusters*, had relevance in the fight against Voldemort—the folk band members stopped leaning against the bar, took their hands out of their pockets, shook their heads in time, and looked around incredulously. The same one who had mentioned the scarves said, "They're kind of like us."

"The first shows were bad," Paul said, and Joe looked like he would have said it if Paul hadn't. Bad, bad, bad. That didn't seem to matter to the fans, though, who gobbled up their concept. Almost instantly the boys were a hot act, selling out local libraries. One librarian began e-mailing her fellows. Soon Paul was getting unsolicited e-mails from neighboring town libraries, asking the Harry Potter band to come play in their town.

Online, where the great and continuously expanding gorge of Harry Potter fans met daily, the Potters' presence was generally below the radar. The Switchblade Kittens' "Ode to Harry Potter" was still making rounds but was considered a quirk and not the herald of a major movement.

At the end of September 2003, the name "Harry and the Potters" started appearing on small blogs, journals, and the burgeoning Live Journal.com. Bloggers talked of this cute little band whose members looked like Harry and who sang melodically simple, sometimes off-key songs about Harry Potter. Then, on September 25, 2003, Cassandra Claire, whose Draco fanfiction was still earning her props from the teen set, made a short post on her LiveJournal, which was usually as comic and pithy as her fanfic and as slavishly read by her fans.

Am I the only person who has never seen this before? she wrote, linking to the band's music download page. *They're kind of catchy, really.*

More than a hundred comments followed Cassandra's post. Her readers who had blogs reblogged, and those who found out about it through those blogs reblogged, and the band was suddenly seen, by the fans who were then the opinion makers of the Harry Potter world, as endearing. Paul's in-box started to fill up.

On September 27 three separate Harry Potter Web sites posted about the band: Veritaserum.com posted and sent the info to MuggleNet.com, who also posted it, while one of Leaky's editors found the band through the LiveJournal circuit, and also mentioned them as news—all almost simultaneously. All the posts were short and simple, no more than a line—*there's a band called Harry and the*

Potters, and one of their cute songs is called "Save Ginny Weasley," and they're fun. But that was enough.

The DeGeorge brothers barely knew any Harry Potter Web sites existed much less frequented them, so when Paul opened his in-box that day to find scores of letters from fans, he was flummoxed. He started working his way through them—some were really positive and flattering; some were full of vitriol and attacked their talent or what the writers saw as a lack of it.

"We were like, what the hell is a LiveJournal? What the hell is a MuggleNet?" he said, laughing.

The community gave him its first gift at the end of that month: a $400 Web server bill for excessive downloads of the 3–5 megabyte files of sample music on their site. Paul panicked and took the files down immediately, but for Joe something sparked.

"That's when I realized we could tour," he said.

By the next summer they had recorded their second record, *Voldemort Can't Stop the Rock,* which was mostly based on songs about *Harry Potter and the Order of the Phoenix.* Their title song, on the surface about the evil characters in Harry Potter, started turning up the volume on their political sides—it contained lyrics like, "and we won't let the Dark Lord ruin our party / just like Tipper Gore tried with the PMRC," referring to the 1980s effort to label and restrict what parents considered "offensive" music. That song became less about Harry Potter than a Harry and the Potters anthem, and they were starting to realize they could really succeed at this effort—if they weren't sued. It was a side thought that had plagued them, and now, with real success looming, it was blossoming into a full-blown worry. Paul was already doing research on parody law and socking it aside like ammo.

They toured lightly throughout 2004, and for the summer, Paul got a two-month leave from work. The guys played more than thirty shows, tracking their way across the country and back, skipping most of the Midwest. Their largest crowd was one hundred fifty people in a children's room in a San Francisco library. The crowds were picking up in intensity, and thanks to some college radio play, people were coming to the shows already knowing the words. In Seattle they met the Parselmouths, a band consisting of Brittany Vahlberg and Kristina Horner, two sixteen-year-old girls who claimed the Potters were their inspiration and in thanks presented them with a Hogwarts toilet seat and sweaters with their initials on them. The girls had taken the Potters' do-it-yourself idea to heart and gotten their music some airplay by leaving it on their answering machine and handing out their number for people to call.

By this time Paul was starting to think he could, perhaps if he tried, make rent out of this gig and live on the band. He chewed on that through the winter of 2005, when, on Joe's break from school, the two-person band decided to hit the road, then the ocean, and try their luck in England.

England, the birthplace of Harry Potter, wasn't as into the concept as the boys expected it to be. They played to crowds of five and eight people. In Manchester the amps blew. The weather gave them a proper British welcome, dribbling rain and just enough snow and sleet to make the moods and the driving miserable. Paul was the only one who could legally drive the car, so he drove them around for eight days.

Their memory of the trip is laced with bitterness, shot through with the irony of being symbolically rejected by Harry's birthplace. Yet it may have just been an outgrowth of their mood, of the rain cloud that was following them around independently of England's shoddy weather. Just before they had taken off for London they had received a letter from Warner Bros. that said, in effect, that they were violating copyrights and trademarks, and that both parties needed to talk.

Paul and Joe bristled with stick-it-to-the-man-itis, fitting handily and happily into the mold of scrappy punks trying to avoid getting stomped on by the giant corporation, a thin rebirth of PotterWar. They weren't going to take this lying down! Fight the man!

Paul sent back a letter written by a lawyer friend, listing several cases that supported their right to exist. It was like David whacking at Goliath's toes with a stick; they set their stance and envisioned legal arguments, a grand fight, and a panel of robed judges handing down a victory for the little guy.

What occurred was far less glamorous. A two-and-a-half-page letter came back to them quickly, listing several case citations to show they had legal grounds upon which to make their claim. However, Warner Bros. was a man to whom it had already been stuck, with PotterWar, and didn't seem too keen on repeating the experience. The company representative asked to speak to Paul on the phone.

Marc Brandon called him a few days later. At the time Marc's department at Warner Bros. was mostly concerned with shutting down bogus eBay auctions, and his main concern with Harry and the Potters was that their online sale of T-shirts and other merchandise would spiral past the point of quirky margin and endanger WB's hold on their merchandising trademarks. After a few rounds of negotiation, he told Paul that they could continue to sell their music online, but anything else was verboten except at live shows, about which WB would simply not concern themselves unless they caught the brothers in the act. Take everything but the CDs off the Internet, and "we'll never talk to you again."

Despite the thrill they had at the prospect of a real fight against the "man," that was a trade the Potters were happy to make. By the end of the conversation they were exchanging pleasantries.

"Man, you've got to come see us play," Paul told Marc, then quickly took it back. "I'm kidding. I don't want you coming. Stay away."

Now comforted by an oral promise, Paul felt the band was only safe as long as it didn't become a huge threat to Warner Bros. He'd gotten the feeling from WB that they viewed Harry and the Potters as a fun curiosity, and would rather the band continued in fun than take action against them. Their merchandise problem, it seemed, stemmed from the $100,000 or more licensing fee that official Harry Potter merchandisers paid to produce related work; those sellers might start feeling put out, especially if children were attracted to "cooler" merch designed by amateurs. Harry and the Potters non-audio business went completely off-line.

Paul quit his job, and Joe planned to defer entrance to college for a year so they could tour almost full-time. But by then others were getting the bug. In April 2005, the Potters played a show at a friend named Matt Maggiacomo's house in Rhode Island. It was the second time they had played there, and this time the friends were planning a little backward surprise for the Potters. Bradley Mehlenbacher (the Potters' future drummer) and Brian Ross, half brothers and musicians from the area, had decided to make fun of the Potters by writing a couple of joke songs and open as "Draco and the Malfoys," who would clearly be the band's natural nemesis. They poked at the Potters' time-traveling joke of being Harry Potter Year 4 and Harry Potter Year 7 by calling themselves Draco Year 15 and Draco Year 19 (to correspond with their true ages). All their songs were about that snotty little Potter boy who gets too much attention at school, and were vicious yet monstrously tongue-in-cheek—such as in "My Dad Is Rich":

My Dad's always there
To open all my doors
You have to call a Patronus
Just to catch a glimpse of yours.
My Mom says she loves me
When she tucks me into bed.
How's your mommy doing
In the Mirror of Erised?
My Dad is rich
And your Dad is dead.

It was all cute and funny and intended as a joke, but as Paul and Joe could attest, you should never do it unless you mean to, because jokes have a funny way of coming true. Matt Maggiacomo, a long-time guitarist and writer of "regular" songs, had decided he'd also poke fun, by "becoming" The Whomping Willow, the violent tree from the Hogwarts school grounds. Instead of writing songs, he simply played "Carry On Wayward Son" by Kansas, and swayed for the full five-minute-plus duration. Neither of the joke bands thought they would survive past the night, though they enjoyed the raucous reception they'd received from their amused friends.

What they didn't yet realize was that more and more Potter fans were taking the Potters' cue and doing what the Parselmouths had done: creating bands based on other aspects of the series. But it was hard to gain a fan following for music online; the Potters had only gotten popular with fans because fans had been able to listen to their "cute" songs. Then their popularity only grew so fast because they were playing shows incessantly and had experience, equipment, and free time with which to do it. Not all bands had any one or two, much less three, of those things. It didn't seem possible for what was fast becoming the wizard rock genre to become one in which any-one but Harry and the Potters got to perform professionally.

But then came MySpace.

By 2005, the social networking site MySpace.com was white hot, gathering more than 25,000 users daily. Growing alongside its main popularity was its popularity among music lovers; the site allowed bands to upload music for free and gave them a tool with which to play the songs right on their site, taking care of all the associated bandwidth costs and providing an alternative to the increasingly common standoffs between record companies and music dilettantes who downloaded too many MP3s off file-sharing networks. MySpace made music easy to hear and easy to spread.

Just as in 2000 the maturation of the Internet prodded a fledgling Harry Potter fandom out of the nest, MySpace urged wizard rock into consciousness, working constantly behind the scenes like the gears behind a watch face. The first band to put its profile online was the Parselmouths, the two teen girls from Seattle; they had started to develop characters for their band, conceiving themselves as popular Slytherin girls who everyone loves to hate. In late 2005, Harry and the Potters put up their profile, and started directing people there from their Web site. The site also provided the Potters with an easy way to directly contact their fans: for the first two years or so that Harry and the Potters used them, MySpace had a feature that allowed bands to target their "friends" who lived in a certain area. Playing a show in Oklahoma? They could send a quick note to who-ever on their friend list was in the area or anywhere near it. They had been carefully collecting an e-mail list at every show—but if two hundred people went to a show, they got maybe ten signatures on the notepad. Now the thousands of people "friending" them didn't know they had also signed up to be notified when the Potters were in their area, but why would they mind an e-mail letting them know when the Potters were in town? It was the kind of direct marketing strategy larger companies would pay thousands to create. With that kind of contact, they could, and did, send out a bulletin letting everyone know exactly where they'd be in each spot and could gather a crowd with almost no notice. With their verbal Warner Bros. agreement, that crowd was necessary, because merchandise sales and performance fees funded most of their operations.

Within five months of putting up their MySpace, they had five thousand friends. In a year, it was more than thirty thousand. In another year, they would be well above the eighty thousand mark. Those numbers are representative of a much larger underlying fan base, and one for which any "legit" band would kill. They were one of the biggest success stories of the MySpace heyday, and their strong identification with the main themes of the books made them naturally attractive to anyone who liked Harry Potter. Of course, their name didn't hurt, either, nor did the fact that they looked like Harry Potter and their music was funny. If Harry Potter itself had started with a stir among young people in schoolyards and independent booksellers, and largely because it was funny, then Harry and the Potters were experiencing a rise similar, but on a smaller scale, to Jo Rowling's.

They were also becoming known for—and identifying the burgeoning genre with—their habit of rocking in libraries. In their earliest shows they found a niche that had been largely unexplored: the fact that not all libraries were the dens of silence that most people associated with buildings full of books. Some had activity centers in them as well, or had theaters and produced shows, or rooms where they hosted author readings or even small local bands. And of course Harry should be playing in a library. It was yet another slight dig at "the man" to be turning up the volume intentionally in a place that wanted you to quiet your speech.

Their summer 2005 tour was sparse, just a few dates on the West Coast and a couple near Boston and New York. But with the advent of a new Harry book came a flood of press and a cadre of reporters looking for a fresh way to talk about Harry Potter; soon they found themselves in the *Boston Globe* and *U.S. News & World Report*, and on Forbes.com.

They spent the release day of *Harry Potter and the Half-Blood Prince* playing at a bookstore in Michigan, and then took a few days off to read. Almost immediately they had two songs that would be on their eventual next album, *Harry and the Potters and the Power of Love*, both of which centered around two of the biggest events in the book. "Dumbledore" became a simple but increasingly complicated song, a paean to the headmaster who dies at the end of the book. The other was the inevitable Ginny love song, which they shot through with bursts of saxophone and a solo section. At live shows, Paul would sometimes use that section to wax for twelve minutes on love and the movie *Ghostbusters*. The song was an instant hit, and soon no show would be complete without a performance of it, or that long monologue. It's their "Free Bird."

Meanwhile, Brian, Bradley, and Matt were doing absolutely nothing. They didn't want to encroach on what Paul and Joe had created, but they were getting antsy: they had ideas and had written songs. Matt, especially, realized that he wanted in on this fun subgenre and had retired the Kansas album in favor of a real Whomping Willow song, about how rude it had been of Ron and Harry to crash their car into his branches. Both of the bands wanted to play shows.

Paul was still paranoid, though, and a bit overprotective. He and his band had just survived a brush with Warner Bros., and he was still feeling the aftershocks; now he had to fund his life, and Joe's college tuition, on their effort, and what if some other band shattered the fragile trust he had worked to build? After all, nothing had been signed; it was simply a gentleman's agreement and for all Paul knew Marc was no gentleman.

The other bands came up with rules to try and ease this fear: they wouldn't play a show unless they were opening for Harry and the Potters; they wouldn't release an album unless Harry and the Potters said it was OK, and they wouldn't sell any merchandise online, as per the agreement with Warner Bros. The Dracos and the Whomping Willows (as Matt was now calling himself, in the plural) would never be projects they could use to support themselves, anyway, the members thought—not without "Harry Potter" in the title. They played a few shows and kept a low profile.

Alex Carpenter, however, knew nothing of the wizard rock status quo when he started his band, The Remus Lupins. The writer/actor/ musician from Southern California could not have presented a more polar opposite to Paul and Joe DeGeorge's floppy, messy, modest scruffiness. In early 2005, Alex wasn't even a Potter fan—he had, in fact, poked fun at kids at release parties—but that would change when he saw the third Potter film, which had been directed by Alfonso Cuarón, a director he loved. And then, to impress a girl, he said, he read the books. His wasn't an all-consuming love, but he liked a lot of the elements of the story, and one night, laughing with friends, he got out his guitar and wrote and sang a quick song about Professor Snape. At this point, he swears, he had never heard of Harry and the Potters or any wizard rock. His friends insisted he put his music online, so he did, goofily naming himself The Remus Lupins because he thought it was funny for a one-person band to name itself in the plural. He made a MySpace account to host his new songs. He put up the Snape song, and another he'd written about Luna and Neville. By October 15 he had a full record.

Alex approached things differently than Paul and Joe. He almost immediately took the band seriously, and, instead of touring incessantly in small venues, he held contests on his MySpace to help spread the word. His album art usually included pictures of himself, and his band description was more self-promotional than others; he was from Hollywood, and his family had ties in the film industry—to Alex, this was just what you did when you had a project you wanted to publicize. He would answer every MySpace comment he got, and because teenage girls found him good-looking, he quickly attracted rapt attention from a lot of young fans. Around Thanksgiving of 2005, he opened his MySpace to discover he had about one hundred seventy friend requests, an overwhelming difference from the week before.

The established bands—that is, Harry and the Potters and the would-be Draco and the Malfoys and Whomping Willows, the latter of whom was languishing due to "the rules"—didn't like this new guy. He was pulling himself away from the pack, and he was playing shows *in Los Angeles*. What if a Warner Bros. person just showed up and saw Potter-themed merchandise on sale? The other bands monitored his online activities quietly. Finally Matt, who's always been a bit of an antagonist—like the Whomping Willow, ready to attack, willing to make incendiary blog posts or write long-winded, brutally honest e-mails that delivered blows—sent Alex an e-mail in which he made it clear that Alex's actions were making them uncomfortable. He explained "the rules," told Alex he was "flaunting" the movement and they would prefer if he would reel things back so as to not jeopardize things.

Alex didn't bite. He thought the rules were "absurd, and the last one [which required he didn't play a show without the Potters] was just unfeasible" for him geographically. "I interpreted this—perhaps incorrectly—as 'stop playing.' Follow these rules or stop playing. And I certainly wasn't going to give in to all these demands."

After a lengthy chain of e-mails, Alex won. Matt started agreeing with Alex. Why were Harry and the Potters deciding what he did with his band? Why was everyone so uptight and paranoid about Warner Bros.? It started to feel like everyone was working too hard to protect the Potters' career, and eventually the Potters, specifically Paul, agreed. Alex was going to play shows no matter what; the age where the Northeast contingent of wizard rockers could control the flow of the movement was over. The only way to stay involved in it was to swing to the other side and start nurturing it. It was either become the grandfathers of wizard rock, or become the type of rock that weeds grew around. They chose the former: Paul (Joe was still in school and mostly uninvolved in anything but creating songs and playing shows), along with the Whomping Willows and Draco and the Malfoys, started to take on a more advisory role, offering the newer bands tips on how to avoid getting stomped out by Warner Bros. and how to best honor the movement and the ideology of Harry Potter.

And then wizard rock exploded. Whether because of the Potters' new attitude or not, because Alex was playing shows all over the West Coast or not, new bands were cropping up faster than anyone could count them.

By the summer of 2007, the genre further distilled itself: there were folk bands, electronica and techno bands, groups that sounded like the Beach Boys or the Indigo Girls, and some that channeled showtunes' lyrical vibe or Rage Against the Machine's guttural screams. Draco and the Malfoys, after a year touring with Harry and the Potters, started doing solo shows and were becoming headliners in their own right. Their onstage personae as Dracos funneled the character's pent-up book rage into song, exhorting about kicking Dobby, killing hippogriffs, and getting back at Harry (whom they always refer to as "this kid at Hogwarts who gets far too much attention for his own good," a mantra that the crowd now routinely chants with them). Matt Maggiacomo quit his day job and is a full-time, touring Whomping Willow; his version of the violent tree is now an activist and (naturally) environmentalist, who has a crush on Hermione and founded his own Hogwarts house ("the House of Awesome"). Even the Switchblade Kittens returned to wizard rock and put out a filly wizard-themed album in 2006 called *The Weird Sisters*.

Yet for all the bands' worrying about the movement becoming far too big for Warner Bros. to continue ignoring, very few bands posed such a threat because few played actual shows. Mostly the phenomenon manifested in hundreds of MySpace profiles in which children, completely new at music, created songs and posted them just for the heck of it. That was true of then seven-year-old Darius, whose parents, Tina Olson and Ian Wilkins, had wizard rock bands called DJ Luna Lovegood and The Cedric Diggorys, respectively. After seeing the Potters perform at a nearby library, Darius recorded a few songs about dragons, one of which mostly consisted of him shouting, "Dragon rock rules! Dragon rock rules!" over a computerized music track, and made a band profile showing off his music. When Paul and Joe found out that they had been the inspiration for a seven-year-old punk rocker, the brothers contacted the Wilkins family and insisted that Darius open for the Potters the next time they were in town.

Now the two bands—the Potters and Darius's The Hungarian Horntails, which consists of him and his younger brother, Oliver—play together fairly frequently, or at least whenever there's a significant wizard rock event at hand. Ian and Tina never miss an opportunity to bring the whole family to a wizard rock show, which often means outings as far as Boston from their home in Pennsylvania. In the first week of June 2007, Tina and her barely week-old daughter, Violet, trekked with the whole family to The Knitting Factory in New York City to watch a Potters show. Darius and Oliver tired themselves out by running around the venue for three straight hours, while three-year-old Holden hung on his dad's leg. Baby Violet sat in a papoose against her mom's breast. Meanwhile the Potters were shouting and strumming and four hundred fans were dancing and drinking. Tina, with her pixie blond haircut and hippie sandals, swayed as though the Potters were singing a lullaby, and Violet slept.

Meanwhile, MySpace was doing the heavy lifting of publicity for Harry and the Potters, but they were getting critically noticed, too. Their shows were praised as being among the top five live shows in 2005 by Pitchfork Media, the Web site that could literally launch bands to stardom with one good review; the site's positive one about Harry and the Potters at the New York Public Library ("The Decemberists wish they could lit-rock like this") meant that they could get booked almost anywhere.

That note is almost entirely how I became a wizard rock fan, because it led the Potters to a big booking at the Knitting Factory in New York, a landmark venue known for the way it fostered music without borders. They played in early June 2006; Cheryl had dragged me there, swearing over and over again that I would like them. I'd heard them and thought they were fun, I admitted, but didn't really like the music. Frankly, I didn't think much of their musicianship. Cheryl assured me it wasn't about that at all. She had her finger far closer to the pulse of the movement than I ever had, but perhaps that was because she worked at Scholastic, whose relationship to Harry and the Potters seemed to be that of the mom who thought her errant child was too cute to punish. The potential for copyright infringement was technically Warner Bros.' lookout, so Harry and the Potters was gaining a secret but ardent following at Harry's publisher.

It was the hottest night of the summer so far, and once I had gotten inside I was glad I'd worn a linen dress. The air was thick and the dance floor an impenetrable mass of people. I had brought my video camera in case the show proved coverage worthy for Leaky. As little girls in Hermione Granger outfits clung to their fathers' hands, and teenage girls in more adult Hermione outfits gyrated to Draco and the Malfoys' opening, hilarious music, I started taping.

I squished myself to the front of the line at the merchandise table; CDs and toothbrushes (and was that floss?) were being sold at lightning pace, hands passing overhead and underhand, exchanging money. When the Potters finally hit the stage, they did so bounding, reflecting energy until the room was buzzing with it. Their opening joke had been heard before by most of this crowd but they laughed anyway, and the Potters tore through an hour-long set that made the already sweltering basement seem like it was pressure-cooking a few hundred pounds of pasta. The floor was slick with everyone's sweat but no one seemed to care. The fandom was alive and throbbing right in front of me, and I hadn't ever seen it so vibrant in the flesh before. The celebratory feel was intoxicating, as the Potters took the joke-and-wink of their existence at the beginning of the set and turned it into an exploration of the awesome force of love on the universe and the idea that moments, small moments, are all that make up our lives. They had a kind of transcendent purity that, by the end, had eviscerated the irony with which they presented themselves. At first they were a joke, and they made a lot of jokes throughout, but by the end they were a vehicle of the messages of Harry himself, perhaps with a clearer mind and louder voice than Harry, at that post-book-six point in the series, had been able to achieve. They were living Harry Potter books. There in the basement of the Knitting Factory, I saw two exhausted and sweat-slimed young men use their simple, self-aware, lyrically sparse, single-ridged melodies and not really on-key voices to persuade a crowd of teenagers to middle-agers to jump in time, pump their fists, and play air guitar to one repeating, commanding chorus—"the weapon we have is love, love, love, love, love." They brought it alive by jumping offstage and into the waiting crowd, by getting right in their faces and urging them to join in as if it were their personal mission to make sure the ground shook with the stomping of six hundred pairs of feet.

By the time they clambered back onstage the crowd moved as forcefully as any mosh pit ever had. The boys grabbed their instruments and played loud and hard, so that above the shouting a triumphant keyboard and guitar blared. At the last, long, trembling note, which wavered off into nothingness, Joe shouted, "Thank you, everybody! Keep rocking, keep reading, keep loving!" There was no encore, though the crowd was primed for it; that last number was the expected end, the usual catharsis that accompanied a Harry and the Potters show.

I couldn't stop raving to Cheryl afterward, and she simply wore her smug grin that I knew so well. Paul, hearing I was from Leaky, had loaded me up with CDs following the show, and when I got home, I went to my trusted friend, the Internet, to discover with some shame that this movement had completely escaped my reporterly notice as it had flourished. Besides the Malfoys and the Whomping Willows, there were bands about Hermione, Ginny, the Weasleys, Remus—basically any Potter character worth exploring had a MySpace music profile attached to it, and songs under its name. Wizard rock was an actual genre.

The last night of the tour was in Montreal, in a small association room for the local Ukrainian organization. The stage had been cut out of the far wall, as though a square hole had been punched through, and on it Harry and the Potters looked like puppets in a diorama. The space was once used for a famous show by the band Arcade Fire, and just the notion of playing there, too, had the guys glowing with anticipation. They had only announced the show a few days prior because of last-minute scheduling, and yet about one hundred people showed up, dancing from the moment they entered. Paul, Joe, Emily, Brad, and I joined in, celebrating the end of the tour. Tomorrow we'd travel back to Norwood and blast "Born in the U.S.A.!" as we crossed the American border, then drive past the first library the band had ever played in and the backyard shed where they'd had their first show.

"It's a pretty good job, you know?" said Paul. "How many people can get other people pumped up on life, music, or art? It's a special thing and also a worthy investment of our time to do that, I think."

He said he felt he and his brother had become better musicians in the times they'd spent as the Potters, and were "grateful to WB in a lot of ways, for letting us continue. We feel almost privileged that we've been able to do what we do. I think that for one instance in the history of copyright law a major megacorporation finally understood the value of allowing certain fair uses of their property, in catalyzing people around that."

They'll stop touring after the summer of 2008, they said, and after that only play a special show here and there. ("You can only be Harry Potter Year Four for so long," Joe said sadly.) They wanted to play the two remaining states they hadn't yet visited: Alaska and Hawaii. Their dream last show is in Jo Rowling's backyard; were she to invite them to do it tomorrow, then tomorrow would be their last show—from their backyard to hers, they said. But then it would be time to pack it in. Paul planned to open a hot dog shop, or become a consultant for youth programming in libraries, or something. Joe had no idea what was next. He wants to continue to study science. He says it's the new magic.

We had dinner at the guys' house in Norwood before going home. Their mom greeted them back from tour with a steaming plate of pasta fagioli and a Waldorf salad. They piled their equipment into the small cellar under the house, which had become Harry and the Potters' warehouse, complete with their first-ever T-shirt silk screens and the panties that had been thrown at them in concerts. Joe and Paul's mom drove Joe and Emily back to college, and Paul saw me off to my train home. I'd had an unexpected amount of fun traveling with them, I said. Seeing people in every city and celebrating Harry Potter through music and community had been liberating and validating.

"It's a shame you guys at Leaky have all this stuff going on this summer," Paul said, almost absently. "You guys should come on tour with us."

CHAPTER SEVEN

Work-Life

our?"

John and Sue were both skeptical when they got my exuberant phone call.

"Tour! It'll be so great! We'll tour the podcast! Has *anyone* ever toured a podcast before? That's how we'll celebrate *Deathly Hallows*! With Harry and the Potters! Rock shows and podcasts together, we'll bring the celebration *all over the country*, come on, it'll be amazing!"

I told them both of my experiences on tour with Harry and the Potters, and of how at each show they'd done, people had come up to me to say they listened to Leaky's weekly Potter-themed Internet talk show, PotterCast, and how often someone wished they could attend a live recording someday. At one point the Potters' drummer and the part-time Draco and the Malfoy, Bradley, flush with excitement, broke free of the knot of fans surrounding him after a show and tapped me on the shoulder.

"Melissa, I just signed a T-shirt that *you signed, too*." I wasn't sure what he was getting at until his face broke into a huge grin. *"Awesome!"*

The day after Paul had brought up the idea of a tour, I cornered him and said, "Were you serious?"

"About what?"

"About touring with us, with PotterCast."

"Yes!"

"No, seriously, you were *serious*?"

"Yes, I'm serious!"

"Hm. Because we haven't really set our *Deathly Hallows* plans in motion, yet . . ."

He sent me the band's list of tour dates, and we started to plan. I sent a proposal to our podcast sponsor, Borders, to ensure they were behind us and would help us finance the cost of renting a van and feeding four people for the duration. For two weeks at the end of June, we'd do podcasts early in the day in the cities where the band was playing shows, and then encourage our audience to go to their nearby concert that evening. We planned for three joint shows, always at libraries (because the Potters were now way too big for any one bookstore to accommodate). We'd open for them. Paul offered to reverse that order but I nixed the idea; no one wanted to settle in for an hour of discussion, no matter how fun, after sweating their butts off at a rock show. After two weeks of shadowing the Potters, we'd break off and do our own podcast-only touring, because they were heading back east to be in Boston for the release of *Deathly Hallows*, and we still didn't have any idea where we'd be. John, Sue, and I put aside the decision for the moment. All we knew was that we wanted to be together for it.

A few months after I met Meg in 2002, she moved to Baltimore to shift her career toward teaching as well as to be near Jennie, one of her best friends and coadministrator on the Sugar Quill. The weekend of her good-bye party, I met Kathleen, a petite, curly-haired girl who was attending graduate school at New York University. She was also a Sugar Quiller, and was someone I'd corresponded with on message boards before. Everything about her presaged her future career as a kindergarten teacher: her clear, careful manner of speech, as though she were constantly explaining the virtue of raising one's hand for potty breaks, the invisible directional lead she always took in group outings, and her youthful enthusiasm over all our shared geek-out moments in Harry Potter, made us an instant match. Soon I was spending many nights with her, her boyfriend Shane, and the rest of our group—a spot-on Ginny clone and artist named Polly, who was so fair-skinned and sweet it was as though the "anna" had been accidentally omitted from the end of her name; Elizabeth, a vice president at an accounting firm whose passion for the superiority of New York among cities surpassed all other things in her life, even Harry; and Mike, a physics graduate student with the twirligig hair and round eyeglasses of a mad professor. At least once a week I saw one or all of them; we went to movies, tried out new restaurants, and watched chick flicks (above Mike's objections). We didn't agree on everything, but we did play by the basic understanding on which we'd formed our Harry Potter–related friendship—canon was better than non-canon, and Ron and Hermione were a fait accompli—we talked about Harry Potter a lot, but not all the time.

I was also falling deeper and deeper into my work on Leaky and the ability it sometimes had to excite the fandom. Every e-mail I got thanking us for a particular news story or providing us with a scooped tip was like fuel. Mostly we were still just collecting links to other news stories, but that was satisfying and necessary work for Harry Potter fans who liked to be kept informed. I was still reporting mostly when I was at work late, or home, or on the bus, though I did check my e-mail more regularly throughout the day. I was becoming almost the only person updating the site, and that suited me fine.

I was also determined to get our fan venture recognized as real press, mostly because I was tired of everyone raising an eyebrow when I told them what I did in my spare time. It was no different than covering any other beat, I thought, and I had a modicum of experience attending press junkets and movie publicity events from my college reporting days. At least, I thought, fans should have access to the big publicity events.

The second film would be out in a few months, so I started e-mailing random people at Warner Bros., whose info I got from the *Hoya*'s old contact list, at least twice a week. I never got an answer, but I continued to repeat the same introductory e-mail over and over again. "Hi, I'm from a Harry Potter fan site; I'd really like to set up a relationship where we report on these movies!" was the basic message, but I filled it with a lengthy dossier on my experience, the site's value to fans, and why I thought they should start paying attention to us.

When, in the course of working on the site, a particular question came up about filming, I would call the studio; the phone offered me even less positive reinforcement. Sometimes the people on the other end of the line suppressed a little laugh when I told them I was from a fan site, but they were mostly polite. However, they seemed not to know what to do with me, and once I was transferred from the original person who'd answered the phone, I knew I'd be transferred four or five times, and then the conversation would end with me realizing that I'd been forgotten, slapping my cell shut and returning from my lunch hour to appease Denise's latest whim.

In the summer of 2002, my bus trips home were usually full of catch-up Leaky work on my laptop. I'd hook it up to the network before I left, download my mail, and work on the way home and on the way to work in the morning. Though I usually sat uninterrupted, there was one persistent middle-aged man who had a habit of sitting down next to me. He waited until I shut my computer and turned to reading, and then would pelt me with questions that made me want to fashion my book into a cudgel and use it to render myself deaf.

"So, is that book good?"

"Work OK today?"

"Lot of traffic tonight, huh?"

I would slowly look over the book and give a polite nod, go back to reading and hope he'd evaporate. One night I was juggling my laptop on one hand like a waitress's tray and had my phone in the other ear while I navigated to my seat; I had finally gotten someone to transfer me to hold at Warner Bros., because there was some sort of lingering question about when *Prisoner of Azkaban* would be filmed, and I decided one more hour of telephone humiliation wasn't too much to ask. I had a strategy for Old Bus Guy, too; I would sit on the aisle until he got on the bus, then transfer to my preferred window seat. This way he couldn't sit next to me without asking me to move, and he usually didn't. He usually was forced to sit elsewhere, in a different row, out of earshot. Tonight he found a seat right across the aisle, and tried to catch my eye but I pointedly ignored him. The bus made all its stops and headed for the highway. I moved over to the window just as someone named Barbara picked up my phone call.

"Hi! Hello! Oh, finally!"

Barbara Brogliatti was the nicest person I'd yet spoken to about Harry Potter. She didn't even sigh when I told her I was from a fan site, and took my question about the filming schedule, which frankly only fans would want to know, seriously. She told me she'd investigate the discrepancy while I held, and all the while I was ignoring Old Bus Guy's attempts to catch my eye.

"Ms. Brog—OK, Barbara, thank you." Yes, it's for the Leaky Cauldron, we're a fan site," I said, though I was trying to keep my voice down because phone calls were generally looked down upon on the bus and I was a frequent breaker of that rule as it was, and this was my normal 7:30 p.m. crew who knew me as the girl with the laptop and the cell phone always blinking. I also kept my voice down because I had just said "the Leaky Cauldron" and "fan site" in the same sentence, and had to also try and sound authoritative about it so that Ms. Brogliatti took me seriously. And the old guy was tapping on my seat to get my attention.

"I'm on the phone!" I shot back, gave him the best fierce look I could muster, and whipped my head around so my hair flung.

And we're all trying to sleep! someone behind me hissed.

"All right, Melissa, well, it seems they're going to take a short break for the filming between two and three after all," Barbara said in my ear.

"And I can report that?"

"Sure!"

"Great! Thank you! So nice to speak with you!"

"And you, too!"

I sighed and clicked the phone shut. The next day Barbara admitted that she didn't do enough in the Harry Potter film world to give me consistent information, so she passed me on to someone else, who passed me on to someone else, who passed me on to publicist Marc Cohen, who treated me nicely and answered my questions. The information was vetted, of course, but it was real information about the filming schedule of the second and third movies. From then on, when we had a question about a filming schedule, or a weird casting rumor, I had someone at the end of the e-mail chain to address it. I was never happier than when some ridiculous rumor surfaced and Leaky got to squash it. We were the only ones who cared about the ridiculous rumors enough to check, and WB was happier than anyone could have ever imagined to help us get the word out. It felt like our information had actually helped.

At the end of the summer Marc had let me know that I would be able to see a screening of the second Potter film ahead of time, which was like manna from heaven. I took a breath and sent him the next question, in very halting, unsure terms: would it be too much, if they didn't mind, because we had proven that we could be responsible so far, to ask for Leaky to go to the upcoming New York press junket for *Chamber of Secrets*? I checked my e-mail obsessively, refreshing every moment until I got a response from a woman I'd never spoken with named Brenda. That was encouraging; it was an indication that my e-mail had been passed around and discussed at Warner Bros. Her words, *Sure, Melissa. Let's make this happen,* sent me immediately to the ladies' room to sneak in a few personal phone calls.

Warner Bros. had gone from threatening fan sites with closures less than a year ago, to inviting them to be within spitting distance of the actors the next. I felt like an experiment in fan inclusion; I couldn't remember ever hearing anything about a fan being involved by the movie studios for any property, especially on a large film like Potter. I babbled about it on the phone to Kathleen, and we celebrated with a movie night.

Every day, though, we were more and more consumed with the prospect of the fifth Harry Potter book. I'd been searching the Internet for information on it since I'd joined Leaky, as though hitting a certain number of Internet searches would make alarm bells ring and reveal the answer to its publication date on my screen. J. K. Rowling and her people had been quiet, and we were starting to get desperate.

Somehow, miraculously, I got the morning off work the day of the junket, most likely because Denise wasn't in that day. As is typical, the junket was held at a hotel. Every time someone asked me what news outlet I worked for, I surreptitiously changed the subject. I acted as much like a perfect professional as I could during the round-table interviews with the director and producers, to show Warner Bros. that I wouldn't scream and faint every time someone from the films entered the room. Only after the press conference, when I got to see the main trio of actors, who looked more like tiny figurines of fully grown movie stars than actual children, did I lose composure and follow the other hundred people to the front table to request an autograph. I got one from Rupert Grint, who was an active BBC message board poster, and who heard me mutter something about my Web site and said, "The Leaky Cauldron, yeah, cool!"

Back at MTV Networks I paced around my little cubicle. I'd already asked for a lot that day. Mimi, my supervisor, who had bright copper hair and a sharp tongue, came by to drop something off in Denise's office, and I looked at her pleadingly.

"What's up?"

I twisted my fingers and launched into the speech I'd been practicing all day.

"Mimi, Dan Radcliffe, the kid who plays Harry Potter, is going to be downstairs at MTV later and I thought I could go down and cover it for the *Pages*. It's big news that Harry Potter is in the building, and I'm sure if I could get inside I could get a little interview with him or at least a picture and use stuff from the junket on the pages and it would be really highly read!"

Mimi gave me a long look and rolled her eyes. "Go. Don't take long."

I squealed and grabbed my tape recorder and ran. I waited in the little internal vestibule that separated the building's corporate offices from its trendy and much-photographed studio. I'd only been in there briefly, once before, to cover a makeover show. Now I stood casually among the hundreds of people rushing in and out for lunch, and waited for someone whose card had the right kind of magnetic stripe. They swished their card through, opened the door, and I rushed in behind them, showing the guard at the door my card as proof that I worked in the building. He barely saw me go by.

The hall was empty and cold, which made me sure I'd gotten there before Dan's entourage. The green room was welcome, empty, open, with just one publicity lady from MTV Networks sitting inside. We knew each other and I hurriedly confessed that I was ostensibly there trying to get an interview for the *Pages*, but I had really sneaked in to try and meet Daniel Radcliffe. She laughed, said she thought my "interview for the *Pages*" was a great idea, and let me stay.

An hour later I was sure I'd made a mistake. How long could it possibly take to get Daniel there, and at this rate would I still have a job by the time he showed up? People kept trickling in, and soon I was one of ten or eleven others in the green room, including some band with weirdly colored hair about whom I knew nothing and didn't much care. I stepped out of the green room to give them a wide berth.

At the end of the hallway the doors swung open once more and I almost didn't even look to see who it was. So many people had come in and not been Daniel that I didn't even expect to see him anymore. However, the sound that came through the door wasn't of one pair of feet; it sounded like a regiment. I looked up to see a diamond formation of huge, black-suited bodyguards, talking into earphones and looking all around them, and at the head of the pack, looking like a child king, was Daniel. He walked through as though alone, and whooshed past me and into the green room; I figured it was over, that I'd never get to meet him now. But to my amazement none of the guards gave me a second glance as I reentered.

Inside, Dan was sipping a soda and pulling at the cuffs of his over-sized jean jacket, once in a while scratching the back of his neck. I didn't dare go near him. My press lady friend and I stood in a corner and tried to look like we weren't staring.

I gathered my courage. No sense coming this far and getting no-where. There was a distinguished looking gray-haired man getting coffee from a table who looked important. I carefully approached him and introduced myself, and winced when I got to the part about—

"The Leaky Cauldron. I do that in my spare time but I work here, upstairs at MTV," I said. To my surprise that was the less important part of the sentence, because the man to whom I was talking bright-ened and extended his hand.

"The Leaky Cauldron? We read that site all the time. I'm Alan, Dan's father."

My hand moved to his, very slowly.

"Thank you," he went on. "Thank you for treating my son with respect. We appreciate it. You guys do a great job."

I looked back at my publicist friend, irrationally expecting her face to reveal that this had been some elaborate practical joke. But she wasn't even looking at me. I turned back and stammered out a thank-you in return, and searched Alan's face, finding only kindness and genuine appreciation, no trace of mockery about the fact that I was a grown woman who worked on a Harry Potter fan site. A few people I knew could take a note from his tolerance, I thought.

I gave my courage another little kick, and explained to Alan that if I could ask five questions of Dan for the MTV magazine, it would justify my being down here waiting for over an hour. Alan sorrow-fully replied that all the interview requests had to go through a specific press person who wasn't there, but that if I could use the information from the junket that morning in my five questions, I could take a picture of Dan now and have a full story that way.

He introduced me to Dan as being from the Leaky Cauldron, and Dan's face arranged itself exactly like his father's had: he emitted a little, surprised "oh!" and then extended his hand to shake and thanked me. I snapped a quick picture of him, and one with him for good measure, said my good-byes to his family, and was back at my desk before my boss arrived after lunch. A few days later my story had been passed back to me from Denise with almost no edits and posted on the Web site to the great interest of the rest of the office.

Two days before *Chamber of Secrets* was released into theaters, I was at Kathleen's, and we were doing the stupidest thing we had ever done in the name of Harry Potter. We were making pumpkin juice. We had roasted several pumpkins and were squeezing them through cheesecloth, thanks to a recipe Kathleen had dug up from the Internet. Her roommate, Mieke, kept popping her head into the kitchen and watching us, skeptically.

"It's for everyone tomorrow night!" Kathleen chirped. "She thinks we're nuts," she added as Mieke left the room, muttering.

"We are," I said, my hands full of pumpkin guts. "Has she seen your room yet?"

Kathleen's room was decked out in the largest vinyl posters of *Harry Potter and the Chamber of Secrets* any of us had ever seen. Marc had sent me three full-sized theatrical posters, leftovers from the ones the company sent to hang from the ceilings in the theaters. The e-mail he'd sent previously had simply said I was going to be really, really happy soon, and we had spent a week trying to figure out what he meant. They were six feet wide and eight feet long, printed on both sides on heavy, smelly rubber; they featured one close-up each of Harry, Ron, and Hermione. Though I was grateful, and they were very cool, and though I could see why he would want to send them to me, I wasn't sure exactly what I would ever do with them. The struggle it had taken just to get them out of the office and to Kathleen's had been epic, as each weighed roughly fifteen pounds. Their combined width took up almost every space on her dorm wall. But we made sure they were hanging before everyone came over the next day—perhaps just to scare everyone when they walked in the room.

That was when I met David. Everyone who was seeing the movie together was sitting on Kathleen's stoop, waiting for me in the cold November air. Denise had kept me late for urgent filing, an oxymoron if I ever heard one, and I ran the three blocks from the subway. My friends were easily spotted: everyone was wearing red and gold Gryffindor scarves. As I arrived, huffing and puffing, David, whom I'd never even seen before but knew from online, unfolded all six feet of himself and offered to show me the interpretive scarf dance they'd choreographed while waiting for me. I laughed but told him it would have to wait, because we were late. And even that ended up being incidental because the movie theater wouldn't let us in for another half hour. We went to a bookstore to waste time, and as we ascended an escalator, David and I both turned left and straight into the musical theater section.

"Oh, yes, we are going to be good friends," he said.

CHAPTER EIGHT

Getting a Clue

n late March 2007, the cover art for *Harry Potter and the Deathly Hallows* was revealed. We'd gotten a few sparse and weird e-mails at Leaky suggesting that something Harry Potter was happening the next morning, and March in a release year usually meant artwork, so I rose early in preparation.

Sure enough, when I turned on the TV Meredith Vieira and her cohorts sat with Arthur Levine on the set of *Today*, pulling a purple sheet from a canvas. There stood a Mary GrandPré drawing of Harry, his arm lifted to the sky, apparently trying to catch something. I'd expected, and half wanted, the cover to be black, but it was orange, the orange of an aggressive morning sun. I took hope; Harry's face seemed free of pain or fear.

Between that cover, the British cover, and the release of two plot summaries, both of which revealed next to no information ("Harry has been burdened with a dark, dangerous, and seemingly impossible task." We knew that at the end of the previous book. "Never has Harry felt so alone, or faced a future so full of shadows." That was true in every book, and the way Arthur had said on *Today* that he

149

sobbed while reading the book, we were set. That was just enough fuel for at least a full month of theory-mongering.

It had been the same in late 2002, when fans were getting truly desperate for news about the fifth book. We were coming up on our second full year without a Harry Potter book, and since any publishing announcement would mean that a finished book was still at least another six months away, we were most likely facing three whole years between books. The original plan had been to release one book a year, of course, but Jo Rowling had discovered that her financial stability wasn't a panacea. She hadn't been able to take any time to enjoy her staggering success. She was working all the time, without full-time child care, and she was getting tugged at on all sides for requests to do everything from charity donations to interviews and appearances.

She felt like she was drowning.

Not that she remained idle: between 2000 and 2003 J. K. Rowling published two "schoolbooks" on the Harry Potter series for charity, got married, had a child, and wrote a nearly 900-page novel. Yet as soon as news got out that the fifth book had been delayed, press reports claimed that Jo Rowling had writer's block and she had given it all up to put on an apron. The thought lit her up with anger, not only because she enjoyed putting on an apron—she often baked—but because she felt a male author would never have had that written about him. No one was speculating that her new husband, Neil Murray, was giving up his career as a doctor to play househusband to his new millionaire bride. Or, rather, they weren't doing it in tones loud enough to reach Jo's ears.

"I didn't have writer's block. I said to Bloomsbury, 'I can't. There won't be a book next year. I need to take some time off.' It was definitely the right thing to do, because I came up for air and realized that life could be good if I didn't kill myself. The truth was I might have cracked up if I'd committed to writing another book but I wasn't cracking up, and I certainly didn't have writer's block, as was proved by the enormity of the book that followed my break."

During this time she was also coming to the end of a more than two-year-long case against Nancy Stouffer, an author who claimed that Jo Rowling had taken the word "Muggle" from her book, *The Legend of Rah and the Muggles*. Not only did the court side with Jo Rowling, they awarded her punitive damages, after her lawyers discovered that documents had been falsified to make Stouffer's case.

In late November 2002, the Children's BBC announced that Jo Rowling had donated a ninety-three-word handwritten card containing clues about the next book, to be auctioned at Sotheby's in London to benefit Book Aid International, a literacy charity in the U.K. Fans positively salivated. Heidi called me at work early in the morning, almost whining with how unfair it was that it would go to someone who could pay the anticipated $9,400. "It's a shame we can't just have people send us money for us to buy it and post it [online]," she said.

I agreed, and hung up, but before my hand had left the receiver I was calling her back.

"What if they *could*?"

The plan quickly emerged: fans could send us money so that we could bid on behalf of all of us, and win or lose, we'd donate all that money to Book Aid anyway. We named the movement Get a Clue, and once we put out the idea, fans responded with an energy and fervor that had previously been flagging during the long wait for a new book. They reposted our announcement across the Net, informed their local media outlets, and did everything they could think of to spread the word, while I created a nonprofit organization under which to collect the money. Within one week we were incorporated and had a bank account, and the week after that I spent every free minute I had on the phone with reporters worldwide.

It was a perfect human interest story; desperate for a peek at the next book, plucky fans worldwide band together to raise money for charity. Our PayPal box overflowed with payments; our mailbox seemed to spew checks and well-wishes. Children taped the coins that made up their allowances to index cards and wrote messages of support in crayon on the back. We were inundated with messages of thanks and excitement that we had brought the Harry Potter community together for such a good cause.

My whole family pitched in to help: when I got home from work each day, my parents had already sorted the mail and prepared the checks for me to sign. Once all that had been done, we entered each name and its donation and address into a spreadsheet. I left two hours early for work each morning, making it to the bank near my office by 7:00 a.m. and doing some extra e-mailing and other work at my desk before the workday officially started. The Leaky Cauldron strained under the increased traffic, and everything was going wonderfully—until the first e-mail from Neil Blair.

I'd seen references to Mr. Blair—for that was all I could bring myself to call him—on court documents. He was Jo Rowling's lawyer, by definition a person to be feared by a lowly fan. A terrifying creature, he could use his lawyer-ness to crush me with one keystroke! Sure, the e-mail just said hello and that he understood we planned to post the contents of the card if we won, and was that correct?—but that had to be a ruse. He was *Jo Rowling's lawyer*. He was *the law*.

I called him instead of answering the e-mail, which seemed to confuse him thoroughly. "Yes, we plan to post the card if we win it," I told him right after I had introduced myself. "Are you going to stop us from doing that if we win?"

"Why don't we just see if you win and go from there?"

"I . . . um." It was the verbal equivalent of letting my fists fall to my sides. "Sure."

Through over a year with MTV Networks, I only told people about the Leaky Cauldron on a need-to-know basis. Mimi needed to know, and some of my friends needed to know, that I ran a fan site in my spare time. Denise certainly didn't need to know. Yet the day I was interviewed about the auction by the *New York Times,* I thought perhaps it was time to come clean. I sent out a floorwide e-mail, explaining that I would be in the newspaper and why, making sure to couch everything more strongly around the huge charity drive and less around it being for a fan site. Then I cowered low behind the white Formica side of my desk and hoped no one would see me as they walked by.

It was less embarrassing than I thought it would be. Most of my colleagues found it fascinating, and admitted to me, in conspiratorial tones, that they also read and loved the books. Mimi came up to my desk, said "Cool!" and walked away. Denise said nothing until the day the article came out. "The power of the fans," she said, and I wasn't sure if it was a statement, a question, or an exclamation. Whatever it was, she said it in a way that clearly made her think she was praising me but instead made me feel like any hard-won morsel of respect I'd earned from her was gone.

Two days before the auction, I came down with a fever, and worse, I had to do Marc Cohen a favor.

"Free Dobby?" I said incredulously the morning he called with the idea. "But he *is* free. He's also not real."

"Just get some friends together and we'll have you guys picked up at three a.m." In December. "You'll do it? Promise?"

I dragooned Kathleen, Polly, Mike, and as many Leaky readers as were crazy enough to join us. It was a blatant attempt at "look at these weird people" publicity for the second film, which had just been released, and it was only a lingering feeling of gratitude to WB for all they'd done for us that made me even consider doing it. We were provided with picket signs that portrayed Dobby in grim cartoon lines, like a haggled-over political prisoner. We dutifully held them while we chanted outside NBC and CBS, hoping for some airplay and wondering why Dobby had to be freed. The newscasters wondered, too; one of them, from their tauntingly warm and cozy studio, turned to us on a commercial break and said through the plate glass window, "But he's already free!" By this time the snow had turned to sleet, and then the sleet turned to ice, and our hair turned into icicles. I actually snapped a piece off. I arrived at work looking like a melting Popsicle.

By the time the auction arrived, thanks to my twenty-hour workdays and our house-elf civil rights march, I had a case of walking pneumonia. All told, we raised $24,000 in less than two weeks for the cause. We were shocked at how much had come in, but told no one the amount to ensure against attracting those who were willing to pay more. I took the day off in order to participate in the auction. It was early in the morning for the East Coast, and though Sotheby's had been kind enough to prep me on the process, I still felt like an impostor sitting on the phone with them. Who was I to spend all this money on this one item, and would I be able to find my voice when the time came to bid? "We're all excited about this," my British auction helper admitted. "Good luck!"

My time never came. The bidding shot past $24,000 in less than thirty seconds, while I sat there, stunned, listening to the whispered updates my phone friend was giving. The whole thing took about three minutes, and finally, when the bidding slowed enough for the auctioneer to go to the phone bids, and my new friend asked if we would like to bid, I hesitated for the smallest moment before saying no. The girl apologized, told me the results, and hung up. As it turned out, we'd shot ourselves in the foot; all the publicity we'd created around the auction had backfired by raising interest in the item. Some unknown American bidder walked away with the card, having paid more than $44,000 for it.

At first I was devastated, but when I stopped and considered what we had accomplished, my disappointment melted away—$44,000 from the bidder and $24,000 from us . . . that was about six times what Book Aid had hoped to get from the auction to begin with. I put on some music and danced around my bedroom with utter abandon. The next day at work, no one but Mimi mentioned it; she read the news and said, "Hey, good job." I waved her off and looked away, eager for my normal and calm life of filing to resume. She planted herself in front of me and said, "Hey, seriously. Good job."

The auction had brought Leaky a lot of attention as well. And though I would learn it much, much later, it had attracted the eye of one particular British author, to whom the extraordinary activity and organization of Harry Potter fans was as yet a mystery.

In January 2003, at long last, we got word that the fifth Harry Potter was due to be released on June 21. The BBC, who had my number on speed dial from the auction stories, had me on a radio show to discuss the announcement.

"After so many years of waiting, it came so fast!" I said, then hit myself in the head as I tried to figure out what I meant by that.

Just before June 19 became June 20—on the stroke of midnight the day before the fifth book came out—I sat at the computer ticking down the seconds. My head buzzed pleasantly, and not just from excitement; David, Kathleen, Polly, Elizabeth, and I had broken into the supply of vodka we'd purchased for the coming weekend, and even though I'd only had one watered-down cranberry infusion, it was enough to plaster a slightly vacant smile to my mouth.

As soon as midnight hit, I pressed Publish on the Leaky post that I had been writing, then rushed to the page to check it out. At the top of the home screen, the counter, which had been maddeningly ticking downward for more than five months, read *0 days*, and my post simply pointed that out.

Hey guys, I'd written, as though everyone who read Leaky was sitting in my living room. *Look up. 0 days. ZERO DAYS.*

"David, come here!" I shouted. The four of us had come here, to my parents' summer home in New Jersey, a day early to set up for the group of thirteen slated to arrive the next day. This house was the realization of my parents' thirty-year-old dream to build a place on the water that would serve as a destination and a vacation, like flypaper to bring the whole family together even after we married. It had become a dreamlike place, a wide and airy expanse of sand-colored tile and earthy furniture. Every summer weekend for the past year we'd hosted a daring number of people for barbecues, poker games, swimming, and crabbing; I'd wake up and find people sleeping in every corner of the house, bunched in blankets on the floor, tucked into the corners of sofas, and piled three and four to a bedroom. At night the pool changed from fluorescent green to blue to pink, and old-fashioned lamps sent glowing ripples through the water and gave the patio the impression of being encased in a golden dome. Somehow I had convinced my parents to let me use this oasis for a weekend without them, to give twelve other Harry Potter fanatics and me somewhere to read the fifth book for the first time—together.

Most of the attendees were friends of Meg's, girls I had met before at a gathering in Maryland during which we'd played Harry Potter–related games, made a large cake in the shape of Harry's face, and written a round-robin fanfiction. They were all people active on The

Sugar Quill, where, with encouragement and help from Meg, I'd also posted my first fanfic. With the New York girls and David, the group was rounded out by B. K. DeLong, my boss on Leaky, and his wife.

But this night it was just the New York girls and David and me, and once our setup work was done, we had time to goof around. David read the note I had posted to Leaky over my shoulder, then bent down twenty or so feet to give me an awkward hug. He turned and lumbered out the door to the backyard, and I heard a splash followed by several feminine squeals. I gave the site a fond last glance, and turned off the computer, following in David's wake. We thrashed and laughed and celebrated that it was finally here after three years of watching and waiting, and that we were together for it, and that we had found each other as friends, and acted that friendship out in immature and glorious ways. We talked about on which page we thought Ron and Hermione would kiss, because surely it was slated for book five, and about how fast we were planning on reading the book, and our words ran out in a rush and we swam until we were tired and talked until we were hoarse, until midnight was gone and the early hours were light in the sky.

The carloads arrived, staggered throughout the next day, but each time I heard a crunch on the gravel driveway I was outside, yelling and jumping. We had all brought one another gifts. Meg had made personalized bookplates for everyone; Jennie, the archivist, gave everyone acid-free paper and pencils on which to record our thoughts as we read.

The Barnes & Noble we visited was full of families. One blond man posed with his white-blond two-year-old son, his hair slicked back and dressed in robes, a spot-on shot for Draco Malfoy. Everywhere we looked there were people in garb, their black robes rolled up to their sleeves and wands in their hands. Some had gone the traditional witch route and looked like something out of *The Wizard of Oz*. We had chosen to arrive a full three hours early, even though our books had been on reserve for months. Something about the festivity of the air was intoxicating, and certainly none of us had ever seen a bookstore this packed.

We sauntered to the back, where we sat in a lumpy and misshapen circle, found paperback copies of all the previous books, and read our favorite passages aloud. Mine was the part in book three when Neville finishes off the boggart, a scene that shows his first foray into bravery and adulthood and is a first triumph for a sweet but betrodden character. Meg's was, of course, a Ron/Hermione moment, as was Kathleen's. As I listened to my friends reciting from my favorite books, I fell asleep on David's lap.

When I woke up, I felt as though I had tried unsuccessfully to crowd surf. People stood around me like tree trunks, blocking my view of anything except their slanted and towering selves. David nudged me to get me up and join everyone else who was standing, brushing off their clothes, starting to bounce in anticipation.

While I had snoozed, the store had transformed. What was just a smattering of costumed fans was now a veritable throng. We had to thrust ourselves around using our shoulders just to maneuver through the aisles, and the volume level had reached a din. The place was full of kids in robes far too long for them, older teens dressed like slightly slutty schoolgirls, middle-aged women who wouldn't be out of place at a Renaissance festival, and parents with children on their shoulders or hanging off their arms, weighing them down like milkmaid pails. These half-pints were brandishing wooden sticks at each other, shouting out random spells from the books, while the slightly older, too-cool-for-it-all crowd was nosing through books that had been placed near the Harry Potter display. We ducked whirling cloaks and wand flourishes and a whisper of the time sped through our group, reminding us: 11:20.

It was my first experience at a midnight launch party, which was a virtually nonexistent event for a book before Harry Potter. I took the crowd at the little New Jersey store to be an interesting case study in fandom: for as many children as were there, there were also teens and adults and even the elderly, wearing costumes and acting just as involved in the fandom as anyone else. But I loved watching the children, who were spending the waiting time either running madcap down the aisles or actually thumbing through other books. By this time Harry had gained a reputation for making reading cool again for children, though some argued that it was impossible for one set of books to have been responsible for such a turnaround. Later, in 2006, Yankelovich, a consumer trend tracker, released a report in conjunction with Scholastic that had been conducted in twenty-five major cities with over one thousand respondents; it found that about half of Harry Potter readers aged five to seventeen said they did not read books before they started reading the series, and now enjoyed reading. About 65 percent said they'd been doing better in school since they started reading the series.

At Leaky, we were always hearing from people who had been taught to love books through their love for Harry. We also heard from dyslexic children who'd fought to overcome their disability in order to read Harry and by doing so realized they could overcome dyslexia almost entirely. Priscilla Penn, a Leaky reader, told me that her niece, Kaitlin, had a substandard reading comprehension level before she started reading Harry Potter in late 1999. By the next year her grade level had been brought to normal, and she was enthusiastic about reading. The same happened for Kodie, a late-teen juvenile delinquent from Terre Haute, Indiana, who was illiterate before he discovered the series; his foster mother Shirley Comer, a nurse, had started reading Harry Potter to him while he was in a juvenile rehabilitation center.

"Now, he wants me to bring him any kind of book on mythology, or Star Wars books. He even tackled *Lord of the Rings*," Shirley said. She even found him a book on psychology that was appropriate for his comprehension level. "It's helping him understand himself a little better, and that's something that I would never have thought he would have been able to read and enjoy."

When it was nearly midnight, Meg grabbed me by the shoulders and made a noise that never escaped her lips but ricocheted inside her voice and vibrated through her throat and shoulders like she was a tuning fork that had just been struck with inappropriate force. This muffled scream brought forth a matching one from me and we jumped up and down on the spot, grasping each other's arms and relishing the opportunity to be among people of all ages and forget our own.

Kathleen made a funny noise and tapped me, to point out in her kindergarten-teacher manner that a sheet-covered pallet had appeared behind the register. No one needed telling what was under the sheet, but making the vision that much more beautiful was the teeniest glimpse of blue at its edge. We stared, mesmerized, open-mouthed, at the book's proximity.

Kathleen took the moment to remind everyone of the game plan.

"Get your book, then go right to the car. *No reading in the car!*" This debate had taken weeks. Should we read aloud from our books in the car on the way back? No, that would be unfair to the driver. That would be cruel. And an accident would become more likely.

Red tickets came next—red tickets with numbers on them determining order of purchase. For the way they were received they might have been the books themselves, or even strips of gold. The attendees buzzed, and the excitement became tangible.

"One minute left!" someone shouted. We counted down. Meg's friend Kristin took a picture of someone's watch.

The book was nearly impossible not to open. At 870 pages, it wasn't *like* a brick, it could have been used as one. Once it was in my hands I was literally eating my lips to avoid opening it. I was the driver of one of our cars; maybe I could just hold it out in front of me while I drove?

While I waited for our whole group to get their books and meet me on the sidewalk, I teased open the front cover and dropped it back down. Then repeated. I peeked under the cover like I was trying to get into a Christmas present without alerting my parents. I surreptitiously looked over my shoulder. I could just look at the title page, just the contents, just maybe the frontispiece, and ooh, was that Padfoot walking out of someone's house?

"You're peeking," Kathleen chirped from behind me, and I jumped guiltily. She had tried to sound stern and failed; it had instead come out as a half laugh, half shout of joy that peeking was possible. By the time all thirteen people had joined us on the sidewalk, we hugged and screamed and then flat out ran to the cars.

Back at the house, we scrambled inside. Some of us changed into pajamas, others into more comfortable clothes, others sat right down on the couch and jumped in. We had set up a video camera in an adjacent room—it was all part of our plan to keep ourselves unspoiled in a house that had to account for thirteen different people's reading speeds. With a video camera and a confessional room, set up if you needed to shout or cry or scream over something in the book, you could just go in the designated room, press Record, and sound off to the camera. Then later we'd watch everyone's real-time reactions, and laugh or cringe.

Within ten minutes of sitting down with the book, Kathleen had gotten up angrily and thrown the book to the floor, attracting all our glares as to why this tiny person held so much rage—and since she was probably the most ardent Ron/Hermione shipper among us, we all shared horribly worried glances. She stomped off to the confessional room, slammed the door, and we could only hear muffled shouts and grunts through it. I had to stop myself from demanding from her what she had seen that had pissed her off so mightily; I was having a very hard time reading as it was, as about eight of us had huddled in the living room and it was proving distracting. Every two seconds someone shouted "Ooh!" or "Whoa!" or "Damn!" or simply cursed in a purple streak and ran off to the confessional room.

A few more pages in, I knew why. The first two chapters of the book completely restructured the entire series. Sirius had a dark past? Dark family members? Incest ran rampant in the wizarding community? Ron is related to the Malfoys? Sirius to Bellatrix? Harry to everyone, in some fashion? I was trying to keep my own gasps and sighs to a minimum and yet they were escaping without my permission. The room sounded like we were recording vocal effects for a production studio. I kept having to stop, backtrack, and reread.

Kathleen had spent herself out in the confessional, and came out with only a slight scornful huff, plopped herself next to me on the sofa, and buried herself back in her book. I kept turning to her as though I expected just a glance would tell me the secret of what had so angered her.

But it wasn't long before I was in the confessional room myself. I switched on the camera and tried to forget that I was essentially talking to myself and acting out the most elaborate display of geekiness in my life. Then I swore loudly.

"What is going on in this book? This isn't Harry Potter! I mean, it is Harry Potter, but this is not Harry Potter. It's so different!"

The door clicked open behind me and Meg and Kathleen appeared. They both looked as weirded out as I felt. So far, Harry had become a whiny bastard and had shouted down everyone who had ever been good to him in his life. Nothing was magic and happy and enchanting anymore. Harry was arrogant and prideful and petulant, and kept doing and saying things before thinking, and, in general, had turned into someone I had little interest in spending eight hundred more pages with. Meanwhile, it was as though dementors had sucked the happiness out of the book.

My head felt full of dryer lint. I needed a break but I desperately feared falling behind my friends and spending the next day listening to their gasps and shrieks while I skipped haphazardly through the pages trying to catch up—missing details and ruining the experience for myself.

"I need coffee," I pleaded. "Will anyone come with me and take a break and make coffee?"

A death pause.

"That sounds great," Meg said. Relieved, I started to move out of the room but turned when I saw that Meg didn't follow.

"Come on, Meg!"

She had sat down again, cross-legged, beer in one hand and her book propped over her legs. "I can't, I'm sorry, you go. I have to read."

Sometime in the wee hours, two of our compatriots, Michael and Heather, finished the book. They were both ridiculously fast readers and while we were still watching Harry's detention with Umbridge, they had gotten through the battle at the Ministry, Sirius's death, and the fallout. Mike sat in the living room looking like he had just emerged from a sleepless week of studying. Heather walked around the house like nothing had happened, cooking for the next day.

Near dawn, my energy was flagging. My eyes were skipping words, until I realized that I had no idea where I was in the text, and had to backtrack and reread. I wandered up to my bedroom, intent on taking a nap, to find Meg and David sitting on top of the bed, books open.

"I have to rest," I said like a war-weary soldier.

They asked what part I was up to, which was the common question all night—people would run by and say, "What are you up to?" and then, depending on your answer (which could only come in page number or chapter number, so as not to give away any information in case the person asking was not that far yet), either they rubbed their hands and told you, Oh wait until you get to X, Y, and Z, or simply said, "I'm not there yet," and scurried off to get there. I told Meg where I was, and she and David shared meaningful looks.

"Oh, wait," David said, reminding me forcefully of Sarah two years ago. "Everything is about to change."

I almost groaned, because now there was no way I could sleep. "Seriously?"

Meg raised her eyebrows. "The whole world changes next, Melissa."

"I guess," I said, sighing, shoulders slumping, "I can't take a nap right now."

"Oh, no, you can't," David said.

The world-changing event they were referring to was Dumbledore's flight from Hogwarts, perhaps the most action-packed and funniest scene of the series. David and Meg were right, the entire scope and focus of the books had changed, but by the time I got there I was nearly dead with exhaustion, yet somehow too tired to sleep. I

The enormous movie posters were a gift from WB and added great ambience to Kathleen's dorm room for our *Chamber of Secrets* viewing party. (Photo by Mieke Toland)

Emily and Susan (and their annotated Harry Potter books) right before the start of the Nimbus 2003 (relation)ship debate.

A fan in her Snape garb at Lumos 2006, complete with wig and hooked nose.

One fan brought a dementor to the premiere of the *Harry Potter and the Prisoner of Azkaban* movie in New York City.

James Phelps, Devon Murray, Megan Morrison, me, Jamie Waylett, and Matthew Lewis in New York before the premiere of the third Harry Potter film. (Photo by John Inniss)

In Dumbledore's chair at the *Prisoner of Azkaban* DVD party—I couldn't resist! (Photo by John Inniss)

Barbara Marcus and Arthur Levine of Scholastic pose in front of a countdown clock on June 16, 2005, one month before the release of *Harry Potter and the Half-Blood Prince*.

With Fiddy Henderson before the release of *Harry Potter and the Half-Blood Prince*. (Photo by Emerson Spartz)

Emerson Spartz, Jo Rowling, and me after our 2005 interview. (Photo by Fiddy Henderson)

A sea of fans at the *Harry Potter and the Goblet of Fire* movie premiere in Leicester Square, London.

Me, Dan Radcliffe, John Noe, and Sue Upton at the after-party for the *Goblet of Fire* premiere in New York. (Photo by Carole Anelli)

Scholastic's double-decker London bus, decorated in purple like the three-story Knight Bus, visited libraries all over the United States in the weeks before the release of *Deathly Hallows*.

Cheryl Klein and me (and Emerson off the picture to the right!)
on our Scholastic podcast tour. (Photo by Dylan Spartz)

After the first show of
the 2007 PotterCast
tour, at the Chicago
Tribune's Printer's Row
Book Fair, we met a
lot of enthusiastic fans.
(Photo by Edward
Drogos)

Our merry Leaky staff group on July 22, 2007, after the last podcast of the tour.
Left to right: Sarah Wilkes, Alex Robbin, John Noe, me, Sue Upton, Bre Bishop,
Edward Drogos, Jeff Zippe, Maryann Penzvalto. (Photo by David Carpman)

Harry and the Potters, with help from Darius of the Hungarian Horntails, perform "The Weapon" on July 20, 2007, for more than 15,000 people in Boston's Harvard Square, which was renamed Hogwarts Square for the evening. (Photo by Stu Sherman)

A child dressed as Harry in Hogwarts Square the night before the release of *Deathly Hallows*. (Photo by Stu Sherman)

Jo Rowling with fans at the London Natural History Museum, about to read from *Harry Potter and the Deathly Hallows* on the night of its release. (Photo by Bloomsbury/ Jamie Turner)

In lower Manhattan, Scholastic celebrated the release with a street fair. Costumed magicians entertained fans. (Photo by Joel Kohen/Wire Image/ Getty Images)

Most of the Leaky senior staff with Jo Rowling at Carnegie Hall, October 2007. *Left to right:* me, Alex Robbin, John Noe, Jo Rowling, Sue Upton, Nick Rhein.

traveled up to the topmost portion of the house, a small loft space, and found Kristin lazily turning pages, sipping a cup of coffee.

"Hey there," she said, her voice as soft and Southern as always. "How are you doing?"

"I feel like a wreck," I confided. "I don't know if people are going to like this book. I feel like she took my best friend away. Harry's mean, nothing's going well, nothing safe is safe anymore, none of the comforts are there."

Kristin made room for me on the sofa, pulled her legs closer into her body, and leaned forward. "I know. I mean, it's brilliant. It's bold and risky and she actually cares to portray real teenagers. We were all like that at fifteen."

I thought about this, and about all the tantrums I had thrown as a teenager and still threw when the occasion presented itself. "You're right. But I don't know. I don't know if people are going to like this series after this book. This is not an enjoyable read. This is not the same kind of fun. It's like anything can happen now and either we're with her or we're not."

As the morning grew out of the long night, definitive snaps heralded more of our number finishing the volume. People were walking around dazed.

The house looked like a train had hit it; I emerged from my reading cocoon and barely saw the piles of clothing spilling out of luggage, or the dishes amassing in the sink. We'd spend the next few hours in recon, reading parts together and revisiting highlights, and watching one another's videotapes, sleeping off the exhaustion it took to expend three years' worth of pent-up anticipation in a twelve-hour period. By late Saturday night Heather had cooked us a Thanksgiving feast even though it was June, and it was only after dinner had been cleared off and everyone was either swimming, staring upward at the midnight sky, or rereading favorite bits, that I went back to my e-mail, and to Leaky.

My guts were in a wrench over book five. I liked it but didn't yet love it, and had expected the same victory and exultation at overcoming the bad guy that was present in all the other books. I expected to cheer through the end and have a great time, and instead I found myself hating Harry, having no fun, and feeling, like him, that all the good things about this parallel world that I had come to love had been stripped away. It was as if I'd spent a year with Snape rather than Harry, or at the Dursleys' instead of at Hogwarts.

Yet we all felt the same: whether we loved it or not, the book had been brave, and we wanted to thank the people behind it for sticking with J. K. Rowling's intentions.

I'd been thinking about doing this since I finished the book, but almost without realizing I found myself riffling through e-mails we had received in the ramp-up to book five. On the Yahoo! Group that had temporarily served as our comments board, I pulled out what we had considered an astonishing e-mail at the time: a posting from Cheryl Klein, an assistant to Arthur A. Levine, American editor of the books. An editor on Leaky had just made an assertion that Levine had made a mistake on an early-morning talk show regarding continuity, and Cheryl had come by to clear up the issue. It was the first time we were made aware of how closely—perhaps even favorably—the publishing houses were watching our site, that they cared enough to correct such a mistake. This Cheryl person had seemed very far off and polite, and though it wasn't the first time she had sent us an e-mail or submitted a link, this was certainly the first time she'd reacted to something on the site. Following the naming convention on her e-mail address, I figured out Arthur's address, and sent them both an e-mail.

Hi Arthur, Cheryl:

I just wanted to write and say thank you for having the cojones to publish that book. I read it in a kind of shocked haze; it's so cold in places, and rightly so, but it leaves you so . . . empty. So grieving and empty. It's a wonderful, brilliant book . . . it keeps you right in line with Harry's emotions all the way through, which explains the coldness. I feel like Harry—I don't want him to have to go through this. I have so much to say and so much to tell but I can't quite get my thoughts straight to do it. I will eventually . . . I finally understand what J. K. Rowling was talking about when she said that she may have only one reader left at the end of this—the giddy, frantic excitement to get this has faded a bit . . . I won't hesitate to buy book six, but I'll feel as though I'm buying a ticket to a funeral. But one thing is sure—the journey is going to be epic and legendary, and I'm glad you have not yet hesitated about presenting it in the way that JKR intends. . . . Now it's a test of who will stick around to see this complete. And all she'll have to say is, "I told you so."

I'm with 13 people right now who agree with me, and send their congratulations. Anyway. Yeah. Wow.

I left it alone, figuring I'd never hear back, and went out to join my friends in the balmy night. Yet the very next time I checked my e-mail I was sent fleeing from the screen and outside to the patio, and my friends all came running back in with me to read the note that had just come from Arthur Levine.

Hi Melissa—

I'm so glad you all enjoyed the book! Give my best to the "Order" who are gathered in your home.

I certainly understand your reactions; it's very raw right now as you've just closed the book. I will only say that other reactions came through more for me as more time passed. I remembered also the wonderful growth of Harry's friends. How Hermione really showed why she was placed in Gryffindor (something Cheryl pointed out) and how others, like Neville, showed a strength of character we'd not yet seen.

It's not all about darkness. It's also about how difficult times will bring out the best in courageous people.

And believe me, Jo's not trying to prove anything to anyone. She's just telling the story as she's always imagined it. She'll be glad to know you liked it, I assure you.

Best,
Arthur

We talked about the e-mail obsessively, as though it had come from Jo herself. And later, sitting with my head on David's lap, I uttered for the first time what was starting to become my most secret, naïve hope: "Someday," I told him, "someday, when I'm a real journalist, I'll interview her."

The Tuesday after book five's release, I slipped behind my white Formica desk at MTV Networks early, dressed casually, just wanting to get through the day and home to my computer, where I had several hours of talking about the book to do.

Already my hands were creeping to my personal e-mail, to Leaky, to the Sugar Quill, to message boards. There had been a virtual storm of e-mails earlier between the people who had been at my house, and they were keeping me laughing while the morning geared itself up.

All my coworkers were giving me excited smiles, for by now I had become Harry Potter Girl. They crept up to my desk when Denise was gone, asking me about the book, regarding me as someone who had just been given a large gift or someone who had come back from her honeymoon. Some were looking at me as though they expected me to have changed. Their inquisitive glances were met with polite smiles as I answered phone calls and juggled schedules. Nice as they were, they were Muggles; they didn't get it.

"Good morning, MTV Networks," I answered cheerily while one hand used my mouse to scan message boards.

"Oh, hello, Melissa, it's Lizo."

"Lizo!" I shouted, attracting stares. I lowered my voice. "Hey! What's going on?"

Lizo Mzimba was a television reporter from the Children's BBC who often reported on Potter and was a fan of the site. He usually called when there was some piece of tantalizing Potter news to discuss, or to tell me that he had a piece for us to link to on Leaky. Today it was just to wheedle me, the way he'd been doing for weeks, by implying that Jo Rowling read and liked Leaky and I should be at her post-book-release reading in London.

"You should come," he said. "The event's in two days. You'll get to meet her."

"Shut up, no I won't," I said, waving my arm as if to shoo a fly. "I can't go off to England now, I have a job," I said, as a pile of filing was slammed on my desk.

Disappointment and disbelief tinged Lizo's voice. "Oh, come on then, just get on a plane. I'm telling you it will be worth it."

"I can't. I'm sorry. I'll see you soon," I managed, quickly hanging up the phone as I heard Denise coming down the corridor. I turned back to my filing and kept my head low, hoping for a pass. She went into her office and I exhaled, and abandoned my filing in favor of e-mail.

"So how was the book?"

The question sounded like it was addressed to a small child, and for the briefest second I looked around the office for one, before I realized that Denise was standing behind my computer and I was the small child. My hand had automatically clicked away from my e-mail and onto my work document. I answered the best I could.

"It was good."

She seemed pleased with herself, then held up a large manila envelope and dropped it onto the white ledge that I usually used to hide behind. I picked up the stack, expecting copyediting or a story idea.

"My shower guests," she said.

My hand paused at the cover of the folder. "Excuse me?" I asked, as though I hadn't understood what she had said.

"My shower guests," she repeated. She turned, went back to her office, and shut the door. I put the folder carefully down next to my phone and stared at it.

I grabbed my cell phone and was thirty floors down and outside within seconds.

The late June heat assaulting me, I marched up and down Forty-fourth Street between Seventh and Eighth Avenues, weighing options. I called Meg.

"Meg, I need convincing."

"All right," she said instantly, her tone brisk and assertive.

"Please convince me to get on a plane in two days to see the J. K. Rowling reading in England."

"Oh," she said, and the briskness left Meg's voice like I had popped a balloon. "Get your ass on a plane. Do it. Do it right now."

"I just took some days off, for the release of the book. If I just disappear . . ."

"Melissa, you don't even get paid for days off. What are they going to do, dock you?"

"I could be fired."

Meg's tone went soft. "Would that really be so bad?" she asked, and a flutter of something like imagined relief coursed through me. "Seriously, follow your bliss, Melissa. Lizo's telling you to go. He's saying you'll get to meet her. Has he ever lied to you? He says she reads the site."

I psh'd.

"Psh all you like, but he's probably right. You know she knows about Leaky. And you're going to get to *meet* her if you go." She paused, probably for dramatic effect, a specialty of Meg's, then went in for the kill. "If you do not get on that plane, will you regret it for the rest of your life?"

My voice felt small. "Yes."

"Then what else do I need to say?"

Nothing. I clicked the phone shut and returned to my desk, then went to Orbitz.com, where I found a relatively cheap flight to London and an affordable hotel. My next bathroom break was used visiting Mimi; she had been transferred to a different department but I still saw her often.

"Mimi, can I stow a suitcase up here in a few days? I have to hide it from Denise so I can say I had a personal emergency while I go to London to meet J. K. Rowling."

She looked at me over her glasses and laughed. "Oh, *hell* yes."

Two days later I stood at the terminal for British Airways in John F. Kennedy International Airport. Operation Get Me Out of Work Unnoticed had gone as smoothly as I could have hoped; Denise left on time, I rocketed upstairs to Mimi's office, which she had left unlocked for me, grabbed my suitcase, and splurged on a cab. I'd called B. K. at the terminal, shot Meg an e-mail before I left work, and informed my parents of my plans. They almost cheered. They'd watched me come home weary and angry for almost two years and were glad I was taking passive-aggressive action. This support above all things made me feel untouchable. It reminded me strongly of the times my mother would wake me up and inform me I was skipping school, just so we could spend time together; I'd go back to school the next day feeling protected by an invisible bubble from any teacher's complaint.

Still, this was the first trip I was taking solely for the Web site. I could momentarily forget that I didn't have a company backing me, that I was funding the trip out of my weekly pittance, and that Leaky wasn't an accredited news organization but a start-up. I felt like a real reporter heading on a business trip. I had packed only business clothes, pajamas, and my computer. I had all my travel details printed in a blue folder that stayed in my hand to make me look more professional. I wore black and folded a sweater over my arm. I had no idea what the hell I was doing.

My hotel room was in a basement in Queen's Park and was a teeny thing half the size of my college dorm room. It was sunny and cool and someone from Scholastic had left me a ticket for the event at the reception desk at a hotel in the chic Kensington district. I'd called Lizo as soon as I got in, and he'd told me to wait at the hotel until he got there.

"You ready to meet her?" he asked as soon as I'd hopped into the black cab.

"I'm not going to meet her. Maybe if I'm lucky she'll answer a question on the press side of the red carpet. I don't know what I'm doing here. Why am I here? What am I doing? Anyway, she won't know who I am."

"Yes she *will*. She reads the site."

"She does not read the site."

"She reads the site."

"That's very nice of you to say"—Lizo laughed—"but she does not read the site."

He waved me off and we sat in silence until we got to the hall.

I'd never been to the Royal Albert Hall before, and expected some sort of theatrical structure, but it looked instead like a walled-off Roman coliseum. Instead of a red carpet, a stretch of green Astroturf resembling a Quidditch pitch stretched from doors to curb. Lizo had a special spot waiting for him inside, so we said our good-byes and I hurried over to the gaggle of press and the sign-in table, looking for someone from Scholastic so that I could get set up.

When she heard my name, a petite, golden-haired woman bounded out from behind a table and grabbed my hand. She was Kris Moran, the publicist at Scholastic with whom I most often spoke. "The Leaky Cauldron!" she shouted.

I offered a nervous laugh, while she introduced me to the other Scholastic people, the other keepers of the kingdom, and I realized for the first time that they weren't palace guards or security trolls. They were people around my age, who worked at a children's book publishing house.

Kris walked me over to the "carpet," and though my feet stopped at the entrance to the press bull pen, hers didn't. I stumbled a bit but rushed to follow her as she led me across the aisle and to the much cooler, more sparse area where a group of twenty competition winners were waiting with their books.

"You'll be over here," she told me, and I barely had a chance to look at her gratefully before another Scholastic person walked me in. "Over here" meant a for-sure signed book, and even just a split second to say hello to Ms. Rowling. Over here meant I wasn't just press anymore, or wasn't press at all.

The competition winners had been flown over from America, and were all well-groomed kids of varying ethnicities, the kinds of teens that always win essay contests, spelling bees, and physics championships—the kind of teen I had been. They were at the geeks' ball, showing ease and confidence they probably didn't always have in school. We talked and waited, my nerves getting more abraded with each passing second. I opened and closed my book, reread passages. The overcrowded press pen looked as messy and sticky as a crumpled wad of used flypaper.

"Ready to meet her?" Lizo was hanging over the barrier looking smugly at me.

"Not gonna happen." But I couldn't keep that up now. "OK, maybe it's gonna happen. Maybe I'm going to meet her." I hadn't ever considered the words long enough to believe them, and coming out of my mouth they felt hollow and numb. I clutched my big blue copy of *Order of the Phoenix* tightly. On the other side of the carpet I saw a petite black-haired woman bobbing up and down, one arm waving over her head.

"Liz!" I screamed. My friend Liz, who was studying in London, had come to see the spectacle.

"You're gonna *meet her!*" she yelled back. I groaned.

A black car pulled up at the base of the carpet and the reporters moved as though one many-legged body, falling over themselves to get to the brightly dressed blonde who had just exited the car.

Everything around me changed. The challenge winners stood in a tense line, giving each other excited smiles and holding their books out for signing. Lizo disappeared into the hall's vestibule, recording his piece. I started fumbling; I dropped my tape recorder, which I had brought because I thought I was going to be press; I dropped my book and fumbled to get the cover on right; I dropped my pen and started shifting through my bags like a bag lady, and all the time Jo Rowling was working her way down the line, having given the obligatory photo op of her with her book to the press and now doing a mad signing that was making her look like a streak of white-blond hair with a hand attached. I had to get ready or miss her.

I gathered myself just in time, and as she signed the book of the person next to me I dropped my pen again—why were my fingers like little sausages suddenly? When she appeared in front of me I put my hand possessively over the cover of my book.

She looked down at the book and back up at my frozen face, laughed a little as if to say, Hey, I'm gonna need that if you want a signature. But if I was going to make a fool of myself in front of J. K. Rowling, I was going to make a fool of myself all the way, so I stuttered out the speech I had prepared in my head. Except I didn't get very far.

"H-h-h-i, Ms. Rowling, my name is Melissa, I work on a site called the Leaky Caul—"

"The Leaky Cauldron? I love the Leaky Cauldron!" she shrieked, and threw herself on me in a hug, shocking me to my bones. She had nearly launched herself over the barrier and now broke away, smiling widely at me, and I was sure that I had somehow actually nodded off at my MTV Networks desk and entered my wildest dreams.

"Turn around, turn around!" I heard from somewhere to my right and looked dazedly to see Lizo wearing an impossibly knowing and smug grin and holding up his camera phone. Jo and I each had one arm around the other and were smushing our heads together as Lizo took the shot.

I finally handed her my book and found a purpose for the tape recorder still in my hand—I asked her if she would say hello to her fans, and pressed Record.

"Hello to everyone who's on the Leaky Cauldron fan site, which is my favorite fan site!" she said, then gave me a final smile and was whooshed away. Only after Lizo had said "I told you so," and Liz had re-created the moment for me several times at my request, did I finally think to open my book. It read: *I love the Leaky Cauldron!— J. K. Rowling.*

CHAPTER NINE

Banned and Burned

ust keep in touch with me," my mother warned. I was packing up my bag, nearly ready to go to the airport. "Keep me up to date on where you are. You never know if she's going to take you hostage or something."

"Ma!" I said, though she had clearly been joking, and we were both laughing. She hadn't been the first, or even the sixth, person to make this joke to me this week—that my visiting Laura Mallory in Georgia was going to result in bodily harm, or that sometime during the course of our meeting she was going to drag me off to view her private crucifix collection. More than one person suggested I could pick her out of a crowd by her horns, and every friend I'd informed of this trip had given me raised eyebrows, or exhaled heavily, or simply said, "Jesus," which at least was on topic.

"I'm sure she's not evil," I assured my mother, and pondered this while zipping my travel bag. "Maybe a little insane."

I wondered what conversations Mrs. Mallory was having in Georgia—were her friends telling her they could pick me out of a crowd by my pitchfork and forked tail? Did my standing in the Potter community mark me as a tainted soul ripe for her attempts at salvation? And wouldn't she look at my life, at the way I lived it, and consider *me* just a little insane, too?

Later that morning I was cursing, driving down the Atlanta Highway looking for the Ruby Tuesday we were supposed to meet in, as opposed to the *other* Ruby Tuesday, otherwise known as the one I'd been in twice and had not found Laura Mallory but a cranky blond woman who didn't take well to being asked twice who she clearly wasn't, and two blond waitresses who had chirruped, "Georgia!" without a trace of irony, when I asked where I was.

When Laura Mallory called, she tried to hide how ticked off she was.

"I have to go pick up my children," she said, and asked if she was supposed to be compensated for her time. I took the request to be true naïvete rather than an attempt to fleece me, and explained that no, it was not common form to pay people for interviews, though I was happy to pick up the tab for lunch. I hoped she could hear the begging in my voice, because I had to leave in about forty hours.

"Well . . ." she said, and there was an interminable pause. "There's this tape I'd like to give you."

"I'll come get it. Right now. You have five minutes?" I didn't even care what was on the tape. It could have been Satan doing a chicken dance.

We met in a parking lot, acting as if we were trading state secrets. Her black Honda was polished so smooth it looked like liquid, and even though I'd seen her picture, when she rolled down a window I was expecting a dour old lady to purse her lips at me and hold a crucifix between us. Instead, she was blond and perky and wearing frosted pink lipstick and a white velour jumpsuit. Perfectly coiffed hair, perfectly manicured nails, and a toddler daughter in the passenger seat, twisting herself upside down and staring at me with tremendous blue eyes sparsely covered by white-blond fringe. I was staring at a pastel-colored soccer mom.

My halfhearted wave was apologetic, and we acted politely, greeting each other and sizing each other up. She passed me a videotape.

"This is the whole reason I started," she explained. "I saw this tape and knew something had to be done."

I nodded and promised to watch it, while Laura's daughter made gleeful smiles and babbled in babydegook. "I'm so sorry it didn't work out today," I said. "Will you have time tomorrow? I'd like to talk to you about this tape and . . . other things."

Laura considered this for a minute, hesitation puckering her lightly made-up face. "I have my kids, and my husband, and things to do," she started, and I did my best to make my face look understanding and like the very last thing I'd want to do is step on her day, even though we both knew it was the first thing I wanted to do.

"All right," she conceded. "You've come all this way."

The tape in my hand was old and had clearly been taken in and out of its package many times. The cover depicted a cartoon version of a black cat, a broom, and a witch's hat in an arched stone window that faced a purply, twilit sky and a yellow moon, with bats fluttering in front of it. *Harry Potter: Witchcraft Repackaged; Making Evil Look Innocent*. Oh boy.

A few hours later I sat in front of the television screen in my room in the airport Hyatt, and watched the tape. The video that started Laura Mallory's trek to anti-Potter infamy played like a pastiche of all the videos I'd ever had to watch in safety assemblies in school complete with early-generation video graphics, cheesy music, dramatic transitions, and the unwavering belief in its own righteousness. Those videos made me believe that the penalty for crossing the street against the light was getting hit immediately by a car, and that one sip of beer would doom me to AA meetings for the rest of my life. Of course, I've crossed on red before, and I've had more than one sip of beer. But faced with those videos, with their cheap graphics, dramatic music, and obtuse visual cues, I became an adherent. Especially after the bus safety one—the bus safety one was the worst, depicting a girl who failed to stand far enough away from a bus and slipped under it as it pulled away. I felt now as if I were watching it again, watching that aerial shot of her head spinning like a top and the camera zooming outward to show her life spiraling into nothingness.

I saw that video as a child and never was irresponsible near a bus again. But if I saw any of them today, I suspected I would laugh at how ineffective they seemed. It was the same with this video. Images of the Harry Potter books (flying by flapping their covers) were cut next to documentary-style footage of Wiccans dancing in a circle, barefoot in the woods, and speaking of the goddess. It spoke of Lily Potter's sacrifice to save her son as "sacrificial goddess magic" and an "inversion . . . of the God factor." Voldemort's sucking of unicorn blood in the Forbidden Forest is taken as an encouragement to perform animal sacrifice; clips from bookstore owners talking about children dying to read the book are played like warning signs of drug addiction. The idea that Harry can talk to snakes is accompanied by crashing music, and the most damning evidence is that Harry's and Voldemort's wands share Fawkes's tail feather as a core, which apparently meant that they shared a power core and somehow, a penchant for evil.

I sat through it, though every word was personally painful and assaulting. If I was meant to believe this video, I was meant to believe that children read Harry Potter and thought, *I can do witchcraft now!* rather than *I wish Hogwarts was real but I know it's not!*

Jo Rowling has said she's never had someone come up to her and thank her for their introduction to witchcraft. The idea of the books being censored never occurred to her, because there are a lot of books about witchcraft and magic, and they're not being banned or challenged. She'd only been approached in person once. In America, while shopping with her kids, a man walked up to her and said, "You're J. K. Rowling."

"I said, 'Yes, I am,' and he said, 'I'm praying for you,' in a voice more sinister than if he had said, 'Die, you evil woman,' " she remembered.

In retrospect, she said, she should have told him she was praying for him, too. But she just backed away, because he was scary.

When I walked into the International House of Pancakes the next day to meet Laura for breakfast, I spotted her immediately. She did not seem remotely scary. Alone in a booth, facing me, immaculate clothing and hair, very little makeup or jewelry besides two necklaces—one small diamond necklace and another, longer, gold cross. I slipped into the booth, said a quick hello, and realized I had disrupted a conversation with the people behind me.

The man in the booth behind me had a friendly face and thinning coffee-colored hair. Laura explained the purpose of my visit to him.

"Ah." He gave me an appraising look. "Are you going to say she has horns?"

For the better part of the previous two years, Laura Mallory's name had been at the forefront of the Harry Potter censorship debate. It's not that she's the first one to challenge Harry Potter, or the last, but there has been a tenacity to her work that has not gone unnoticed. Her story certainly plays well in the press: mom worried for kids' welfare, tried to pull books from shelves, and took her humble case to the school board. Rejected, she tried again. And rejected, she tried again.

That's been Laura Mallory's calling card: the relentless pursuit of a goal that, if she ever reached it, wouldn't really affect her anymore. Her son has since graduated from the elementary school whose Harry Potter books offended her, but that hasn't stopped her quest. She took the fight from the actual to the symbolic, from concern for her family to concern for all humankind—from the classroom, to the school board, all the way to the Georgia Superior Court. In doing so she has been stoking the fires of the Christian fundamentalist antagonistic attitude toward Harry Potter, bringing it under regular waves of nationwide, and perhaps even worldwide, scrutiny.

The town of Loganville is a six-square-mile crumb off Gwinnett County, one of its encasing counties. Gwinnett is a stretch seventy times bigger and home to the largest school system in the state and a population boom of 50 percent since the year 2000. The county, part of Atlanta's metropolitan area, has been listed among the fastest growing in the nation.

Yet the cotton-white Loganville, where almost two-thirds of homes consist of two-parent families and 85 percent of residents have a high school degree or more, is more of a suburban relic of its surrounding model of urban growth. It's not a quaint town in the way of New England, with rustic town squares. It's more the last vestige of its rapidly changing surroundings. It gets busy at the center, bisected by Atlanta Highway, which continues west into the more dense Snellville. The highway seems to repeat in sections, like a real-life Möbius strip: Staples, IHOP, Ruby Tuesday, Eckerd, Staples, IHOP, Ruby Tuesday, Eckerd, with maybe a Wal-Mart thrown in. This road branches off into shrubbed and flowery communities consisting of white-slatted or redbrick houses, with sweeping driveways, rambling yards, and almost no fences.

On one of these back roads, a hooked lane called Brushy Fork, is J. C. Magill Elementary School. It looks more like a barn or ranch than a school. The schoolyard features a tennis court, a basketball court, a covered shed, and a small soccer field. The mixture of mud and rambunctiousness during recess turns the kindergartners to fifth-graders into sweaty carriers of odor and muck. The faculty members smile as they point out the dust the children bring back into the clean, sparse, muraled hallways. The children stop at intersections to make way for the faculty to pass, and it's easy to remember the gesture as a salute.

This is the school whose moral compass Laura Mallory thought was askew, thanks to the presence of Harry Potter on its shelves. I came to Georgia to try and understand. I was holding out hope for her. I knew most of my circle considered her a nutcase, and there was no shortage of times I'd called her nuts myself. But she was the leading voice on banning Harry Potter for some reason, and I was determined to find out why she was so hell-bent on criticizing what I and so many I knew loved so madly.

And I knew both of us were thinking we each stood a chance at changing the other's mind.

Everyone in the area seemed to know who she was; I tested my theory on the hotel clerk and was met with an eye roll; a librarian in greater Gwinnett said, "Oh, her," with heavy disdain.

Laura Mallory began her campaign against Harry in 2005, when her son came home and told her that his teacher encouraged them to read the series. After doing some research, and with assistance from the *Witchcraft Repackaged* video, she decided that the books were dangerous, and asked the school to ban them. She was denied. She appealed, and was denied. Finally she took the case to the State Superior Court and, again, was denied. The press took notice, the way they usually did when someone challenged such a beloved series on such a vehement and grandiose level.

The appeal to the school board, in April 2006, brought ninety-five people to the small hearing room that was usually reserved for school disciplinary hearings. Laura held up a brochure for "witchcraft camp," and swore that Harry Potter teaches that it's all right for children to practice spell making, potions, and other types of magic. She also trotted out Jordan Fuchs, a fifteen-year-old girl, as a witness; Jordan said she and her friend had tried spells and performed a séance after reading Harry Potter.

Several students left high school early to attend the two o'clock meeting, some of them wearing shirts that read Censorship Destroys Education, and others wearing stickers featuring the face of Daniel Radcliffe, who plays Harry in the movies.

Challenges to Harry Potter began in 1999, but boomed within a year. By the 2000s, the Harry Potter books were those most often requested to be removed from school and library shelves. No one requests that just one, and not all, of the Harry Potter books be removed from shelves but that the whole series be banned.

The American Library Association's Office of Intellectual Freedom deals with the challenges on the public school level, often providing assistance to those who fight against the books' removal. They offer documentation and information, and occasionally provide assistance if the case gets taken to court. The director at the Office of Intellectual Freedom, Judith Krug, remembers the 1990s as the good ol' days, when the most hotly challenged books were about homosexuality. In 1999, the ALA received only 472 cumulative challenges; the office estimates that the figures represent less than a quarter of all those reported and recorded. The Harry Potter books, said Judith Krug, left "everything in their dust."

A lot of the complaints around Harry Potter were really calls for moderation and amendments to school policy. There had only been a few book burnings (to which fans usually didn't object, since the person who burned the book first bought it, which defeated their aim), and usually parents just requested that teachers give them reading lists so that they could tell their children they had the option to leave the classroom when certain books were read aloud. And sometimes the complaints had nothing to do with witchcraft or religion: the parents simply complained that the content was scaring the child. But those had never been the hotly contested incidents.

The books were most heavily challenged between 1999 and 2003, coinciding with Harry Potter fandom's incubation period. In 2000, the ALA alone received 646 challenges, a 50 percent increase from 1999, which Krug says was largely because of Potter.

Challenges don't mean bannings: at most challenges are the record of a complaint, or the attempt by a parent or anyone else to get a book banned from a shelf. Laura Mallory had made plenty of challenges, but had not succeeded in one banning. A lot of libraries, including one in a school county near Galveston, Texas, the same county for whom an issue of school prayer led to a Supreme Court ruling against it in 2000, have instituted restrictions requiring children to get permission slips from their parents before they could check out any of Jo Rowling's books.

In 1999, one attempt to ban readings of the Harry Potter books resulted in a civil student revolt. The fourth-graders in Zeeland, Michigan, who were subject to the ban wrote letters to the superintendent, asking him to repeal the restriction. When they learned how many other children from other locations shared their outrage, they formed Muggles for Harry Potter, an anticensorship group that almost immediately saw thousands of adolescent members grow from a grassroots campaign of Internet postings and paper petitions.

The challenges aren't just restricted to Christians; some in the Jewish and Muslim world have opposed them in small sections, too. They were banned from use in private schools by the Ministry of Education in the United Arab Emirates because they were found to have values opposite to those of Islam, and there have been minor flare-ups from the Greek and Bulgarian Orthodox churches as well.

One of the Christians who sees Harry as a positive moral influence is Father Stuart Crevcoure, a Roman Catholic priest with the Diocese of Tulsa, Oklahoma. A passionate Harry Potter fan, Crevcoure said the use of the occult in Potter doesn't constitute a recruitment program for young pagans.

"I read stories about witches and fairies and leprechauns and magic growing up, and I seemed to have turned out okay. There are a lot of themes that I think are very compatible with Christian understanding . . . the themes of death, love, and sacrifice—these have been a part of good storytelling for ages and ages and ages, and certainly they are also very Christian themes. I don't think we're going to see Pope Benedict write an encyclical about Harry Potter any time in the near future, but his first encyclical was on the theme of love."

When I told Laura Mallory I was Catholic, she invoked the Pope and Father Gabriele Amorth, the Catholic Church's chief exorcist, who have both spoken against Harry Potter in the media (the Pope did so before he became Pope, when he was Cardinal Joseph Ratzinger and was a prefect for the congregation for the Doctrine of the Faith, a position frequently described as the Church's devil's advocate). I waved her off, explaining that neither of them spoke for me and their arguments had not convinced me differently; in fact, there were any number of priests and clergy, one of whom was on my own staff on Leaky, who believed differently, and who had even used Harry Potter to illustrate the morals evoked in the Bible.

That's when Laura started in about her vision. She rarely talks about it, she said. It came to her like a dream, perhaps a waking one—she couldn't remember exactly what she was doing when it happened, which was at least three years ago. In her vision, she watched a grim procession of oblivious people, marching toward a deep chasm. She saw it clearly in front of her eyes even as she was talking about it—or at least she did a convincing job of seeming to be watching an invisible screen. In the dream, hundreds, thousands, maybe millions of people walk to their doom without ever knowing, walk mindlessly off a cliff and into a pale blue, iridescent fire. Flowing like a river, she said, winding around, making a human waterfall as they descended into a lake of blue flame, as predicted in the Book of Revelation. She's there, too. She's the one person trying to stop it. Wielding a white rope, trying to use it to hold them back. Trying to stem the flow.

She was a curious woman, full of contradictions. Slight, but capable of eating heartily; mild-mannered, but sometimes hard-faced and white-knuckled; polite and yielding but at other times abruptly dismissive of alien opinions. She's cagey about her history, about names and dates, because of the verbal lashing she had received from a small portion of Potter fans: what she will reveal is that she grew up in Atlanta, and she described herself as solely an evangelical Christian, with no other denomination associated. Her family went to church when she was younger but she had no real ties to religion, and she had virtually no memory of being associated with any one sect; she remembered only one "big Presbyterian church."

She spent less than a year at Oxford College in Emory University before she dropped out and tried some classes at Georgia State. Peer pressure and a "need to be accepted" turned her into a poster child for the Georgia party scene, she said, complete with a nicotine addiction and a boyfriend who sold "good time" narcotics like marijuana and Ecstasy. She never tried Ecstasy or anything "worse than that," she said, though she admitted to some experimentation.

The scene was "getting old," she said. Her friends would backstab her, given the chance. "Drugs were getting old. The whole party thing was getting kind of old, too. It was fun for a while but it just lost its flavor."

Then her boyfriend went away to a Bible college and claimed his life had been turned around. She visited him and found him among people who welcomed her, even though she "didn't have the right clothes" and "probably reeked of smoke." They told her about Jesus. They told her He had a plan for her, and the prospect spoke to her spiritual void. She spent the return trip home crying and asking for providence.

She didn't say what exactly happened to bring her what she feels is a more enlightened state. She just said Jesus opened her eyes, and acted as though that was the most comprehensive explanation for which anyone could ask. Suddenly she could quit smoking, cold turkey. Drugs and alcohol were banished for life. She claimed the Holy Spirit came to her, and opened her soul and spirit.

"You have emotions and the will in your body, but there is something underneath," she said.

But most of all, she could hear God's voices. Clear as day, clear as anything, and she can repeat the things He'd said to her; she can recount it as though He were someone she spoke with on the phone last week. And she can instantly sense my disbelief.

I was a person of faith, I told her; I believed in God. I had religion. And I had no idea how she managed to treat her beliefs as more important than mine, which don't see Harry Potter as a danger to them.

I wanted to know on what authority she could claim that I was wrong, and she was right; that Harry Potter wasn't a call for moral righteousness or argument for ideals that closely followed Christian morality but was instead a dangerous portal to secular and pagan belief systems. For that matter, I told her, I wanted to know how she could call pagan beliefs inherently evil, or how she could transfer that belief system to the public school system, which is supposed to be free of religious influences.

"We pledge allegiance under God," she said fiercely. "Church and state has been taken out of context. America's roots are clearly Christian and anyone who says any differently has done no homework."

In October 2006, six months after that infamous school hearing, Laura made some of her most explosive comments about Harry Potter to date: that books that promote evil, like Harry Potter, promote a culture in which tragic school shootings occur, like the one at Columbine High School in Colorado, in which two students opened fire on their class and killed thirteen people. Laura's April 20 hearing coincidentally had taken place on the seven-year anniversary of that shooting, and Laura had planned (but never had time) to read a quote from Darrell Scott, whose daughter, Rachel Joy Scott, died in the shooting. Mr. Scott spoke before the House Judiciary Subcommittee on Crime in Washington, D.C. The quote she intended to use from his speech was:

> *Your laws ignore our deepest needs*
> *Your words are empty air*
> *You've stripped away our heritage*
> *You've outlawed simple prayer*

> Now gunshots fill our classrooms
> And precious children die
> You seek for answers everywhere
> And ask the question "Why?"
> You regulate restrictive laws
> Through legislative creed
> And yet to fail to understand
> That God is what we need!

I've no doubt that Laura feels great pain for the victims and families of victims of Columbine, but I wasn't alone in my outrage the day she made that comparison. Nor was I prepared for the e-mail we got from Lindsey Benge.

> It is not her opinion that Harry Potter is evil that
> grates me so, it is the completely insane accusation that
> Harry Potter and similar material is the cause of school
> shootings. As a survivor of the 1999 shootings at
> Columbine High School I feel that I should know a little
> bit about this topic.

Lindsey Benge isn't simply a survivor of the Columbine shootings; she was standing right on the edge of the worst damage and has had to live with the fallout.

An hour before Dylan Klebold and Eric Harris entered the school bearing guns and bombs, Lindsey was passing notes with her friend Dan Mauser, a skinny, blond fifteen-year-old who wore round glasses, and whom she had known since elementary school. Lindsey wanted to ditch her class and go to the library with him next period, a move Dan was trying to block. "I don't want to see you until after lunch," he told her. A movie was playing in class, and they whispered and bickered until Lindsey, resigned, walked Dan to the library and then turned to go to math.

"Bye, Moose," she said.

"Bye, Linds. See you later."

The library became the nucleus of the tragedy. As the two shooters made their presence known, students fled there and hid under the tables and inside rooms. About ten minutes after he first started shooting, Eric Harris entered and screamed at everyone to get up— those in white hats (most likely jocks) first. Dylan Klebold followed after Eric. They went on a rampage through the library, destroying display cases, throwing bombs, and injuring or killing nearly thirty people. The gunmen asked at least one girl, survivor Valeen Schnurr, if she believed in God; she said yes and was not killed, though there were reports that another, Cassie Bernall, said yes and was shot immediately afterward.

Daniel Mauser was shot in the face, at close range, by Harris. He died immediately.

In the melee caused by the shooting, Lindsey had been pulled out of the school; a friend tugged her out an exit via the back of her shirt. Before she left she got one look at Klebold, turning, with something dark in his hand.

"Moose," as Lindsey called him, wasn't her only friend who died in the gunfire. Rachel Scott, the girl whose father's words Laura Mallory was going to use in her testimony, and a few others who were wounded, were also friends. But it was losing Moose that shut Lindsey down. She didn't react. She barely cried. She stared at the news reports dispassionately. Friends would call, and she would just tell them she was fine. Everything was normal. Later in the year, a friend of hers who was paralyzed from the waist down in the shooting would lose her mother to suicide. Lindsey and her friends found Rachel's abandoned car. The media rehashed and recycled stories about the shooting. Lindsey's grandfather passed away in June. And outside of a few isolated incidents, Lindsey refused to come to terms with the tragedy.

"I completely shut off," she remembered. "I pretty much shut down and went about business as usual." She got some closure the following year, when the school installed a skylight in the library to honor the victims; she did some gun control work; she considered a future in law; she tried to talk about the shooting and deal with it properly, on all the emotional levels. But it wasn't working; there was a certain numbness about her activities. She'd go to the movies with friends but couldn't let herself enjoy them. She felt like she was walking through mud.

After the first Harry Potter movie came out, Lindsey found herself with a coupon for the books; her friends were fanatical about the series but she refused to get sucked in. But finally she gave in. And then she fell in.

Like so many others, she became immediately entranced with the series. At that time there were only four books, so for her the story ended when Cedric, a kind and just classmate, was killed in a random act of violence. The themes of loss, and of relying on your friends and doing what's right over what's easy, struck deep chords within her. In Neville Longbottom, she saw her sometimes bumbling, sometimes geeky, always determined friend Dan, who, like Neville, could and would stand up to his friends when it was important. "Dan was one of those friends who, in the early parts of your life, kind of went underappreciated, much like I think Neville was," she said. "You didn't realize how important he was and how much of a good friend he was."

Soon she was on the Internet, looking up any information about the books she could find and discussing them for hours at bookshops.

She read them repeatedly. She dressed in wizard gear for parties. It was like a veil had been brushed back from her consciousness, leaving everything more vibrant; she hadn't felt as immersed in anything since the shootings. Even as time passed and more books came out, she felt more in tune with Harry's messages, and they helped clarify her feelings around the senseless shooting and the deep loss she and her community had suffered. When Harry, at the end of *Half-Blood Prince*, has an irrational urge to laugh during Dumbledore's funeral, Lindsey remembered all the times that "silly things" made her laugh in what anyone else would see as some of the saddest memorials and tributes around the Columbine tragedy.

"It brought back an innocent sense of joy," she said, "as well as providing me with something I could relate to in terms of struggling through hardships and loss. I can only hope this woman [Laura Mallory] realizes that she is not proving a point. She is merely insulting the people who she is using as her examples. How dare she?"

The e-mail from Lindsey clarified one of the real ironies about Laura Mallory, and while sitting across from her at an IHOP I felt the thudding presence of that irony. I really thought she could love Harry Potter. If she could just get over the witchcraft part, disregard the spells and potions and creatures, I thought, and gaze into the clear and moral core, she would fall into it the same way I, Lindsey, and so many others had. The thought weighed down our conversation and muddled my thoughts. Just like the sadness and fondness she expressed for the souls she claimed were "lost" to Harry, I felt my disdain for her dissolving into a deep sense of regret that she was denying herself the experience.

The centerpiece of Laura Mallory's argument is not that the books scare children or that she has a problem with the idea of witchcraft in general practice (although she clearly does). It's that she believes the books actually promote real witchcraft: that children read the books and turn to what she terms the occult. Within five minutes of our meeting she brandished a list at me with eleven types of magic found in the real world that are in Harry Potter, including divination, outer-body experience, and traveling through space and time. I didn't really know this before—that is, I knew it was part of her argument, but never guessed her belief in magic as a reality was so ingrained, was making her eyeballs widen as she pointed at each of the names on the sheet as if they were revelations—but they're written here, see how true they are! I choked back the urge to point out that she believed in magic more than I did, and that she was probably doing more to spread the idea that magic can be practiced using Harry Potter as a guidebook than I am with my Harry Potter Web site.

Fans have seemed particularly eager to make sure everyone knows that the fundamentalists who oppose Harry Potter don't speak for all Christians. In fact, people of all faiths have embraced the books. They maintain that the morality of the series cannot be questioned. Harry consistently makes choices that can be considered to be in the Christian spirit: he risks his life to save others, he stands up against prejudice, and he considers fighting evil his most important task in life. In January 2000, *Christianity Today*, the flagship evangelical publication started by Billy Graham, ran an editorial asking parents what they should do, given all the reports of Christians fighting school boards to have Harry removed from their shelves, then answered its own question:

"We think you should read the Harry Potter books to your kids."

While asserting that Christians should "never apologize for rigorously scrutinizing what influences our children," the editorial calls

Harry Potter a "Book of Virtues with a preadolescent funny bone." The literary witchcraft of the book "has almost no resemblance to the I-am-God mumbo jumbo of Wiccan circles," and contains "wonderful examples of compassion, loyalty, courage, friendship and even self-sacrifice."

I could not get Laura to understand this.

"There is a good message at the core of these books," I said, insisting that message is much stronger than the urge to pick up a wand and wave it around.

"But what about all the kids that come away feeling they do want to pick up a wand and have gone into witchcraft?"

"They are in the extreme minority, and there are other factors there including interaction from parents. Their parents have a responsibility to know what their kids are reading."

"And there's no responsibility from the books or Scholastic or Rowling?"

Not to make sure they don't start practicing Wicca, I said. They are free to publish what they want, within reason. "No one's going to publish *How to Murder, 101.*"

She crossed her arms. "Do you know the books were turned down by nine publishers?"

"A lot of books are."

"Oh."

"It's common."

She looked punctured. "Is it OK to use witchcraft to fight evil?"

"*I* don't think so, but—"

"But that's what Harry does."

"But it's *fictional!*"

"It is not. It is sorcery." Her Bible was already on the table and open to Revelation 21. I waved my hands to try and stop her.

"The way it's *practiced* is fictional," I objected, but she was already reading aloud, about the cowardly and unbelieving and abominable and murderers.

"I just want people to know my heart," she said, beseeching me. "My heart is in the right place, and I love kids—I love them, and I think they're righteous to God and He loves them so much. They're getting into witchcraft because of Harry Potter. What about their souls?"

"I believe my—and your—reasoning is imperfect," I told her. "I believe all human reasoning is imperfect. It's not for me to say. And the difference between us is that I'm not a missionary."

"You could be a missionary with your book. You could use it for good."

" 'For good' is a very loaded phrase," I said, nearly to myself, feeling almost weary at this point. I tried again. "It's just such a shame, because I think if you would just read them, the way I do, and get over the idea that there's spells and magic, you'd really love these books. They're about being moral and honest and just and *good*."

"You can't fight evil with evil," she said, and her face went waxen, one perfectly polished finger pressed so hard against the tabletop it turned white. "He is a wizard. Witchcraft is evil. And if you don't believe that, then that's your choice. You're allowed to believe that. But one day everyone will know that witchcraft is evil."

Her face was steady, despite the hand on the table, still white where she had pressed the blood out of it. There was pride under her words. Pride and something else I had been searching for the whole afternoon—a belief in her own righteousness. I'd never seen such stalwart righteousness up close like this before. It was the first time I'd met someone who had used the wall of faith to block every line of logical reasoning I could find. That hope I had carefully constructed shattered and dispersed inside me; Laura was convinced that she had all the answers, because she believed God had already told them to her or would offer them whenever she asked. I envied her surety.

"Is everyone allowed to practice any religion they want?" I asked.

"Sure they are, but you don't have to indoctrinate our kids into witchcraft at school."

"So what would you say," I offered, sitting up further as I realized I was on to something, "if a Wiccan person came into school and said, 'Such-and-such book is indoctrinating my child into Christianity, and it's got to stop.'"

She hesitated. "What book?"

"An imaginary book! Just say one existed."

"Then they'd have a case just like the atheists have done."

"Would you support their attempts to get it off the shelves?"

"That would depend on circumstances. That is just too raw of a question without having a specific book."

I cast around for some obscure title to make my point. "One of your books on your shelf at home, one of the Christian books you say your children read, about the Bible. If they put those books on the shelves."

She visibly brightened. "What about the classroom? Harry Potter's in the classroom."

"In the classroom, fine, and a Wiccan person [objects]. What would you say to that?"

"They have a right to do that. America is a free country. They have their right to oppose it. Would I help them? No, I don't agree with Wicca. Witchcraft is an abomination to God."

"Then how," I asked, because I was truly confused, "how can you ask the school system to support you and your wish to get the books off shelves, if you won't support this Wiccan person?" She doesn't answer. "Do you follow me? If you're asking support from our system—"

"I know you want to pin me down."

"No, I want to understand, I'm trying to understand, how you cannot say to this fictional Wiccan person that your Christian books should be taken out of the classroom."

"They've already done that! The Bible has been taken out."

I pointed out that the Bible is actually a Christian text, an officially recognized one. No one has designated Harry Potter an actual instructional book in wizardry, except her and those who share her beliefs. She latched onto this, claiming the presence in the classroom, and the teacher's recommendation, says otherwise.

"They were being used as *texts*," she insisted. She repeated it to try and shake the reaction out of me, but I didn't bite.

"As reading texts, not as practice-these-spells texts," I said.

She straightened up. "Well. I would *hope* the teachers aren't like that."

J. K. Rowling came in at number four on the list of authors most challenged between 1990 and 2004—even though only five of her books (plus two textbooks) had been published and, at that point, she'd only been a published author for half that time. Challenges to Harry Potter, at that point, had only been coming in for five years, so she made up for quite a bit of lost time.

Mainstays on the ALA list have included fare that had been considered timeless: *Of Mice and Men* by John Steinbeck has virtually set up camp on it. So have books by Maya Angelou (for "sexual content, racism, offensive language, and violence"), as well as *The Catcher in the Rye* by J. D. Salinger. The last series to make a continuous splash on the list were Harry's much-touted predecessors: the Goosebumps and Fear Street series by R. L. Stine. Harry initially took the title of most challenged book from *Heather Has Two Mommies* and *Daddy's Roommate*, two books that explain homosexuality to children.

I presented Jo Rowling with this fact at her house in Edinburgh; she was in the middle of pulling the curtains, and before it was half out of my mouth she raised one hand in the air and said, "Well, there you go."

Mostly, she seems bemused by the whole affair. She never expected her books to sell well enough to gain fame, never mind notoriety, or to gather an ardent following, never mind an active picket line.

As soon as I brought up Laura Mallory her face grew pensive and her chin tilted, like she was trying to figure something out. "Has she read them yet?"

Laura Mallory's central contradiction—and it is one she shares with many of the people who fight her case—is that she has never actually read the Harry Potter books. Many of those who are against Rowling's work are against it before they read it, and seem to use the books chiefly to mine them for satanic gems. Harry's mother's sacrifice is portrayed in the books as an instrument of good and of the power of love, and the video from which Laura Mallory takes her mission is crafted to make us believe that such a sacrifice is bad and wrong, because it takes away from Jesus' patriarchal role as the Savior of Mankind.

The one time the American Library Association had to go to court over a censorship issue, it was because of a case in Cedarville, Arkansas. In July 2003, Billy Ray Counts and Mary Nell Counts, parents of a fourth-grader, challenged the city school board's placement of the series on a restricted list that requires students to submit permission forms in order to get the books. A chief argument was that it violated a 1982 Supreme Court decision that forbade the restriction of books based on content.

The case was quickly decided in the ALA and the Counts' favor and never appealed, and not at all to the ALA's surprise, no one on the school board had read the Harry Potter books. They had simply "heard they were bad books," Ms. Krug said, and put them on the restricted list.

That's the thing that most galls me, and Jo as well: that anyone could go on such a worldwide mission to ban the books without ever having read them.

"She's severely misguided," Jo said. "The view I would take in my own life would be to say to my children, 'Let's discuss it, let's talk about it honestly.' I'm not going to lock away a popular children's book and tell you it's evil. That's nonsense, and I would go further to say that it's damaging. Fundamentalism in any form, in any religion, is intolerant, and tolerance is the only way forward. For all of us. I cannot imagine, in my life, shouting and screaming about something I didn't actually know about. That's insane to me."

The fact that Laura Mallory hasn't read the books was the biggest source of my frustration. I couldn't help but feel that being so outspoken against Harry Potter without actually reading the books is like being against baseball just because players use bats.

She knew I was thinking it. When, unable to wait for a better moment and bursting with curiosity, I blurted out, "Now, a bit of a sixty-four-million-dollar question for you," she simply looked at her half-eaten eggs and breathed, "Oh, no."

"Why haven't you read the books?" I felt better as soon as I said it. I wanted to scream it.

"I knew you were going to ask me that."

I barely breathed, waiting for her answer. For years, as she's claimed publicly that she didn't need to read the Harry Potter books to make her case, we as fans have loudly wondered how she could make such a ludicrous claim. As much as her refusal to read the books seems to be proof to most fans that she's simply intolerant, or a fool, it's chiefly upon this that I've spun my fragile web of hope for her. She just hasn't read them. Once she reads them, she'll see.

"I repeatedly prayed," she said. "I hope you can understand this, but many people don't. I said, 'God, I need to read these books because the criticism is unbelievable, and how can I do what I'm doing and not read the books?' He always let me know, 'Don't read them. I don't want you coming under the influence of these books. There's demonic assignment on these books,' and that was what He showed me."

I'd traveled to Georgia almost entirely just to hear her answer to this question, and that was it? God told her? What if I told her that God had urged *me* to read the books? I certainly couldn't quote Him verbatim but I wholeheartedly believed, at that point, that something larger had brought me to this series and the changes it had made in my life and my ability to contribute goodness to the world. Wasn't that the same thing? I was tempted to lie and tell her that God had given me opposite instructions, but I couldn't bring myself to mock her faith. There was something admirable about how unshaken she was, and I didn't want to be the one to rock her. Not that I could.

Besides, Laura is out of the game. On May 29, her appeal to the state's Superior Court was denied. Her faith alone couldn't win this one. She has apparently given up.

"It's in God's hands now," she said.

CHAPTER TEN

High Seas

here were four cameras and six media outlets waiting for dinner to begin. I was in the final throes of preparation for the live podcast scheduled for after the dinner; everyone else was anxious to see the wave of fans, dressed as Bellatrix and Voldemort and Snape and even Dobby the house-elf. We had a final sound check before the doors opened, and then the hordes descended for the opening of the Phoenix Rising Harry Potter conference in New Orleans.

It was May 17, 2007 already. Time was speeding by faster than we could believe it, and as July approached, excited as we were, part of us desperately wanted to stop it.

The way Harry Potter was getting covered, it seemed it was all anyone was talking about anyway. Borders had sent a seven-person team to the conference to film enough coverage for its Web site to last them the next nine weeks until the publication of *Deathly Hallows*. They were filming our podcast, interviewing people on the street, and having round-table discussions with fans, and would be streaming it all in broadband to their seventeen million subscribers. *Dateline* was there collecting information for a series of specials about

J. K. Rowling, and Salon.com used the event to launch a long piece on the character of the fandom.

About a thousand people were at the conference, and almost all of them were waiting to get into dinner. When the doors opened it was like bridal-dress sample sale day at Kleinfeld. They flocked to their assigned seats and cameras flashed and the red lights of recording video cameras scanned the crowd. Already it was easy to spot fans with tears in their eyes, or those having a conversation about the first time they read the books or what they would be doing when they read the last one, or how they were twelve when they had started and twenty-two now, and how they had grown up with the series. This was our last chance to be together before the end, the last large conference before the release. A thousand people had come here and most of them had done so in costume. Later tonight, Sue, John, and I would be hosting a podcast to entertain some of them and discuss final theories and, mostly, whether Snape was good or bad. That was the big question and had been for two years; this conference was featuring a live Snape Debate that was the hottest ticket around. At the opening dinner there was even a shiny, leathered Dominatrix Snape who went around smacking people. These days it was all about Snape, Snape, Snape, which was, in some ways, a tremendous change from just four years earlier.

I had come back from the Royal Albert Hall event and my first encounter with Jo Rowling in June 2003 to a hostile work environment. I was grilled on where I had been, but I dug in my heels, said it was personal, and wouldn't budge. I wasn't really lying. That trip had been nothing but personal. After I'd met Jo, I'd sat in the basement at my small hotel and done what I said I'd never do: sent an e-mail to

Fiddy Henderson, Jo's personal assistant. I'd gotten her address by accident and was holding back from using it out of some sense of propriety. After the reception Jo had just given me I chucked that propriety out the window and sent an unsolicited e-mail to her and Neil Blair, effusing and telling them how much the moment had meant to me.

All my employers had to do to discover the truth was check the Leaky Cauldron. I'd rushed to an Internet café right after the event to tell Leaky readers what had just happened, and that report, my pictures with Jo Rowling, and the scan of my signed book cover were there, surrounded by ebullient messages from longtime Leaky readers who had been overjoyed at the validation. I almost wanted my bosses to get fed up and fire me, but even after two years under Denise's rule, I held slimly to the desire to walk out under my own steam. So I snubbed my nose, jutted my chin, and stayed silent. The interrogation over, I returned to my cell and worked studiously on the things I found least inspiring, digging through all my filing. It was easy, even enjoyable work; the secret of my trip, of the welcome I had received from Jo Rowling, of the overwhelming excitement my parents had shown on my return, and of the signed book, now lying carefully covered in towels in my bedroom, surrounded me like an invisible bond, defending me against the place like a Patronus.

Still, I decided not to push things any further, so I at first declined Heidi's insistence that I attend Nimbus 2003, the first-ever Harry Potter fan conference, to be held in Orlando the following month. I'd never been to any kind of fan conference, convention, symposium, or whatever they were calling it, and so had no idea what to expect. Fans were so excited about it that the idea tugged at me, though, and curiosity overcame me two days before the opening ceremonies. One more cheap air rate later and I was taking my second trip in as many months. I wouldn't have to miss any work for the weekend trip, so on a balmy Friday night I found myself on my way to Florida.

The conference was at the Swan & Dolphin Resort in Orlando. I got there late in the evening, so I stowed my luggage at the hotel desk and walked to the main room of the conference, the hotel's green-and-amber coloring making me feel like I was swimming through a cartoon ocean.

Unease tugged at me as I walked; these weren't my people, weren't my online friends, except for Emily Wahlee, whom I'd finally be meeting after two years of talking with her on a message board. The fans going to this conference seemed to be primarily from the big fanfiction sites or LiveJournal. I knew a few of them but had really only spent time on the Sugar Quill and Leaky and in all honesty had no idea what I was doing here. I had a camera and my laptop; at least I could write up a report for the site. I'd never felt part of the physical fandom aside from my few real-life friends and the Leaky people I talked to every day. I didn't express my Potter love in non-digital ways. I concerned myself more with everyday happenings and news rather than detailed academic papers plumbing psychological inferences and societal conventions as referenced by Potter. Though I had nothing against it, I never dressed in costume, and I owned no themed Harry Potter clothing or merchandise. Just one glance around the lobby of the hotel had revealed four Dracos and a Snape; it made me feel like a bit of a fraud.

And the opening day of the conference made me feel like an impostor. It was a six-hundred-person costume party. Never before had I seen such an assortment of people of all shapes, sizes, and costumes. There were girls dressed as Lucius, way too many people dressed as Hermione, and surprisingly few dressed as Harry. Minor characters outnumbered the major ones at least two to one.

This was different than it had been when with other fans, like hanging out with Meg or with Kathleen and David, and doing silly Harry Potter–related things like baking cakes or making pumpkin juice. This was fandom concentrate. I ducked a few duels in the hallways. A gallery featured rich, detailed pieces of art depicting the Harry Potter universe. The presentation topics looked like a college registration catalog: "Narratorial Control: Harry Potter Joins the Three Investigators," "Hermione Granger and Issues of Gender in the Harry Potter Books and Films," "The Seven Deadly Sins/Seven Heavenly Virtues: Moral Development in Harry Potter."

Except for the book five release, I'd never been in a room with more than twenty Harry Potter fans at one time; here the only reason I was being looked at strangely was because I didn't look *enough* like a fan. No scar tattoo, no wand, no robes. I was a freak.

I got my first physical display of what Leaky meant to fans when I visited the room in which Steve Vander Ark was giving a lecture on the geography of canon. Steve's site, the Harry Potter Lexicon, was an online encyclopedia of the books, restructuring the information inside them so that they were researchable; it was of great use to fanfiction writers who wanted to keep their stories true to canon as well as for Potter trivia buffs and anyone trying to piece together the details of the plot. Our sites were partners—B. K. and I had written Steve about a year earlier suggesting we form the Floo Network, an online collection of sites affiliated with one another, to be a complete fan resource—but this was the first time I'd ever met him.

He had a bowl of graying hair and thickish glasses, as well as a booming voice and a polished presentation style. It was clear he'd given many previous talks and spent a lot of time in front of people, which made me cringe remembering my awkward high school acting and my stumbling attempts during my college public speaking class. I was always behind a camera or a notepad; it wasn't that I lacked vanity, but I simply felt most comfortable being busy and looking at people instead of watching them look at me. So when Steve decided to alert the one hundred or so people in the room to my presence, I was quite busy.

Up to that point, no one had really known what I looked like. This group of people probably all read the site, but online pictures of the staff were scant; the one picture of me and Jo Rowling that had circulated in the past month was grainy, and I looked different in person. So no one knew who the girl at the front trying to get a picture of the entire face-on group was; I was crouched low to stay out of the way of the projector, and was sneaking left to get the shot in focus when Steve swept his hand to his right and announced that this was Melissa, that girl from the Leaky Cauldron who had just met J. K. Rowling. The appreciative roar that followed surprised me so much I fell right on my butt.

Scrambling up and blushing hard, I waved, took the picture, and got out of the way. But after that a strange thing started happening: I was stopped more frequently in the hallways and asked to sign people's program books. I'd had my own signed by all my friends, like a yearbook, and it didn't occur to me to think of it as anything other than that. It was flattering, anyway, to think that I was in a strange world where a lot of people knew who I was. It was a nice antidote to toiling anonymously on unglamorous things like HTML code for the Web pages and shot-by-shot analyses of the films.

I spent most of the conference wandering around semi-aimlessly but attempting to soak up as much atmosphere as I could. The costumed people, I soon learned, were "cosplayers," or role players in costumes, who roamed the hallways, using their just-bought wands to hex and Stun people. At midnight on my first night I roamed the halls, and found scattered groups sitting on the paisley carpet. One was having a fierce discussion on canon, on Snape, and whether we had any more insight into his nature after the fifth book, which still hadn't revealed his loyalties. Another was a motley fan-art group, and I nearly drooled over the luminous and textured depictions of my favorite characters.

But the thing that kept making itself apparent all weekend long was a profound sense of relief. It had been three years since the true online fandom had begun, since the community of hard-core fans had started to find one another in earnest. All of us led other lives, with work and school and families who didn't understand how we could love anything as much as we loved Harry Potter, who even, at times, made fun of us for devoting so much time and energy to it— but then would spend six hours shouting themselves hoarse at a football match, and five after that shouting themselves hoarse at each other as they discussed the same game. Meeting someone in the "real world" often meant that the question of whether they knew and/or liked Harry Potter became a crucial one, the same way anyone else wanted to know if someone liked music, theater, or sports. Here, finally, was a community of people who understood. People formed friendships based on love of Harry Potter plus something else. They loved Harry Potter but they also were artists, or enjoyed the same television shows, similar authors, and clothing styles, or also wrote fanfiction or their own fiction. In other words, everyone at the conference was out of the closet.

Which did not at all mean everyone was getting along.

The most anticipated event of the conference, by far, happened on the second day. I'd been delayed at a different panel by someone who wanted to show me her Snitch tattoo, so I had to run to make it in time, before they closed the doors. My dear friend Emily, one of the first people I'd ever met in online fandom and the most ardent R/H supporter I'd ever known, had been practicing for this; I didn't want to disappoint her by skipping it.

A year in the making, some worried that the release of *Harry Potter and the Order of the Phoenix* would render this panel useless, but as we had discovered over Kathleen's frustrated screams the week before, they were wrong. More than 870 pages of new material had only served to polarize the parties, deepen the controversy, and convince each side that it was the righteous one.

Chants and cheers were already going as I entered. At the front of the room, two teams of two people each reviewed notes and rehearsed opening speeches, their copies of the fifth book blooming with hundreds of colored tabs.

Latecomers filled gaps in the room by clogging the aisles, lining the walls, and queuing up out of the door into the hotel hallway. Those who had lined up for hours beforehand sat on the floor, and had naturally split themselves down the middle, like guests to a wedding. They hissed at one another and threw dirty looks across the table.

"You have to wear one," Emily said, thrusting a T-shirt at me, guilting me with her eyes. I wavered; I was there to represent and report back for the Leaky Cauldron, armed with a camera and notepad and supposed objectivity. But I had met Emily on the first message board I'd ever frequented in Harry Potter fandom, and she was presenting in person today the same way she'd been fighting eloquently and passionately for years online. This day was huge for her. I was on her side anyway, and had been since the beginning.

So I gave her an encouraging smile and donned the shirt, then tried to hide my biased self among the devotees on the left side of the room.

"Welcome to the first ever live Harry Potter Ship Debate: Ron/Hermione vs. Harry/Hermione!" an emcee announced, and the room exploded in cheers.

This Great Debate at Nimbus 2003 was the first-ever physical manifestation of a fight that had been going on since 2001. The "ships," short for "relationships" were, in this case, the potential coupling of Harry and Hermione versus Ron and Hermione. The "shippers" at this debate were those who thought that Jo Rowling was actually intending to pair their favorite couple up in the books. Some shippers simply favored one couple over the other, but at the debate, that feeling didn't matter. This debate was for the facts. Not what *should* happen, but what *would* happen, based on facts from the ultimate source—the Harry Potter books themselves.

There comes a point in the growth of every community where it gets too big to maintain the peace, and in fandom, disagreements over interpretations of the source material on which the fandom is based are the easiest way to get a good civil war brewing. That started happening to Harry Potter fandom in 2001, among the adult fans, who were then just starting to coalesce online. The Internet had reached the point where there were an abundance of places— message boards, LiveJournal groups, fanfiction sites—for them to gather, but one of them, the one most simply and aptly named, had become its standard-bearer. Harry Potter for Grownups was the first significant canon-debating battleground.

Between 1999 and 2002, more than 4,000 people joined Harry Potter for Grownups, where they mostly discussed the series' main plot questions. Fanfiction writers made up the core of online fandom at the time; FanFiction.net, a relatively new site, often ran slow and lagged under the swift rate at which Harry Potter fanfictions were added to its database. Its aim was to archive all types of fanfiction, but from about 1999 on, its portion of Harry Potter–related stories grew exponentially, doubling and tripling the number of its closest runner-up. Most fanfics were short and simple, and had little depth or development, but a small core of competent writers had risen above the grammarless masses. Usually these popular fanfiction writers were adults who had their own creative agendas as writers of other work, or an interest in exploring Jo Rowling's characters in different scenarios.

Jo Rowling would never become comfortable with the idea of fanfiction, but it was somewhere around this time that her lawyers asked her what she wanted to do about it. Some writers, like Anne Rice, prohibited fanfiction. Jo didn't love the idea—she thought it was like someone going into her house and rearranging her furniture—but didn't want to interfere with her fan base's expression of love of the series, either. She set up simple guidelines with her lawyers: never for money and nothing pornographic. Other than that, leave it alone.

As we had just spent years salivating for new canon—that is, new information about the books straight from Jo—in the lull between books fanfiction writers who wrote long and epic pieces were starting to be considered something like demigods in Harry Potterdom. They posted chapters online in Dickensian fashion, and their audiences, just like Harry Potter's had, gained speed and size exponentially with each posting.

Before the Internet, fanfiction was usually confined to adults who wrote stories about their favorite television or movie characters and collected them in printed, often mimeographed, fanzines that were sent out by snail mail at what now would be considered an interminably slow pace. With FanFiction.net, all anyone needed to share their fanfiction with the world was an Internet connection and an account. Within minutes, readers could start leaving reviews, and the instant gratification was like a drug.

The popular fanfictions in 2003 had actually little to do with Harry Potter. They started there—the characters and magic spells were there. The author's great gift to fanfiction is the work she's put into creating characters and landscapes; with that original setup work out of the way, fanfiction authors are free to play and experiment in characterization and plot. So a Harry Potter fanfiction is easily recognizable by the names of characters and places but sometimes by little else. Popular fanfiction versions of Harry Potter characters were a little more hip, a little more sardonic; they had more pop-culture references in their arsenal, and their evil counterparts tended to have secret good sides that would be revealed by cunning yet sensitive witches who teased it out of them. There were swooning, exaggerated romances as well as disciplined and detailed adventure romps, but the number of the latter paled in comparison to the former. Harry Potter slash started to come into its own as well, and while the term "slash" generally denotes a male homosexual romantic pairing, it was generally written by adult (usually straight) women portraying their romantic scenarios in a preexisting fictional world.

On the Harry Potter for Grownups list, a main set of authors emerged, vocal and passionate in their discussions on the Harry Potter texts and just as serious about their fanfiction. Beyond a doubt their leader was Cassandra Claire, who wrote three novel-length stories forming a trilogy about Draco Malfoy in which he's a twisted but redemptive soul, more sardonic than sadistic. Before *Order of the Phoenix* one couldn't enter fandom without being told they had to read the Draco series! I'd been told that, too, but never got truly caught up, partly because Draco seemed different and partly because the series seemed to be featuring Harry/Hermione.

In fact, back then, most popular Harry Potter fanfiction depicted Harry and Hermione as romantically involved. Writers either believed they *would* get together in the series or that they *should*. Sometimes they believed both. The writers of the most popular fanfics were almost always young professional women or middle-aged married ones, and whether they were filling in what they felt the canon lacked or were creating a tabula rasa with Hermione didn't matter; they had gathered a following of people who felt the same way.

The review boards for fanfiction, even if the story is genuinely poor, are havens of glowing praise. It's almost not a fanfiction if there isn't one review that says, OMG *are you sure you're not J. K. Rowling?*

The Harry Potter for Grownups list, however, wasn't a place where teenyboppers tried to get in fanfic authors' good graces by complimenting them heavily. It was a place for discussion, often deep and theoretical discussion, about politics and religion. These were adults who were proud to love Harry Potter, and the level of discourse had to reflect that. So when the issue of shipping came up on Harry Potter for Grownups, it was never going to die quietly.

It all started with a semicolon. When the stunning Fleur Delacour smiles at Ron at the end of *Goblet of Fire*, a semicolon stands between her action and Hermione's resultant scowl. For Ron/Hermione shippers, this meant that the smile caused Hermione's scowl, and therefore Hermione's affection lay with Ron. Harry/Hermione shippers argued that the entire scene—which features Fleur also showering affection on Harry—annoyed Hermione. From a study of detail as minute as punctuation sprang endless and vicious online debates tackling character, psychology, and what can be inferred from a sidelong glance or blushing cheek in literature.

Although Jo Rowling had, at that point, been deliberately cagey about many aspects of her series, she has seemingly been very clear about relationships. In a radio interview in 2000, when one child asked, "Do Harry and Hermione go on a date?" she said, "No, no, they are very platonic friends. But I won't answer for anyone else, nudge-nudge wink-wink!" Instead of taking her words at face value, Harry/Hermione shippers argued that because this interview took place before the release of *Harry Potter and the Goblet of Fire*, Jo Rowling meant that they were very platonic friends only prior to that .

book. Long after the release of that fourth book, a fan asked if Hermione had romantic feelings for Ron; Jo Rowling said, "The answer to the question is in *Goblet of Fire!*" Still, thanks to that infamous semicolon, each side of the debate claimed that the statement proved that they were advocates of the right relationship.

Lori Summers, a fanfic author well known for her Paradigm of Uncertainty series, in which Ron dies and Hermione and Harry spend lengthy chapters getting over it before consummating their love for each other, asked in mid-2000 for members of the Grownups list to contribute to a list of Harry/Hermione clichés most often found in fanfiction (such as Harry dying and leaving Hermione pregnant). She got a healthy response, including, *Ginny confesses her love for Harry/Draco/Neville in her diary* (Ginny's diary, possessed by Tom Riddle from *Chamber of Secrets,* would make frequent appearances in Ginny fanfiction). Or *Harry dates Cho, who cheats on him, leading him to find true love in Hermione.*

She wouldn't say why she was collecting these tropes, but the list responded with some mostly harmless, some slightly pointed comments about fanfiction and the relationships in question.

At the end of 2000, Kathleen MacMillan, apparently tired of all the Harry/Hermione discussion, felt the need to post a long rant entitled "H/H and why it's just wrong." She asserted that the obvious romantic tension in the books was between Hermione and Ron, and that the large majority of Harry/Hermione fanfiction ineffectively dealt with Ron as a character. She admitted that some list members had effectively argued that there may be evidence that Hermione has feelings for Harry, but argued against the idea of the reverse being true.

"Harry cares more about Ron than he does about Hermione," she wrote. "If I read one more H/H fanfic where Ron says some variation of 'I knew you guys always liked each other, I'm so happy for you, I'm glad I got over that little crush in our fourth year,' I am going to scream! . . . I am just tired of Ron getting shunted aside."

Kathleen's e-mail naturally led to even further discussion on the list; long-standing members posted part-by-part analyses and line-by-line rebuttals, quoting evidence from the books of Harry's concern for Hermione, while conceding that few H/H shippers thought they would date in the context of the seven published books. The conversation was light enough, with only a few outraged moments to speak of. Otherwise the debate remained civil, and calm, and though the conversation certainly kept moving through the month and intensifying through the next, it was no more heated than the debate over whether Sirius was a proper godfather or how effective Dumbledore was as a headmaster.

Then a new user named Zsenya appeared and declared her dismay for the many treatises in the list archives that insisted that Ron was going to go over to the dark side. She wrote a post called "Ron in Shining Armor," and engaged in a long tussle about whether Hermione kissing Harry on the cheek at the end of the fourth book meant anything.

Zsenya, or Jennie Levine, runs SugarQuill.net, the fanfiction site whose main goal is to keep all the characters as close to their canon incarnations as possible. The archivist is in her mid-thirties, and her hair is an explosion of black curls shot through with angel hairs of gray and one bolt of white near the top. She, like Jo Rowling, worships Jane Austen, and spent years visiting and partaking in the Republic of Pemberley (Pemberley.com), a site that housed Austen fanfic, most often based around the plucky and sardonic heroines of Austen's tea-and-corsets world.

She met Meg on July 8, 2000, the same day that the fourth book, *Harry Potter and the Goblet of Fire*, was released, at a Pemberley.com meet-up. The girls had both bought their copies of Harry Potter ear-

lier that day and were dying to get home and read them. But first
Meg, Jennie, and several other Pemberlians, as they called themselves, were meeting in the city to see a play featuring Jennifer Ehle,
who played Lizzie Bennet in the much-lauded BBC adaptation of
Pride and Prejudice. It was a group bonding activity, like making the
pilgrimage to Platform Nine and Three Quarters. Meg and Jennie
kept their side passion for Harry Potter away from their Austen
group, as though it were a breach of etiquette to move the discussion
in that direction.

It was at their next meeting, in September, at an English tea in
Manhattan with the same group of people, that Jennie finally blurted
out, "Has anyone read the Harry Potter books?" And the only person interested in talking about them and answering questions was
Meg. They had their first geek out, kvelling to each other about the
characters, and broke from the rest of the Austen group. They spent
the rest of their time walking around New York, talking about the
series, and playing an official Harry Potter trivia game they'd bought
from a nearby store.

They discovered that each of them had been writing Harry Potter
fanfiction on her own, secretly. They started e-mailing and swapping stories. They searched out places where they felt comfortable
online, where they could meet and talk with fans who were similar
to them, and found few. HPforGU was one of them, and in December, Jennie made her entrance as Zsenya, not realizing she was entering an established world with different rules than she thought would
apply.

"I was totally naïve, and, you know, it's a really funny post, like,
'Hi! I'm Zsenya and, I love the Harry Potter books and I think Ron
and Hermione are meant to be together and isn't it great? Don't we
all love each other?' and got totally attacked," she said in retrospect.

The flame war didn't flare immediately following Zsenya's post, but the message definitely sparked a slow burn. Eventually the careful, half-grinning war between the Ron/Hermione shippers and the Harry/Hermione shippers began to gear up for what it was: a showdown between the old guard, the popular fanfic writers (who were mostly of the H/H persuasion and who had basically set up the structure for the fandom), and the new, who saw things differently. The arguments became laborious, and intense, and centered around the tiniest of details, in ways usually reserved for ivory-tower types.

After a while the R/H defenders got tired of living the same arguments every day, having to keep on top of what was quickly becoming a war, feeling the urgent and ill-inducing need to answer everything and make their points repeatedly. But there was nowhere online for them to gather. So they started quietly planning a Web site that would suit their needs. The R/H defenders now included Kristin Brown, Maureen Lipsett, Kathy MacMillan, and someone who went by the name of Jedi Boadicea. They started e-mailing one another and passing a document back and forth containing their plans for the Harry Potter version of Pemberley.com: a place that valued civilized literary discussion and celebration in a different way from what was being offered on the Grownups list, and where moderators were careful to remove anything that was trash-talking, crude, or full of Netspeak.

Just as Pemberley.com strove to re-create the careful and polite world Austen's characters inhabited via the Internet, so did the Sugar Quill aim to keep discussions and fanfiction true to book characterizations. The site was ablaze in orange background and red text, and with in-jokes about the books and a whole page devoted to the adoration of Ron Weasley, it was clear they were either modeling themselves on the Burrow or the Gryffindor common room, if not exactly in looks, then in attitude. The founders stated their devotion to the canon, to representing fanfiction based on what actually happened in the Harry Potter books; they also made a page called SPEW or the Sugar Quill's Purpose of Existence on the Web, that established the Sugar Quill as a biased site run by a group of individuals who set up their site a certain way for a certain reason. It said, in effect, that the people who ran the site were young professionals passionate about literature and writing and that they had no wish to pick the books apart but rather examine them, problem solve, discuss, and attempt to predict the future, but not to "host discussion that cannot be justified by the books. We're not interested in hearing that Ron is going to the Dark Side unless you have a pretty damn good reason why you think so. And even then, we're not so sure."

The statement also made it clear that one of the site's aims was to archive "our own humble Harry Potter fanfiction," as well as provide help to those trying to do the same thing. "We've found fanfic to be a great boon to our learning processes as we grow into our skills—it gives us a ready-made world and characters on which to cut our teeth. . . . Our hope is that this experience will give people the courage and confidence to branch out and start writing original stories." There was a beta service for young writers to avail themselves of, in which the six founders of the site would carefully edit stories and offer suggestions and critiques.

The statement also made it clear that the people on the site were fans of the Ron and Hermione ship and the Harry and Ginny ship, and that the idea of Hermione and Draco together was "smut" (which it technically wasn't, but the administrators found the idea so objectionable that they labeled it trash).

"In addition, since some of us are pushing thirty, we may also freely fantasize about Sirius Black and Remus Lupin, two of the sexiest wizards of their marauding generation. We are very prone to mushing and giggling, though we will do our best to back up these Lavenderesque tendencies with solid evidence from the books (if you read them the way we read them, you'd agree that our pairings are correct . . . let us convince you . . .) In any case, much of what happens on this site may be very crushy. If you don't like it, find another site."

"If you don't like it" has never been a popular statement in fandom. It's never been a popular statement in life, either. But online, where everyone is freed from the bonds of facial recognition, they can rail and scream in much greater numbers than in real life. Something about the Sugar Quill's attitude never quite fit in right with the old set. Maybe it was their willingness to call H/H wrong, when many H/H shippers were making pained attempts to be diplomatic. The site's Daily Affirmations became salt in the proverbial wound.

They ran down the side of the page and were meant as jokes poking fun at the fan theories and fanfic clichés with which they most ardently disagreed. "Ginny doesn't spend all her waking time giggling." "Ron will not betray Harry." "Hermione is NOT whiny."

But it was the first one that did it.

"Harry and Hermione is a ridiculous impossibility."

The thin veneer of civility was starting to heat and crack on the list. The shippers were starting to take their names seriously, and had started to label their ships accordingly. The Ron/Hermione ship became the Good Ship R/H, while, potentially in response, Penny Linsenmayer started to sign her posts with Captain of the Cruiseliner H/H.

Jennie posted the SQ's Daily Affirmations to the list, because she thought they were funny and wanted to share the joke, and maybe share a little snark with her sympathizers. She was immediately criticized for admitting that she and her admins wanted to be "dictators" over their own site. In one note Penny signed, "Captain of the Cruiseliner H/H, where we trust our members and their freedom of thought & so have no need for such things as Ship Rules or Daily Affirmations . . . <g>."

And so it went. There was a lot of talk of "R/H types" and "H/H people" and what a person's shipping said about her personality and accusations that R/Hers couldn't stand to see Ron criticized in any way, and accusations that H/H couldn't stand to see Harry criticized in any way. It was all conducted cheerfully, with a "come visit and hang out with us on *our* site and we can all be friends!" mentality, while the seething was happening privately. A lot of back swatting, and a lot of <g>s.

Later, Jennie and Meg unveiled "After the End," a fanfiction about the summer after Harry, Ron, and Hermione defeat Voldemort; the relationships are clearly drawn from the outset—Ron/Hermione, Harry/Ginny—and the opening chapter even contains a fake-out, in which Hermione tells Harry she loves him. It's later revealed that the declaration was for a friendship element in an important spell. The whole style of the fic seemed to contradict every popular Harry/ Hermione fanfiction. The girls posted it on FanFiction.net, partly as an antidote to the monstrous popularity of H/H-based fics, partly as an exercise in characterization, and partly as a way to have fun with characters that Jo Rowling hadn't updated for us in a while. It was met with a remarkable amount of sniggering and disdain for a new piece. The negative reviews persisted for the first two chapters, and datewise coincided with exactly when the online ship debate had intensified.

Simon Branford, a popular poster on Harry Potter for Grownups, told them the girls characterizations were "totally OoC," fanfic-ese for "out of character," one of the worst insults you could throw at fanfic writers. One poster said that Hermione was a "priss" for having still had only limited physical contact with Ron by her eighteenth birthday. They were criticized by Heidi for not launching the trio directly into jobs, and for leaving Hermione with a bossy attitude as a grown-up. By the second chapter Heidi wrote, "Oh, poor Sirius—what have you done to him?" Other, more vicious comments appeared from "anonymous," which rarely ever happened on fanfiction from new authors. They were being review-bombed. But Jennie had done her share of review-bombing, too, so she mostly let it go.

Eventually, sparring on the Harry Potter for Grownups list got so bad that the Sugar Quill members simply left it. Meanwhile, in the wake of all the warring, fanfiction sites were splintering and growing according to preference: there was Gryffindor Tower, a distinctly Harry/Ginny–based site in which the most popular fic featured a teenage, pregnant Ginny, who had allowed herself to have Harry's child at seventeen years old because Dumbledore had soberly informed her and Harry that they needed to procreate to save the world. There was also the Werewolf Registry, which had been set up partly to fully celebrate the wildly popular "fanon" (a spin on "canon," meaning an idea wasn't completely supported by the original text but was more of a fan convention) ship of Sirius Black and Remus Lupin; they were perfectly tortured souls, one wrongly condemned (and according to canon, not yet dead; many pieces of fanfiction indulged in overwrought exonerations and public displays of retribution for Sirius's wrongful incarceration), the other stricken with a condition that turned him into a beast once a month. They were angst incarnate. RestrictedSection.org housed more "adult" (read: sexual) fiction, and was the subject of a cease-and-desist letter from lawyers for Jo Rowling, and now exists with warnings to those who are under eighteen, redirecting them to Leaky or FictionAlley.

When the Harry Potter for Grownups ship discussion died off, it moved over to FictionAlley, the site that Heidi set up after Cassandra Claire had been banned from FanFiction.net for including large, unsourced patches of other published material in her fanfic. FictionAlley became a site for, pointedly, *all* fanfictions and not just the ones the administrators deemed site-worthy. The ship discussion continued ad nauseam, but without the original players it seemed to have less hanging in the balance; it was like a schoolyard fight that had gone on so long they brought in alternates. Its tone, however, was clear in its message-board title: Deathmarch. New debaters for each side joined the fray. The four of them who emerged near the top of the pack—for the sheer number of posts they made, the essay length of each post, their snarky panache, and for having in spades the intelligence any member of an online forum needs if their printed words are going to become respected—were my friend Emily, Angua (also known as Susan), Zorb (Sara), and Pallas Athena (Linda).

The players had seemed to come off my computer screen for this debate at Nimbus 2003; I'd followed it fairly closely for a long time, marveling at how long the argument could go on, or how often people who posted could offer new material or a new twist on old. The main players were known to me, before the conference, as extraordinarily well-read people who wrote with sophistication but often engaged in sophistry.

The twitters in the conference room at the live debate died down to whispers after these players were announced; I tugged at my stiff cotton shirt and sat cross-legged on the left side of the room. Someone had put a pro-R/H shirt on a life-sized model of Dobby the house-elf; it hung on him like a nightgown, and his wide, confused eyes seemed to make silent comment on the proceedings.

The opening statements for each side summed up each stance

within a few sentences: R/H shippers thought that Jo Rowling was showing her hand and directing us solidly down the R/H path, while H/H shippers felt books six and seven would reveal a hero/heroine model that had only been hinted at all along. Though it was clear each side had spent a long time preparing, the crowd seemed most excited when one side made a snipe or hinted at an in-joke only those who'd been following the debates could get. When the H/H side suggested that Hermione's status as the frequent voice of reason in Harry's head was proof of their relationship, Emily shot back, "Do you know who the voice of my conscience is? My mother," and the crowd erupted. When the R/Hers said that Harry was shocked that Hermione looked "so incredibly different than she usually does" at the Yule Ball, the H/H shippers chimed in with "and pretty," bringing more laughter. I was fairly sure I'd had arguments like this with my sister—when she wouldn't give me a turn at the Easy-Bake Oven.

All told, I thought Emily and Susan had fought bravely, but moving an online debate to an in-person argument deflated it somehow, diffusing all the pent-up anger you could infer from the tightly polite online arguments. At one point Linda rubbed her hands and said that Hermione was a "crafty" witch and would get whatever she wanted, and I completely checked out of the conversation. Somehow the image of Hermione, who at that point was still only fifteen by Jo Rowling's estimation, resorting to crafty means—what did she mean, would she start slipping love potions into Harry's pumpkin juice?—did more than anger me, it befuddled me. The whole exercise had befuddled me; wouldn't it all come out in the books anyway? Why were we doing this, again? No one could say they won the debate; no winner was declared, though both sides claimed victory later. In the end it was simply an entertaining literary prizefight.

After the debate, I was sitting by myself near a fountain in one of the hotel lobbies, just finishing up a phone call, when a tall African American woman sat down next to me. I'd seen her at the con and knew exactly who she was, because Emily had pointed her out to me—Angela from the old Grownups list squabbles. I was supposed to hate her. She'd been mean to my friends online, and if she knew me she probably wouldn't like me on principle, since I was an R/H shipper. But then, I hadn't been a shipper when I came into the fandom—I hadn't even heard the term before—the fandom told me that I was.

Angela was a fiercely H/H fanfiction author. Hers was the kind of fanfiction that sprawled out in episodic fashion, catching new readers with each posted chapter until there was a sea of devotees clamoring for new postings. She and others like her—Cassandra Claire the most notable example—were also loosely called BNFs, a term new to me, but which I naïvely thought might refer to writers of Big and Numerous Fanfictions. I learned at this conference that BNF meant Big Name Fan, and I was being treated as one, too. I worked on a popular Web site, and Jo Rowling had knighted me with her touch. That was all that was required, apparently. BNF-dom didn't come with a golden key, either, just a sense of discomfiture, like I was standing in to accept someone else's award or, worse, had been given one I never wished to get.

Angela and I sat in silence for a few tense moments and then she smiled at me. And it seemed so genuine, and so unlike the person I read about, that I smiled back. She told me she'd read my reports of my Royal Albert Hall experience, and again my grin and nervous laugh came unbidden. She was not the first, second, or tenth person to look at me as though they could see Jo Rowling right behind me, just out of reach. When I'd met Jo I'd rushed to the nearest Internet café to post about it out of a genuine, incomprehensible excitement and the need to share it with the readers of the Web site—not out of the desire to be invited to the cool kids' table. The people here had a remarkable way of making me feel as though that had been my prize, and expecting me to love it. Angela was not acting toward me the way she'd acted toward my friends online.

"You're going to interview her one day," Angela said with hard clarity, surprising me. She was the first person ever to say that out loud.

I started, and gaped. Had I had some imaginary conversation with Angela in which I'd told her that this was, secretly, my dream? "I could only hope," I said. "No, I don't know, I can't think that far—"

"No, you will. I'm sure of it. It's coming. One day."

I jumped a little at her surety and started to reply, trying to think of some way of dissuading her without extinguishing the teeny flame of hope that had started burning inside me. I was about to tell her that what she had said was flattering but I couldn't possibly imagine it would come true. I was about to tell this smiling and clearly nice person how I felt, how everyone in this place was looking at me with expectation and a secret knowledge of my future that I wasn't in on; I was about to tell her how I felt that even their well-intentioned hopes were making me nervous, like it was cursing my chances. But then some other BNFs came along, and I was invited to dinner.

CHAPTER ELEVEN

Access

n the first day of June 2007 I traveled into Manhattan to the Jacob K. Javits Convention Center for the annual BookExpo America, the publishing industry trade show. Scholastic was sponsoring a booth, and there were rumors of *Deathly Hallows* merchandise giveaways, which I couldn't miss.

As I approached the building I noticed a large, lurid, purple inkblot on wheels in front of it. I got closer and realized it was the Knight Bus: Scholastic, to celebrate the release of the book, was sending a double-decker bus, covered in Harry Potter–related imagery to look like a triple-decker, around the country as one of the similar purple buses depicted in the series. The bus in the books is useful as an emergency transport vehicle; witches or wizards can summon it in an instant, so long as they are not underwater, and for a small fee they can travel almost anywhere with enormous speed and the whirligig motion of a runaway train.

The real-life version was certain to obey speed laws, but effort had been made to give it the same sort of charms as its namesake: the tartan driver's seat was ratty, as though it had never been changed; the inside had been fitted with purple, squashy cushions, old lanterns, and a pattern of gold stars; the recently revealed *Deathly Hallows* artwork stood behind a glass frame, while bookshelves held all the Potter books and a countdown to July 21. In the front, a golden chain roped off the stairwell to the upper level, with a placard hanging from it reading No Muggles Allowed! At the back, visitors to the bus could record a thirty-second videotaped message, all of which would be compiled and sent to Jo Rowling. Publishing professionals, in business suits and jackets, lined up, sweating as they waited, craning their necks to peek inside before they cycled through and left their messages.

The bus would stop at ten libraries, allowing school-aged children to leave messages for Jo. I had to laugh as I imagined this thing skittering down the Iowa interstate, raising suspicious looks from cows and tractor drivers.

I was about to go on tour as well; in about a week John and I would open our six-week run-up to the release date with a podcast at a book fair in Chicago, then travel out to California and double back, meeting up with Sue and the Potters in New Mexico for our first joint show. Cheryl came over for dinner before I left, trudging into my apartment with a huge brown box under her arm. She opened it to reveal a life-size Harry cutout of the type that was appearing in bookstores—he was in his full *Deathly Hallows* artwork pose, arm outstretched toward God knows what. It also featured another countdown, with each day a tear-off featuring a piece of colored art by Mary GrandPré, the illustrator of the American editions. I shrieked and clapped, and we amused ourselves by putting flowers, towels, and even a glass of wine in Harry's outstretched hand. After Cheryl left, I burrowed through the countdown to see what the powers that be had chosen for the last day's image. It was Dumbledore's empty desk, and Fawkes's empty perch. My chest seemed to constrict with the foreboding message it implied, and I stared at it for a while, pondering the day when the Hogwarts in my mind was similarly quiet.

The crowd in Chicago was the largest ever for a live PotterCast, spilling out of the white tent that had been set up for us. Since my Harry Potter work usually involved sitting quietly at home on my computer, it never failed to shock me to see our readers gathering in the flesh. It had only been two and a half years since Leaky had started to expand, and I had originally fought against that change, objecting loudly that we didn't have the manpower to become a supersite and should remain just a smaller news source. By that time, in 2003, I was doing most or all of the reporting work and was the de facto head of the site, and feared the responsibility and work that would come with redefining its borders. I'd also scurried out from under Denise's thumb at MTV. My new day job, as a reporter for the *Staten Island Advance*, was going amazingly well; within a few months, thanks to a few "enterprise" stories (articles I conceived, reported, and wrote with only nominal instruction from editors) I had been catapulted from the role of glorified stenographer on the night shift to frequent daytime feature writer specializing in offbeat, colorful slice-of-life pieces. I'd also been part of the reporting team on the worst transportation accident to hit the borough in recent memory, the Staten Island Ferry crash of October 2003. I'd only been three weeks into my job and fully expected to be left out of the coverage; my editor, however, sent me to the hospital to get stories on the victims, and, when I actually returned with some, kept me on the team covering the aftermath. I could feel my work and abilities expanding, and for the first time in my life loved my job. I used to be paralyzed at the thought of trusting my instincts to report a full story without direction, but the reception I received from my few enterprise stories was making it easier to do so. Now, the two types of reporting in my life were facing off: day vs. night, real world vs. Potter. For the most part, I let the day job win. Potter was great fun, but still a hobby.

In the fall of 2003, a WB rep invited me to visit the film set for *Prisoner of Azkaban*; I would become the first fan site representative to do so, and I jumped—literally, up and down in my work cubicle—at the chance. When the day came, and we arrived at the Leavesden lot where Harry Potter is filmed, I experienced a Capraesque thrill with none of the appropriate scenery; the lot is on a tract of endless, dry land, and looks like nothing more exciting than an airplane hangar. Yet by the time we'd gotten there, the other reporters knew I was "the fansite girl," and weren't only excited for me, they were excited to rely on my fannish expertise to tell them what Honeydukes and the Shrieking Shack were.

When I got off the bus that brought us to Leavesden, Lisa St. Amand, a publicist with whom I spoke occasionally, grabbed my hands and started jumping up and down. "You're here, you're here, you're here!" she squealed, and I returned the gesture, because never in my life did I think that when I fought for Leaky to be treated as regular press that I'd find myself on an overseas junket along with big film sites like DarkHorizons and SciFi.com. I'd just wanted us to be able to secure an interview here and there. A production assistant ran out from the shed and urged us to quiet down, and we giggled like children who'd been caught passing notes. The traditionally jaded expressions of my fellow reporters melted into kind, if slightly disbelieving, smiles.

I'd never been to a movie set before, never mind a Harry Potter one, so I was having a full-on geek attack as I traipsed through the elaborate structures. I kept pointing to things and noting how they differed from canon, with accidental but nonetheless tactless disregard for the feelings of the craftspeople ("Where's the section in Honeydukes with the blood lollipops? It's supposed to be right here!"), or running up to random props in the warehouse and shrieking at them ("The *velvet poufs!*" I shouted, when I saw the little footstools being prepared for Trelawney's divination class. "They're velvet and poufy!"). The other reporters assaulted me with questions on the plot and intricacies and accuracy of the representation, but otherwise seemed to be buoyed by my naïveté.

It had been a year since I'd seen any of the actors, so I was delighted and surprised to spot Daniel Radcliffe, who played Harry, and Rupert Grint, who played Ron, sitting in two directors' chairs between takes, punching each other and laughing loudly until an assistant director sharply told them to cut it out. The chagrined looks on their faces matched, identically, the one I had worn so often in elementary school when caught sniggering during assembly, and that made me laugh. Throughout our interviews that day and every time I met them thereafter, I came away stunned at the normalcy of the young actors. I supposed it had something to do with filming in an area of London that looked like Dorothy Gale's Kansas, or because assistant directors were willing to snap at them when they were being rowdy, that the set was always swarming with parents and chaperones, or perhaps it was because Vanessa Davies, the head publicist, acted like a mother to the actors and a bodyguard to the press.

The main trio of actors in the films—Daniel, Emma Watson (Hermione), and Rupert—were all cast in late 2000, all of them relative unknowns. Jo Rowling had insisted that the cast of her films remain British, and she got her wish: soon a veritable who's who of the English acting community joined its ranks. Robbie Coltrane, Alan Rickman, Dame Maggie Smith, Sir Richard Harris, Emma Thompson, and so many others. Some had jumped at the chance to play in *Potter*; Richard Harris, who played Dumbledore in the first two Potter films, said he had been bullied into it by his grandchildren.

A book's success has never guaranteed the success of a film; there'd been enough flopped comic-book movies to prove that. In 2007 *The Golden Compass*, a movie based on a fantasy series that became popular around the same time as *Harry*, had a similar budget and grand scale of production, but earned only $70 million in the United States and disappeared from the marquees quickly. Yet the Potter films had already become some of the highest-grossing films of all time, at least partly because they were produced during the era in which the actual book releases still surpassed all other kinds of excitement, and fans would have watched three hand puppets and a squeaky toy act out the series if it meant entertainment between books.

There was a real fear, when the movies were released, that the previously unknown kids' catapult to stardom would leave them embittered, selfish, and too rich. Rupert Grint and Emma Watson had done hardly any acting—Emma had done some acting for her school play and Rupert for a grade-school class. Dan was the only one of the three who had film experience. He had played David Copperfield in the film of the same name, and had attracted the eye of director Christopher Columbus. It wasn't until film producer David Heyman ran into Daniel and his parents in a British theater that they started to seriously court him for the part.

By 2007, Dan had spent about seven years with the Harry Potter franchise. Try though they might, the British tabloids couldn't find anything significant to throw at him; no scandalous drug stories, no wild parties, no inappropriate spending of his fortune. Press reports of Dan seemed to match my, and every other person's I knew, experience of the teen: he was smart, quiet, polite, and seemed much too normal to be an international superstar. I said the same to Jo, who laughed and said the spoiling of the children had been a fear of hers as well.

God, let it not mess them up, she had thought when the children were cast, thinking of Jack Wild, the child who played the Artful Dodger in the musical version of *Oliver!* and became a bit of a cautionary tale for young, rich celebrities. "It feels like being a godparent or something," she said. "We took [Dan] out to dinner recently, and I was saying to him, 'I used to be so scared about the boy we found to play Harry Potter,' and he cut across me. He said, 'Oh, everyone mentions Jack Wild!'" She mimicked his exasperated and dismissive tone when referring to the former child star whose later life spun into drinking, smoking, and an early death from oral cancer. "I said, 'Yeah, for a reason, Dan, for a reason! But they are, all of them—I'm touching wood as I speak—grounded people and I credit all of their families with doing an amazing job. And I have to credit Warner Brothers, because they've been very protective. In the right way. It would upset me so much if I thought that any of them felt that it hadn't been the right thing for them to do."

Toward the end of my day on set, we were brought to the Great Hall at Hogwarts. Lisa and Vanessa stopped outside the grand oak doors and turned to me.

"Close your eyes!"

I was absolutely ready to oblige; nothing said Harry Potter quite like the Great Hall, and I wanted to have as immersed an experience as possible. They led me in by my arms; by this point all the other reporters were watching me more closely than they were watching the set, so I was sure, without seeing it, that I looked like a blind person being led around by eight of her closest friends.

When I opened my eyes, it was as though I'd entered the books whole. The scratched, long, wooden tables, Dumbledore's chair at the head of the hall, the fire-charred gargoyles and flagstone floor; it all made my head light and my arms heavy. I half expected Professor McGonagall to emerge from a side entrance and call me to be sorted.

This was the first set Jo Rowling had seen, once it came time for her to visit the movie filming. She had shown the filmmakers a rough sketch of the hall, and then months later walked right into her drawing.

"It's a real room—it's not all plaster and spit holding everything together," she said. She walked down Diagon Alley, and went right into the shops. Privet Drive, she noted with no small measure of surprise, was laid out exactly the same as her own childhood home. But the real shock came when she saw the Mirror of Erised.

"I went into the room . . . and for a second saw myself reflected in the mirror. There you are—the happiest man sees himself reflected exactly as he is—there I was and my books were successful and the film was being made in Britain with an all-British cast, and I really believed by that point they were going to do the right thing by the books, so, yeah, that was kind of spooky. It was almost too symbolic, standing there."

By the time I returned from London with my exclusive set report, John was positively twittering to allow me to let Leaky expand.

"I don't have the time!"

"But it's what the fans *want*," he insisted. At that point I didn't know John very well at all; a few instant messaging conversations and a persistent attitude were all I had to go on. But the site was expanding whether I liked it or not, if just on the interviews page. That November, Meg, who had moved back to New York and was helping out on the site, and I interviewed Jamie Waylett, who played Slytherin thug Vincent Crabbe in the films, during his family's trip to Manhattan. John Inniss, who I thought was Jamie's father at the time (he turned out to be Jamie's mother's boyfriend), e-mailed me to let me know they were going to be in town, and I wrote back what I thought would be a joke for someone like him, who was used to his son doing interviews. I wrote,

> *Does Jamie have time to chat or is this going to be a "get the journalist in, get the journalist out," 20 minutes kind of thing?*

I knew that I meant the comment as a silly quip, but the Internet has no inflection, and at the time I didn't realize how brazen it could have come off. Lucky for me, John Inniss deals in cigarettes and sarcasm, and the cheeky response only endeared me and the site to him. We decided to meet up for pizza and a thirty-minute interview.

The interview lasted over two hours, as Jamie told us more anecdotes about his life as a *Potter* actor than we'd ever heard, and did so with unfettered glee. Halfway through he started doing impressions of Rupert Grint (Ron), Matt Lewis (Neville Longbottom), Chris Columbus (director of the first and second films), and Alfonso Cuarón (the director of the third film). It turned out Jamie had an interesting personal story to tell, too: He had been in a car accident when he was ten, and doctors said he wasn't going to survive, but he'd somehow made it through. About a year later he walked into his family's home after film scouts had visited his school and said, "I'm going to be in *Harry Potter*," and no one believed him until they got a call from Warner Bros.

But the interview was more than a good scoop for Leaky: Meg and I realized we genuinely liked this kid, who had a chubby face and eyes that disappeared when he laughed. We liked John, too, who had a thin rim of gray hair, wore a Queens Park Rangers jersey, and cracked sarcastic jokes between smoke inhalations throughout the entirety of the two-hour interview. His son, "Little John," who was Jamie's age and much more laconic, even shared a few smirks.

We were finally saying our good-byes when we ran into Jamie's mother, Theresa, and his grandparents, who were balancing loads of shopping on each arm and looked like they were ready to assault some more retail outlets.

I don't know what made me say it. "There's an arcade around here; why don't I take the boys there and you guys can shop, and we'll meet you for dinner?"

Later, Theresa would tell me we walked away and she panicked, wondering how on earth she could let her son leave with a total stranger. Jamie, Little John, Meg, and I played air hockey, Skee-ball, and fake hunting games until we were out of quarters, then went to a Chinese food dinner and dessert with the entire family. John told dirty jokes that seemed all the funnier in his British accent. Theresa, who had tightly curled hair, smoked as many cigarettes as John and had an endearing dialect that turned her "ing"s into "ink"s, displayed the truckload of clothes she had bought and taunted me about how badly the exchange rate favored visiting Brits. Jamie regaled us with more impressions. They seemed fascinated by my and Meg's absorption in the Harry Potter culture, so we told them stories of the ship wars and clued them in about what was going to happen to Jamie's character in the fifth book, which he hadn't yet read.

When they returned to England, we kept in touch via John Inniss, and to the tune of sixteen one-line e-mails a day. The interview and all the footage, video clips, and stories had gone up on Leaky to a tremendous response, and we extended the coverage to include a question-and-answer between the fans and Jamie, something that was only possible through John and which thoroughly excited our read-ers. Jamie wrote candid and anecdotal answers, and the entire piece felt like a series of letters between friends. When one fan asked, "Did you get to keep your Slytherin ring," he wrote back, "I WISH!!!!" He also told stories of the time he had to go to a casting for his "bum double," for a scene in which his pants got pulled down; the fans' overjoyed reaction to Jamie's stories was proof, to me, that they had been dying to feel personally involved with the film franchise, and Jamie was providing them with more than a standard interview clip. I wanted to do more and more of that, every day, for Leaky and the fans, and John Inniss—who was even more amazed by the response than I was—said he'd help.

Meg, Kristin, and I planned to visit with the Wayletts at the end of May, coinciding with the premiere of the third film. I hadn't been to England in a while, and we thought we could see Jamie off to the event, take some pictures in Leicester Square, and then tinker around in museums. At the end of April, John called. He sounded excited, despite his usual faintly droll tone.

"Hello, there!" he chirped. I could hear the slight thwap of his lips as he then took a drag of a cigarette. "Bought your tickets yet?"

"Yes! What's up?"

"Oh, nothing, girl," he said, too lightly. "Right. So, we were won-dering, what were you going to do while we're at the premiere?"

"I don't know. Go to a pub or something."

"*Right,*" he said, slowly. "Well, right, how's 'bout this—I've got this extra ticket in my hand, why don't you just use that and come with us?"

It took me a full ten seconds to process what he was saying, and another five or so to stop screaming at my phone.

"Are you sure? Really? Are you sure? Don't you have other family to give it to? Really? You're sure? Honest?"

John laughed and called to Theresa to come hear my freakazoid episode. "Thought you'd like that," he said, satisfaction dripping off his voice.

"But wait—why? Why? You've got to have twenty people who'd kill for that."

I could almost hear John shrug. "Does it mean the same thing to any of them as it'd mean to you?" I fumbled for an answer, but John cut me off. "Thought not!"

Within two weeks, Theresa had somehow managed to snag two more tickets—for Meg and Kristin. When we got to London, I asked how she had done it, but she just looked mysterious and disappeared to the kitchen to make coffee. The three of us were positively twitching in anticipation, and not just because we would get to wear pretty dresses and walk down a red carpet. Jo Rowling regularly attended U.K. movie premieres. I was desperate to try and actually form words to her this time, and I desperately wanted Meg and Kristin to meet her, too.

I wore a pale blue dress that I'd bought for $20 at the Gap. I threw a shawl over it and put on white heels, and Meg did my hair, and I felt glamorous. On top of everything else, I'd be going in the car with Jamie and his family. When we rounded a corner near Leicester Square and I heard a roar, I thought it was thunder. John laughed.

"That's the crowd," he said.

We pulled up to the front of the theater, and as Jamie got out of the car with us behind him, it was as though I were trapped in a thick current of noise coming from all sides, capable of carrying me along its waves. I dazedly reached for John and followed him along the path as Jamie did his interviews; only when I saw Meg and Kristin, who had been in another car, come bounding toward me with stunned looks on their faces did it feel like any of it was real. I'd seen the movie already, so I spent most of the screening squirming in my seat and waiting to get out of there and go to the after party.

When we left the theater, most of the fans were gone but a thick group of them still remained. Jamie walked down the barrier, signing autographs. I stopped him at the end so we could get a picture together outside the theater, and someone off to the side yelled, "Hey, Jamie, give 'er a snog!" We laughed the whole way to the bus, which was waiting to take us to London's Natural History Museum for the party.

The museum had been transformed from the last time I'd been inside it; the entrance seemed to have been bathed in blue. We entered under amber spotlights and walked right past the life-sized, moving model of Buckbeak the hippogriff, a prop from the film. In the main hall, the full-scale dinosaur model that was always there now looked like a Harry Potter prop; the room had been pinpricked with white lights that looked like stars, and Mylar ribbons hung over entrances, giving the appearance of walking through a shimmering waterfall to get in. In every corner there were different types of food stations, and near the back, in theme with the film, were fortune-tellers, palm readers, and handwriting experts, all prognosticating for guests. Honeydukes had clearly been plundered, because there was a full wall of candy, looking like a rainbow against the dark backdrop.

Someone wearing a headset directed us to a VIP area and gave us all bracelets so that we could move back and forth between there and the rest of the party. My eyesight seemed to sharpen as we entered, triggered by Jo Rowling's presence. I knew she was in here somewhere. I had decided I would say hello to her, but that was it, would try hard not to burden her with my geekiness, when even in this roped-off area she was completely surrounded by well-wishers and admirers.

For the second time now I was prepared to see her but completely unprepared for the moment. I didn't see where she'd come from or what knot of fans had loosened their grip on her, but suddenly she was in front of me and I was squealing louder than I intended and moving to hug her again. I had started to cringe at my less-than-suave manner, but then realized she had done exactly the same thing. At least my arms worked instead of sticking out from their sockets like chopsticks, the way they had last time—I tried to make my tongue move in proper word formations, but it wasn't happening, so I settled on something like "Aye, ow are u?"

She politely complimented my outfit then asked me what I thought of her new and updated Web site, which she had just revealed about a month earlier. The concept was meant to go beyond the idea of a fan club, an idea with which she was never comfortable because it usually meant fans had to pay for information and were subsequently let down by the content therein. Instead, the impressive Flash site, which was designed by Lightmaker, had been made to look like her real-life desk, littered with hidden puzzles, concealing prizes like first drafts of chapters and hand-drawings of characters. Kathleen and I had obsessed over each detail, and Meg and I had explored the site together for an hour over the phone. It was a haven for a Potter fan, and I wanted to tell her how cool it was to know more about Dean Thomas, and to see her drawings of Harry, and where she had dropped coffee all over her notes. Standing in front of Jo, however, all I could say was, "Yeah, it's great!" then lapse into my special brand of awkward silence.

We nodded at each other. All my thoughts rushed up to the front of my brain and had gotten themselves into a traffic collision, and by the time one or two of them had disentangled themselves from the wreckage, Jo had smiled at me and moved away. In a stall in the ladies' bathroom, I pounded my head against the wall. *One day I will talk to her*, I thought and smacked myself again.

A week later, in New York, John Inniss introduced us to Devon Murray, who played Seamus Finnegan; James and Oliver Phelps, who played Fred and George Weasley; Matthew Lewis, who played Neville Longbottom; and their families. We went out to dinner at a Scottish pub, and Meg and I interviewed the actors while the parents ate separately. They were all in town for the New York premiere of the film, and were happy to answer our questions over some food. I was continually impressed with Matthew, who displayed more ready knowledge about the books than any actor I'd met so far; in the fan world, that meant a lot. When he spoke about how hard he studied the character because he was so intent on getting him right for the fans, I felt he was being honest and taking his role as a true responsibility.

Later, Jo backed me up: he remains, she said, the only person to turn down information about the series because he wanted to read about it in the full, published book. She had sauntered up to him at a movie premiere, about two weeks before *Deathly Hallows* was released, and offered, "You know, there's great stuff for Neville coming in—"

"*Don't tell me!*" he shouted at her, loud enough to make her re-creation of the event boom through her house. "*I don't want to know!*"

At the *Prisoner of Azkaban* premiere in New York the next day, Matt was whisked past us on the red carpet before we could do a quick interview for the site. Later, John, Jamie, Meg, and I jokingly took him to task for that and he happily played along. We threw a red shirt on the floor of the hotel hallway and Matt stood on top of it;

Meg videotaped and John hid behind a door, playing the fans, screaming, "We love you, Matt!" every other minute and emitting assorted
"crowd" sounds the rest of the time. Jamie shyly moseyed up to Matt
and asked him for his autograph, and Matt pretended to be aloof and
snobby about it. I played a reporter, naturally.

"Mr. Lewis! Mr. Lewis!" I said in a pitiful imitation of the typical
shouting on the red carpet, because I was laughing too hard. "What
is it like, being here at the *Harry Potter* premiere?"

Matt laughed, and in his Leeds accent enthused about how great
it was to be where "everyone's shouting your name." He gestured
around to the empty hallway as though he believed it.

I promised myself I'd learn how to speak to Jo properly, and when,
in 2005, the date for the sixth book was announced, I decided it was
time to take action. In February I sent Jo's assistant, Fiddy, what can
only be adequately described as an application to interview Jo Rowling. I had a well-thought-out plan: Jo would choose whatever news
outlet she wanted, and have a fan interview her! It would be perfect!
I sent a résumé, clips, and a long letter explaining why I was the perfect person to pull off this job.

Fiddy and I had developed a halting correspondence in the eighteen months that had passed since the Royal Albert Hall event, after
I had written her from the basement of my London hotel room,
hours after Jo had shrieked at me that she loved my Web site. I
e-mailed occasionally to ask her to clear up a rumor, but mostly just
to say hello or to let her know about a piece of news she'd enjoy. I felt
comfortable enough to send her a proposal—a proper, businesslike,
official proposal. I'd give credentials. Make my case. Detail it all so
there was absolutely no chance they could say no. I didn't even imagine the interview going on Leaky. No, I imagined it would go in a

publication, a "regular" one, because Jo Rowling could decide what publication she appeared in, right? Right. It was a perfect plan. She had to see my way of it!

I sent the proposal off with the same feeling that had become second nature to me, whenever I handed in a story I particularly liked or was important. Nauseated.

Fiddy wrote back almost immediately, just to let me know she had gotten the e-mail. She said barely anything—nothing to ease my nerves or give me any hint of a positive outcome—but there was an excitement and urgency under her words nonetheless. All she said was to sit tight, that everything would work out in the end. In the back of my head, where I kept secret hopes and dreams, something flared. I smothered it and went back to preparing the site for the release of the sixth book. We had just opened a message forum, thanks to a terrific proposal by Nick Rhein, and now had six times the amount of staff we'd had before. I was struggling not to micromanage, and losing the struggle. I got irritable; I yelled at people who had done nothing wrong, and generally displayed an amount of naïveté that would look, in retrospect, embarrassing. I'd come onto the site as an editor, and somehow, unofficially, taken over everything; I didn't even know, looking back, when the change had occurred. I was worried about coverage and interviews, not personnel and morale, and didn't do any of the things that good managers did, like get to know my staff. When John Noe, still then just a designer for the site, told me I was driving everyone mad and needed to relax, I took that to mean I should stop reading or posting in our staff forum or getting involved below the administrative level at all, which only made things worse.

In late April I got another e-mail from Fiddy, asking for my telephone number, because someone from the Harry Potter camp needed to talk to me. I shrugged and sent her the information without thinking about it, because unless she asked me to break a law I was likely to give Fiddy anything she wanted. It was only later that evening, watching a movie, that I allowed my thoughts to wander, and unwittingly give room for a new idea to spring up and swell. Hang on a second. Every day, every week, I talked to tons of Harry Potter people via e-mail. They seemed to live in my in-box: Jo Rowling's lawyers, her editors, her representatives, Warner Bros., Fiddy—all corresponded there and hardly anyone ever needed the phone. For what purpose, possibly, could someone need my number? Like a little freight train, the chant *Jo, Jo, Jo* meandered through my brain. I made myself laugh out loud at my unwitting arrogance. No way.

I couldn't rid myself of the thought, and didn't try, because to do so would be admitting that the thought was feasible. It was only when I was daydreaming that the potential outcomes came to me, and I indulged in a little internal game, making them as ridiculous as possible. Jo wanted me to look over the manuscript to spot continuity errors. Jo wanted me to babysit her children. Jo was going to fly me to Edinburgh to interview her on the occasion of the release. I'd laughed right out loud at that one.

On May 4, at 8:00 a.m., my beat-up cell phone woke me with its shrill ring. I seriously considered chucking it out the window until I remembered what day it was and Fiddy's e-mail of the previous afternoon, warning me that something was happening today. The caller ID said Unavailable. I flicked it open and sat up.

"Hello?"

"Hello—is this Melissa?"

"Is this Fiddy?"

"No—no, this is Jo."

She had barely gotten through her name when I shouted loud

enough to make the house shake and wake my roommate: *"I knew it! I knew Fiddy was up to something!"*

She laughed, and I thought, *I've just made Jo Rowling laugh. Finally! I'm sitting here on the phone in my apartment and I'm in my pajamas and I've just made Jo Rowling laugh.* Something had to be done to bring this conversation back to earth.

"How are you? How are your children?" I winced. I was back in the bathroom at the premiere, banging my head against the wall.

"They're fine," she said, and we shared an awkward pause, which was fast becoming a specialty in our relationship. "I was wondering, as you know the launch of *Harry Potter and the Half-Blood Prince* is coming, and I was hoping you could come to Edinburgh, to interview me."

I blinked. My roommate snored.

"What? I mean, yes! Yes, of course, yes-sure-yes!"

"Oh, good." She explained that Fiddy had said something about my interview request but that she'd had this idea before I sent it, and I tried to will myself into a normal, casual conversationalist before we hung up. It didn't work. She explained more details of the excursion, how she was about to call Emerson Spartz from MuggleNet and invite him as well, and how we had to keep it strictly between us until the big announcement ten days later. "This is—this is really—I mean, you honestly *don't* have to be done with the book, I don't expect that, but the interview will be Saturday afternoon." That left us with about fifteen hours to read the entire novel, but I didn't even pause.

"Jo," I said, for the first time aloud ever, "we will be done with the book. Don't worry about that."

When we hung up, I stopped pacing and held my phone tightly to my chest. I wasn't allowed to tell anyone. I wasn't allowed to tell anyone. I wasn't allowed to tell anyone. Except my family, and Emerson, who would be sleeping. After I told my mother and had hung up while she was still yelling, I ran down the stairs and sent Emerson an e-mail, the subject of which was *Call me* and the body of which said, *when you know what this is about.*

The house was quiet, and I couldn't take it anymore. I text-messaged David and Kathleen and told them to call me right now. David answered first, and I blurted it out: "You can't tell anyone but I can't, I can't, I can't not tell you—J. K. Rowling just invited me to her house to interview her on the day that *Half-Blood Prince* comes out."

There was an interminable pause and then David just laughed, a slow, rumbling, infectious laugh that caught me in its wave. I fell onto my bed, cradling my phone, enjoying the unrestrained laugh of someone either insanely happy, or just insane. At that moment I didn't care which.

The day of the announcement, Jo Rowling had also awarded Leaky her Fan Site Award, the e-trophy she handed out to good and devoted Potter sites. The comments section on Leaky exploded in cheers, as did many of my fellow reporters at the paper, when I told them. I was much freer about telling people about my hobby at the *Staten Island Advance* than I had been at MTV Networks, because by the time I joined the *Advance* I had plenty of real journalism experience associated with the site under my belt. The site was even on my résumé. Not a single reporter heard the words "interview" and "J. K. Rowling" without looking at me incredulously and demanding the full story of how it had come about. I'd cowritten a series about a cultural center on the island, I'd done reams of reporting on the biggest ferry crash the island had ever seen, and I had been on the reporting team for stories that won two Associated Press Association awards, but the thing that gained me the most respect around the newsroom was the Leaky Cauldron. If I'd been a painting, the smile couldn't have been rubbed off my face with turpentine and terry cloth.

I asked David and Kathleen to come with me to Scotland, because we had been planning on reading the book together and that didn't have to change. Besides, I knew that if I didn't have them with me right before, and after, this interview, I might well and truly go insane.

CHAPTER TWELVE

The Interview

ur Tucson, Arizona, podcast, in late June 2007, was my favorite live show up to that date. Sometimes crowds seemed willing to laugh at anything, whether we had made a joke or not, and Tucson was one of those crowds; it seemed a giddiness had touched everyone now that the summer was in full bloom and the book was so close. We gathered in a Borders, where we held most of our shows, and the audience sat on the floor around our three chairs; it was like story time with an adult audience who had complete mastery of the fiction at hand. We played trivia games and tried to puzzle out the series' mysteries.

Two girls had come dressed as Slytherins and brought a graphical depiction of Earth's antipodes, to illustrate a point about the Antipodean Opaleye, the only dragon in the Harry Potter universe that had no pupils. This was central to all debates recently, because the cover of the deluxe edition of *Deathly Hallows* had been unveiled, and it featured Harry, Ron, and Hermione flying over a pastoral village on the back of a scaly and milky-eyed dragon. Some said the dragon was clearly an Antipodean Opaleye, and raised complex theories regarding antipodes (which were diametrically opposing spots on the Earth), and whether the dragons had to come from England,

Australia, or France, and what that meant for the kinds of magical worlds we'd see in this final book. Some said the dragon looked more like a mix between an Antipodean Opaleye and a Chinese Fireball variety. Some said it was Draco Malfoy, in his animal form.

And John and Sue were still fighting about the Hogwarts house-elves. They had started this argument so long ago I could no longer remember exactly when it happened: at some point, Helga Hufflepuff was revealed by Jo to have been good in the kitchen. From that day, John, basically to get at Sue, who identified strongly with the house of the badgers and thought all good things in the world shined Hufflepuff yellow, started saying that this meant all the Hogwarts house-elves, who work in the kitchens, had been enslaved by Helga herself. The logic didn't even follow, but John could stir Sue into a frenzy about it with a word; during the recording of one show, I sat quietly for ten minutes, filing my nails, while the two of them went at it. When a fan in Tucson mentioned Helga, I knew exactly what was coming.

"That hardworking Hufflepuff, who has all the house-elves do all the work behind the scenes—" John started.

Sue immediately went on a rant, her pure defense of Helga as passionate as if she were doing it in front of a judge. "No! I think that she was the first person to save the house-elves from persecution out there, and gave them an environment. Because at Hogwarts they're safe. Dobby gets paid. Why would you pay someone if you're keeping them prisoner? Hello?"

"It's Willy Wonka–esque." John adopted a female voice. "We'll find the Oompa-Loompas and bring them to my factory! And I will enslave them to make my chocolate."

"Willy Wonka does not wear glasses and is not the Boy Who Lived!"

At this point, I knew, the argument did not matter to John at all; he simply enjoyed saying ridiculous things to get Sue going. He, like so many of our listeners, enjoyed hearing her earnest debate on this topic. "Well, maybe she borrowed that from Willy Wonka."

"Oh, my God," I groaned.

"She does not say, 'Ooompa, Loompa, doopidy-doo!' " Sue insisted.

"This is the point in the recording when I go make a sandwich," I told the audience, "and I come back and they're still doing it."

It seemed the closer we got to release the sillier things started to get.

Meanwhile, Jo was preparing for her release event, an all-night signing at the London Natural History Museum, the same place that had seen several *Harry Potter* premiere parties. The plans hadn't worked out the way she wanted them to. Originally, she wanted to sign all night long. For the first time for one of her releases, she offered her idea to the publishers assertively, at first insisted on it. It was how she wanted to spend her night: she'd show up at midnight, do a reading, and sign all night, for however many people showed up. She still talks about the idea with longing, as though perhaps if she were a tad bit less famous, she could have done it.

"Wouldn't it have been great?" she said, almost four months later. "Wouldn't it be great to be semi-spontaneous and just let it happen?"

Her people talked her down to a twelve-hour signing, but not even that was doable: memories of long-ago riots for signatures in Boston still lingering, they had to redouble their doubts. What if a child ran away to get his book signed? And how good of an idea would it be to have this event go on all night in London—what if someone got hurt? J. K. Rowling could no longer be a woman of spontaneity, at least in this arena. The entire continent of Europe, most of North America, and probably a couple of Siberians and a native Papua New Guinean would want that signature, and there would be chaos.

The final details emerged in mid-June. Jo would do a midnight reading at the museum for about two thousand contest winners and their guardians. Most of the contest winners would be chosen by her British publishers.

It was a grander spectacle than she'd had for book four, when she rode a Hogwarts Express–style train through the United Kingdom, signing hundreds of books at every stop. It was a much bigger event than for book five, when she arrived unannounced in a Waterstones bookstore to give out books, and half the people in the store didn't know who she was. And it had more people than the event for book six, at Edinburgh castle, which had a full audience of children and a reading by Jo, but was over within an hour.

Emerson and I had been hiding in the wings at the castle that night in 2005. A few minutes after midnight, a chipper Bloomsbury employee handed us our copies of *Half-Blood Prince* and expressed amazement that we were intent on reading them through the night. We then ran the whole way back to our hostel, with me panting in the very-tall and long-legged Emerson's wake. He seemed to have a boundless amount of energy, even if belied by his lanky frame, slow-eyed movements, and terse, sarcastic speech. He was between high school and college at the time, and had enough business savvy to create and maintain a Web site with traffic two to three times my own and twice as much staff—yet everything about him still resolutely said teenager. He would only eat fast food, and it seemed the only clothing he had brought with him on this trip were several MuggleNet.com T-shirts in varying levels of cleanliness and one pair of jeans.

We both finished the book overnight, barely making it, taking

short naps and checking on each other throughout. Cheryl had instructed me to call her after "the chocolate cauldrons," a scene which
turned out to be one of the most hilarious I'd ever read in the series,
in which Ron downs Harry's love-potion-laced chocolates and falls
head over heels for Romilda Vane. I woke Cheryl up with my phone
call so we could giggle together.

David and Kathleen braved the night with me, sacrificing their
own leisurely reading time to race through, making sure they would
be able to help me prepare questions in the morning. We'd spent the
night on the tiny bed in our room, checking to see where each of us
was in the reading and taking pauses to let whoever was lagging
(usually me) catch up. When we finished around 10:00 a.m., the
three of us trundled out of the Grassmarket hostel, bleary and with
post-Potter shell shock stamped on our faces, and walked to one of
Jo's established café writing haunts. Hunched over our coffee and
eggs, we had our first discussion of the sixth book, in which we
learned that Severus Snape may, indeed, be evil after all. We were
still mourning Dumbledore; his death felt real and fresh, as though
he had been a favorite teacher of ours in elementary school.

I had a sixty-six-page document of questions with me, culled from
fan questions on the other books, and we were adding our new book-
six questions to it as fast as we could. While I showered, David and
Kathleen ironed my skirt and printed out my new questions, and
wouldn't let me leave the room without taking a good-luck shot of
"Ginevra," a Dutch liquor David had brought from Amsterdam, that
smelled like witch hazel and went down like knives. They insisted I
needed it to wake me up from the night before and take the edge off
my nerves, and they were right on both counts.

While I was dressing for the interview, Emerson appeared at the
door to my room, looking worried. One glance at him said he had
just finished reading; he had that vague struck-by-a-truck look.

"Should we, uh"—he started, then yawned—"go over what we're going to ask her?"

I stared at him incredulously. Had he prepared at all?

"I'm getting ready," I said, and indicated my toweled state. "I already printed my list of questions." His face widened in slight panic. I sighed. "We'll go over stuff in the car. OK? Go shower."

In the car Emerson goggled at my sixty-six-page document. I and several amazing volunteers from my staff had trawled a one-hundred-or-more-page forum-discussion thread to pull out the best questions. It had taken days, and one very kind staffer named Heidi D. had taken all the chosen questions and organized them by category, color-coded them, and put them in a Microsoft Excel document. I think Emerson had four questions scribbled on a scrap of paper torn from a notebook and that was it. Looking at his face I suddenly knew exactly how Hermione felt when Ron came beseeching her for last-minute help.

"All right," I said, sitting up straight. "The first thing we need to ask her, the *very first thing,* is whether Snape is good or evil." Emerson nodded, and I laughed grimly. "She's probably just going to say the answer's in the book."

Fiddy, freckled and grinning, met us at the gate of Jo's home. Fiddy and I had met for the first time at the event the night before; she'd been dressed up then, but today she gave a perfect example of what I'd later learn was the standard breezily casual dress code for Jo's office. She showed us to the shed at the side of the house that had been converted into Jo's business office and Fiddy's nerve center. I was slightly disappointed not to go inside Jo's actual house—I was dying to see how she decorated, for one thing—but the office was still a Potter fan's geek-out dream. It was golden and airy; all the wood light, the windows floor to ceiling. There was a small kitchen on the top level, which also housed two workstations for assistants; a small stairway led to a second level that had views of the backyard and Zen-like garden, and was dotted with all kinds of interesting or wacky Potter paraphernalia, like a picture of the plastic cow statue dressed like Harry that had been in Leicester Square. There was one computer, which was where I was told Jo worked. I had sent her and Fiddy Leaky Cauldron stickers some time back and was overjoyed to see one of them stuck to the wall.

I'd dressed with respect for what the occasion meant to me and wore a linen skirt, soft brown top, and faux snakeskin shoes. Emerson, as always, was in his MuggleNet shirt, but when he'd seen my outfit had thrown a striped button-down shirt over it, leaving it open so his logo showed. When Jo came in, she was with her husband, Neil, who was holding their newest daughter in his arms. Mackenzie Jean Rowling Murray beamed and gurgled at us.

"You dressed up," I heard Jo say, as though we had complimented her by doing so.

Jo would later say the start of this interview was like sitting down to a three-sided blind date, and she was right. We awkwardly exchanged gifts; Emerson's mom had secured a key to the city of LaPorte, Indiana, which I thought was a beautiful gift, while, based on Jo and my shared insatiable thirst for caffeine, I offered several pounds of flavored coffee. Jo gave us a gift bag each, and begged us not to open them until later.

We chatted nervously about the night before, the event at the castle, and the reading she had done for the schoolchildren, and Emerson and I recounted the way we had sprinted across the cobblestoned streets to get back to the Grassmarket hostel to start our read-athon. While I wired up her microphone, she asked what we thought of the book, and I nearly spit on her trying to hold back from screaming how much I had loved it, for the Harry/Ginny kiss alone. Still, we were tiptoeing around the edges here; someone needed to flag a start to this interview soon or an hour would pass and we'd still be exchanging pleasantries.

"Who do you talk about Harry Potter with?" Emerson asked, and though he probably meant it as small talk, he had begun the interview. Whatever nerves he had been showing in the car were gone, and prepared or not, he began spouting off insightful questions with what I would have thought was practiced ease, had I not known better. His great opener led easily into other topics and it was a full five minutes until I got to what I thought would be our first question.

"Is Snape evil?"

Jo adopted a sly look that would reappear whenever she had a secret. "Well, you've *read the book*, what do you think?"

I glanced sideways at Emerson, and started laughing. "Told you!"

And now my nerves were gone, too. The rest of the interview went by in a blur; Jo, Emerson, and I burrowed through answer after answer, clearing up a lot of misconceptions about the canon and finding out more about the books in one interview than fans had ever done before. I could already imagine the fans exploding with glee, as our answers were hitting almost every area of fan favorites—Sirius's state of mind after the Potters died, Dumbledore's history, parallels between the Death Eaters and Nazis, even nitty-gritty things that some of my more canon-obsessed friends would love, like how many wizards were in the world and why Peeves can't be kicked out of Hogwarts. I was almost jumping in my seat to get the interview transcribed and online, even before we had finished. But the best part about it all was how hard we laughed at certain moments—at one point Jo laughed so hard she accidentally snorted her soda, and I had to work hard to suppress a laugh-turned-burp thanks to my can of the same.

So we were slightly giddy when we got to talking about romance in the books.

The interview wasn't scripted, and we had no preapproved questions or discussion topics. Ships came up very naturally—it seemed like all of us had been dying to go there. I asked Jo how much fun she had writing the romance in *Half-Blood Prince*.

"Oh, loads. Did you enjoy it?"

Emerson and I squeaked in response, telling her that we were high-fiving during the Gryffindor party scenes, where Jo had made it clear that Hermione favored Ron, not Harry, and that Harry favored Ginny, not Hermione.

"Although, we thought you made it painfully obvious in the first five books," Emerson said.

Jo pointed to herself and whispered something nearly inaudible.

"What was that?" Emerson pounced.

"Well so do *I*!" Jo repeated, nearly pounding her fist on the table.

It was like five years' worth of stress cracked open, right there on her bleached wood table. We all let out huge guffaws, a release that came from years of contending with the ship wars in our own ways. For her part, Jo had watched, agog, as the shippers conducted mass debates online; Emerson said flat out on his site that Ron and Hermione were destined and anyone who didn't believe so was insane; I pressed my lips shut every time I wanted to argue with the Harry/ Hermione shippers who stirred raucous discussions on our comment threads. I had made it Leaky policy not to deem Ron and Hermione factual until proven in the books or until Harry/Hermione was irrefutably shot down by Jo, though oftentimes I wanted to shout it from the rooftops. The attempt at impartiality had caused me more than my fair share in headaches, and trying to keep the peace between quarreling parties was maddening. Now, Jo had done it. It was over.

"Harry/Hermione shippers," Emerson said, the way he'd done so many times on his Web site, "they are delusional!"

I clapped a hand over my mouth, but even the insult couldn't hold back the glee. The argument was now over.

Jo adopted an admonishing tone to Emerson.

"*Emerson*, I am not going to say they're delusional!" she said. "I will say that, yes, I personally feel . . . it's done, isn't it? We know. Yes, we do know now that it's Ron and Hermione. I do feel that I have dropped heavy hints. *Anvil*-sized, actually, hints, prior to this point."

"She nailed it down," I said later, still amazed at what happened. "Nailed. It. Down. The ship wars are *over*."

Wrong. And Jo knew it.

"As soon as Emerson said what he said, on tape, I knew we were in trouble," she said later.

We left Jo's house around 5:30 p.m. Fiddy called us another taxi, and we both sunk into the seats with the satisfied sigh that usually comes after a full meal. I rested my head against the seat back and stared upward.

"That was—"

"I know!" Emerson said.

"When the fans read—"

"*I know!*"

We had driven a few minutes in silence before Emerson poked me in the arm and gestured down to our unopened gifts. I told him to go first, and he unwrapped a gorgeous silver cup with the date and *Love from J. K. Rowling* engraved on its side.

Mine was in a small green box with a leathery, reptilian feel, and the embossed gold words, *Joseph Bonnar, Edinburgh,* stamped on the top. What was inside was true to theme: I stared for almost a full minute before removing the corrugated gold ring. Shaped like a snake, his tail wrapped innocuously around him and his emerald green eyes flashing, it was, Jo had said in the accompanying letter, modeled after the engagement ring Prince Albert had given Queen Victoria. She said it was a thank-you for the *hard work and your invaluable protectiveness towards Harry and his fans*. I put it on and swiped at my eyes and unlike the night before, as he would say later on his Web site, Emerson didn't laugh at me for doing so.

We started working almost immediately, and well into the next day, which was the second-to-last day I had in Edinburgh. I was just reaching the bleary point with the transcription when David and Kathleen, who had been spending the day loafing around Edinburgh without me, walked into the room where Emerson and I had our laptops set up, with very serious expressions on their faces.

"Melissa," Kathleen said with the air of someone about to break up with her boyfriend. "We're staging an intervention."

"A what?"

"We want to see *you*," David chimed in. "Stop working. Now. We're making you stop. We're in Edinburgh! Come on!"

I frowned; my editor from the *Advance* had called me two days ago to ask me to write a story about my experience. I hadn't started it, and the deadline was in a few hours. And I was in Edinburgh to *work*, after all, this wasn't a leisure trip no matter how fun it was— but the puppy-dog eyes on my friends . . .

"Give me ten minutes?"

We performed a similar intervention on Emerson, who needed absolutely no convincing; in a blink he, his friend Jamie, his mom, and we were at the Last Drop, a pub in Edinburgh's Grassmarket district. Emerson and I high-fived as we relished and relived the interview. We later walked miles through the town, over a few bridges and down unknown alleys and streets. I danced as we went, twirling; Jamie and Emerson fake kung fu fought the entire way, all of us shouting at inappropriate volumes for the dead of night. By the time we made it, sated and exhausted, to our hostel, we dropped right onto our beds and into a slumber that seemed to seal the events of the weekend in my mind forever.

The next morning Emerson woke me up, by knocking hard on the door, to say good-bye. I waved to him tiredly, and before I knew it, I, too, was on my way home.

Emerson and I posted our reports from the night of release right before each of us left the hostel. They both told the same story from two different points of view—of how we had gotten our hands on our books at midnight and sprinted, how my feet had been aching so badly Emerson insisted on carrying my shoes so I could run faster, how we had gotten lost, and how we had slapped hands while reading the book through the night. Our twin reports mirrored each other's feelings, and showed, I thought, a bond of friendship we'd formed over this event that rose above the small rivalries of which we sometimes were accused (and in which we sometimes gleefully participated).

My mother greeted me at the airport with the fiercest hug I'd ever gotten and the widest smile I'd ever seen. She immediately started babbling about all the people she'd told, everyone who'd called her up to ask how I was doing, every interview of mine she'd taped or read.

"Everyone's calling me to ask how you're doing, and I keep sending them to Leaky to read all your interviews, and here, call Daddy and tell him you're home!" She tossed me the phone, but I was more interested in the still-out-of-reach Internet. I'd been out of touch with the online world for almost a day and I hadn't any idea how our reports had been received; my mother only said that the fans seemed to be loving it.

When I walked in the house, however, my sister was there, and had a much different reaction waiting for me.

"*Memerson, Memerson, Memerson!*" she chanted like a schoolgirl, throwing her hips from side to side with each repetition. She was dressed in sweats, like she had just returned from the gym, and her ponytail was flying left to right in her childish dance.

"What?"

"Memerson! Melissa and Emerson!"

"What?"

"They're talking about it on Leaky! Memerson! They want you two to get together! They think you already are!"

I still had my carry-on luggage in one hand and my purse in the other, and stood like a very confused statue in my mother's bright foyer. My sister seemed to be speaking a foreign language.

"What?"

She snickered and filled me in on how the fans, upon reading our reports of Emerson's chivalry and our friendly experience, and our similar personalities to Ron and Hermione, had taken it upon themselves to infer that we had become romantically involved while in Edinburgh. The notion was ridiculous; Emerson was seven years my junior, I had nothing but sisterly feelings toward him, and we hadn't, in any way, indicated that anything had gone on between us. And nothing had. And why did they care?

The idea caught fire on the message boards, and within a day there was fanfiction posted about us (some of it written jokingly, some not), most of which guessed at behind-the-scenes moments about our joint set reports. I couldn't read it; every time I got sent a link to a story my curiosity made me click the text but I always had to stop when I reached my name. I couldn't take seeing myself written as though I were a fictional character, with made-up thoughts ascribed to *me*. Every time, my eyeballs froze in my head and my neck cramped. My "weird" threshold had been upped significantly since entering such an intensely devoted fandom, but this kind of weirdness just didn't compute on the normal scales. Once, I simply forwarded the link to my close Potter friends, including Kathleen, David, Meg, B. K., and Kristin, with whom I spoke regularly on an e-mail list. I told them to read it and tell me what was in it because I couldn't get through it; they had a grand time dissecting it and laughing as they did so. Even those messages got hard to read, especially when someone mentioned that I had been described as having "chocolate brown eyes," one of the most classic and off-putting fanfic descriptions for Hermione.

For better or worse, I was incidental in all of this. Most of the fervor was coming from MuggleNet, and Leaky was catching the overflow. I knew why they were semi-obsessed with Emerson. Prior to the release of book six, the first picture of Emerson had made it onto the Net. It was taken by a photographer from the *Chicago Tribune,* and it showed a grinning Emerson holding a copy of the fifth Potter book that appeared to be glowing, lighting him from underneath. The entire picture had an eerie blue tint to it, bathing its subject in a cool and mysterious hue. It also revealed that Emerson was not the twerpy kid everyone thought he was but a strong-armed teenager with a wide white smile and big blue eyes. The little girls went wild. He ran their favorite Web site, had a sense of humor, *and* had the nerve to be cute? Instant Internet stardom. Fan sites and fan clubs went up in his name, and to the teens who were Harry Potter obsessed, he might as well have been a demigod.

In the wake of "Memerson" and the strange insistence people had on believing it was true, I landed, to Emerson's fangirls, in a position totally unfamiliar to me and instantly ridiculous: as *that girl*. The one whom all the other high school girls wish would sprout eczema. Or antlers. Soon, I found myself decried by the teens who wished they could have had my fictional smooches with Emerson. Another helpful fan sent me a link to an online photo album where I was depicted rather unflatteringly as a Sim—a character in the popular video game where users create digital avatars. The person who had posted had played the game with me as a character in it and had taken pains to portray me as an unemployed, unwashed, and sexually promiscuous character with a bad temperament and predilection for out-of-wedlock pregnancy, while the boys from MuggleNet (for now that Emerson had fans, so did the top portion of his staff list) were employed, kempt, and as devastatingly good-looking as low-resolution digital characters get.

It was all engrossing, the way horror movies are engrossing, but I couldn't spend too much time wallowing in my paradoxical popularity; I had enough to deal with—the interview was being posted piecemeal on both my and Emerson's sites, and we were mentally steeling ourselves for what was going to happen when the second part of it hit the Net.

I sat at my computer hitting Refresh for ten minutes straight when the second part of the interview, the part with the shipping comments, was posted. I didn't have to wait long at all for the first wave to come through, and by two hours in I was staring at the rapidly populating comment thread in abject horror.

It was worse than I imagined. Worlds worse. The e-mails came in immediately. Some seemed to hold us up as modern-day heroes; others cursed our very existence for sinking their "ship." As celebrated as we instantly became in the Ron/Hermione community was as reviled as we became among Harry/Hermione shippers. They called Jo Rowling foul names and wrote her letters—one man, in his thirties, wrote her one that said, *Excuse me for thinking you a better writer than you are.*

But that was nothing compared to what was happening to Emerson. I'd come out the least scathed; some vile person suggested that I did unclean things with relatives, but that was the worst comment. Emerson's insistence on calling a certain faction of fans "delusional" gave his detractors a rallying point. He was mean and had insulted them, they said, so they were offering the same courtesy back. Emerson received repeated death threats (I only got one); his line of reasoning was compared to that of slave owners; he was depicted in vile fan art, and fans wrote vitriolic missives cursing his name. He only made it worse when he issued an "apology" to the H/H shippers—that is, the ones who weren't suggesting that Jo was actually going to pair Hermione up with Harry. The others, he said, rubbing enough salt in the wound to defrost a city block, were still delusional.

Meg, who had been only involved in the fandom peripherally at that time, went back to the Sugar Quill to read the reactions to the interview. She responded privately to a poster named Devin who had made a pithy comment about how good it felt, finally, after all these years, to be gloriously, wondrously, *right.*

Two weeks later they were dating. He was scruffy and black-haired with green eyes and glasses, and with Meg's bright red hair, the two of them together would have seemed ridiculously contrived were they not so instantly, and clearly, in love.

If nothing else, the controversy showed me exactly who I could trust. Publicly, some H/H shippers, like Angela, the girl who'd so brazenly predicted this interview and with whom I'd kept up a cordial relationship, were being nice and polite to me on my personal journal. She assured me that she hadn't been hurt by the interview at all, and made herself out to be above it. A lot of people bought it, too, including me. A week later a friend gave me a login to an H/H community and showed me something different: a post where Angela had just called Emerson an eighteen-year-old twerp and me a Rita Skeeter wannabe.

I just laughed and rubbed my thumb against my left ring finger, where a golden snake rested benignly.

More than two years later, I sat in Jo's office again, wearing the same ring and, despite the lack of one Emerson Spartz, feeling immense déjà vu. *Deathly Hallows* had been published and digested, and Jo and I were nearing the end of an eight-hour interview. We both laughed a little, remembering what had happened here last time.

"I tried very hard to soften it, I suppose," Jo said. "Just because someone had a view on Harry/Hermione didn't mean they weren't genuine, or that they were necessarily misguided. In fact, I will say this. Steve Kloves, who has been the scriptwriter [on the Potter films], who is enormously insightful on the series and a very good friend, after he read book seven he said to me, 'You know, I thought something was going to happen between Harry and Hermione, and I didn't know whether I wanted it to or not.'

"I had always planned that Harry's true soul mate, which I stand by, is Ginny, and that Ron and Hermione have this combative but mutual attraction. They will always bicker, there will always be rough edges there, but they are pulled together, each has something the other needs."

I stared at her, sensing she wasn't finished, and a sense of foreboding crept in around my edges.

"[Kloves] felt a certain pull between them at that point. And I think he's right. There are two moments when [Harry and Hermione] touch, which are charged moments. One, when she touches his hair as he sits on the hilltop after reading about Dumbledore and Grindelwald, and [two] the moment when they walk out of the graveyard with their arms around each other."

I was holding my breath by this point. She wasn't done.

"Now, the fact is that Hermione shares moments with Harry that Ron will never be able to participate in. He walked out. She shared something very intense with Harry.

"So, I think it could have gone that way."

I could hear the shippers' cries of woe—H/H and R/H alike—reaching me all the way from the future.

CHAPTER THIRTEEN

Independence

 e'd finally decided where to spend our *Deathly Hallows* Eve, and I couldn't be happier about it: Jan Dundon, a manager at Anderson's Bookshop in Naperville, Illinois, had called me up and asked us to join her for Anderson's party, a two-town, tens-of-thousands-of-people event. We'd hemmed and hawed, but decided that the Chicago area offered us a great central location for fans, and the size of this party made the perfect ending to the podcast tour.

One June evening, while I was on a break from touring, Jan picked me up at the Naperville train station so we could discuss plans for July 20. She and I walked around the town and the neighboring Downers Grove; kids were twirling in the streets as a Jamaican band played, and old-fashioned streetlamps lit the lanes. Naperville and Downers Grove would stop traffic for the event, commandeering streets and involving hundreds of vendors in what they were now calling The Party That Must Not Be Named. (Their previous name, Muggle Magic, had been changed by request of Warner Bros.)

Anderson's is a highly respected bookshop, with two locations in town centers; it had survived the proliferation of chain bookstores like Barnes & Noble and Borders, which had become more and more of a feat. But after Jan picked me up from the train station, as we walked around the town, there was a bit of a saddened tone to her voice.

"This should be the biggest sales day for all bookstores," she explained. "Instead, we're going to be lucky to break even."

Independent bookstores had once whispered life into the Harry Potter series, but with the series' popularity a raging retail war had sprung up around the books. Deep discounts cut at the stores' sale prices, until the competition meant booksellers essentially would have to pay people to take the book. Anderson's went as low as it could, and stopped at a 25 percent discount—and they could only manage that because they were selling two thousand copies. Some stores would only sell a few, maybe a hundred copies (like the Hungerford Bookshop in the U.K., which sold seventy-four). Yet to take part in the experience, most or all stores were staying open until midnight and staffing parties, which meant a lot of money they weren't making on a book that was supposed to have been the easiest seller they ever had.

Publishers sold the book at a discount somewhere between 40 and 50 percent to resellers, so at a suggested retail price of $34.99, that meant stores could buy them for $17 or $18. Yet by *Goblet of Fire*, and increasingly with each release, wholesalers, supermarket chains, and eventually the big online retailers like Amazon.com and Barnes & Noble, started using the book as a loss leader, which basically meant they were losing money on the book in order to generate revenue from other sales. They would have the lowest price, so they would attract the most interest, and the difference would be made up elsewhere. This fierce competition all but ensured that independent stores had to either offer the same price as competitors and thus take a loss on the book, lose their sales, or charge full price and depend on customer loyalty.

"Losing money on a book that is a guaranteed best seller is bonkers," said Vivian Archer from Newham Bookshop in London. If everyone in the U.K. sold *Deathly Hallows* at the suggested retail price of £17.99, or somewhere between wholesale and retail, everyone would make money. Yet independent bookstores were ordering carefully, or underordering copies to make sure they weren't stuck with any extra. With most books, sellers can return what goes unsold, but as Harry Potter gained clout, Bloomsbury stipulated that only 10 percent of stock could be returned.

There used to be a different playing field in Britain under the Net Book Agreement, a publishers' agreement dating to 1900 that allowed for a shared minimum price on books. The sale price would be set by the Publishers Association, and further discounting would only be allowed in book clubs, libraries and schools, or similar outlets. The agreement was decreed anticompetitive in 1997, following the withdrawal of several major publishers from the arrangement; thereafter retailers were free to set whatever price they liked on any book. Some said the change in practice resulted in overall lower prices on the book market due to more competition; others said it burdened books that sold fewer copies to pick up slack, because best sellers were so heavily discounted they weren't bringing in money. Supermarkets like Tesco and Asda, which were growing their libraries—regularly offered books for the same price as a magazine or a few loaves of bread. Harry Potter books could be bought cheaply, for 50 or 60 percent off. Similar deals could be had online from Amazon or Barnes & Noble.

But there was also, with Harry Potter, a saving grace for bookstores: no online seller could get your book to you by 12:01 a.m. the day of release. For that you had to be in a bookstore. And online sellers couldn't throw you a big party.

Jan excitedly told me about her costume for the big day—she was going as Madam Hooch, and with her short stature, spiky gray hair, tough sheen, and sparkling eyes, I saw no better fit. There would be people acting as live portraits, human chess here, and a costume contest over there, she said. The party was clearly her baby, from the way she was gesticulating and seeing the future mayhem before her eyes. "The town just comes alive. It's so special." Over the course of the day more than fifty thousand people were expected to roam in and out through the scene. It would be an all-day carnival.

"Perfect," I said, getting swept up in her enthusiasm.

The following day, at our next tour stop, fan predictions came unbidden, furious, because time was running out and everyone had to get their position heard. Especially when we asked who would die in the last book.

I'll never fully understand why the deaths were so important to us, or what we stood to gain by guessing them. On the one hand, it was something hard and definitive, a prediction you could write down and claim credit for afterward; on the other, the simple fact that one character died or survived revealed little about the circumstances under which such a thing would occur. To bookies it was just another thing to bet on, the way they might have a standing bet on whether it will be a white Christmas or when Tom Brady will score his next touchdown. It felt different to fans. We knew how seriously Jo Rowling planned her deaths, so we took it seriously as well: if you thought someone was going to die you had better offer up a good explanation why, because it affected the plot, which affected your theories, and sometimes a good theory was all someone needed to establish their cred in fandom.

For years on PotterCast we had been polling fans on who would live and die in the different Harry Potter books. We called the game, ingeniously, Live or Die. It was easily one of our most popular features and most popular game, and on the road or at live shows it became easy and fun to play huge, shouting rounds. We'd name one character and the audience would shout "LIVE!" or "DIE!" After almost ten years of speculation about the books it seemed a remarkably simplistic distillation of our complicated theories and predictions.

All the wild speculation about character death had started off innocently: Jo Rowling had said in response to a reporter's question way back in 1999 that a character we care about would die in the fourth book. There are deaths in the first three books, but of people we never knew or cared about. A character we actually know well dying? That was big news.

The first recorded instance of the statement is innocuous enough. Yes, someone dies in the fourth book. That's all. One quote from Jo Rowling. She said that bit was hard to write.

"I couldn't contradict it," she said recently. Anything she revealed about the book would be considered a spoiler, and fans were mightily against spoilers. "I would be establishing a precedent of flagging up major plot points before they happened. I think there was a degree of disappointment when it turned out to be Cedric Diggory but I never meant to mislead anyone. Even worse, I'd started a hare that just wouldn't stop running."

She had been trapped by her own intention of keeping the plot details sacred. Meanwhile, a whole new and ruthless element emerged: money.

The U.K.-based betting company Blue Square was one of the first to make Internet betting available, instead of relying on bets physically placed in stores. When J. K. Rowling suggested there would be a death in the sixth book, bookies at the agency felt it was "the natural thing to do" to open a book on whose death it would be, "especially with the extensive press coverage of Harry Potter." And they were right; the idea of bookies taking down names hit the media in a big way.

Their idea backfired, thanks to the people of Bungay, a curiously Pottersque town in Suffolk, England, off the Eastern shore of the British Isle. The town was home to a castle that appeared to be in ruins; it has a Godric Way, and local custom keeps alive the belief in the Black Shuck, or a large black dog, the sight of whom portends death and destruction. If there was ever a place where Harry Potter should be printed, this was it. The local Clays publishing plant played midwife to hundreds of thousands of copies of Harry Potter over the years.

Blue Square was taking bets on the book at a normal rate, until a huge amount of wagers started coming in suggesting Dumbledore would die. Had this happened before the Internet, there would be no way to prove the origin of the bets, but online forms meant addresses and credit card numbers, and soon, it was easy to determine that all the bets for Dumbledore were coming from one town: Bungay, Suffolk. More than six thousand bets came in over less than a week.

Blue Square cut off the betting, but not before contacting the *Sun*. The story carried widely, and ensured them against the potential monetary loss stemming from the security breach.

Considering past books' history at the printing stage, it wasn't an unbelievable reach to believe that the gamblers had inside information. Dumbledore's wasn't the least likely death anyway, and when the press reports came out revealing this character as a probable favorite, most fans shrugged and said, "Yeah, we thought so."

Bets had been limited to fifty pounds, so those six thousand people netted 250 pounds each.

"We paid out the money, at five to one odds, so around thirty thousand pounds of liability," said Alan Alger, a spokesperson from Blue Square. "We probably got about one hundred thousand pounds of press coverage, so in that respect it didn't feel like we were losing money."

I posted the story on Leaky when it happened, but barely lifted my eyebrows when I saw Dumbledore's name. Though somewhere inside I felt it was a genuine leak, I forced myself to allow for the possibility it was merely the result of a very concentrated group of Harry Potter fans who all placed bets together. With a little willpower, and a touch of denial, it was possible to remain unspoiled.

Within a few days of the Blue Square story, statements had been made by Bloomsbury as well as Jo Rowling (via her Web site), reminding us to have an extra few grains of sodium lying around for stories like these. However, there were a *lot* of stories like these, and few provoked a response from the author; this made us all pretty sure it was Dumbledore who was going to buy the big castle in the sky that time around.

The funny thing about the book six betting, and all the talk of deaths around book six, was that Jo Rowling never once specifically said, in any of the thousands of articles, interviews, or anywhere on her site, that book six would contain the death of someone we loved. She mentioned that there would be further deaths in the series, and she certainly never *denied* that there would be a *big* death, but as far as book six was concerned, everyone could have been alive, well, and playing Parcheesi at the end. Somewhere between books five and six the general populace stopped wondering whether someone would die and whether that person would be a character known and loved to us, but started assuming that big and important deaths would just be part and parcel of the remaining books in the series. In short, they stopped being shocked about the very thing that used to be played for such shock value.

Even so, the death derby never faded, partly because it was so much fun. It entered a cycle of ask-and-answer that continued with each installment. Undoubtedly in some interview or other, Jo Rowling would be asked about the next book and which characters we could expect to die. Then the lead story on the wires the next day would be all about how she promised a bloodbath, and we fans would roll our eyes and remember that she did promise a bloodbath, years ago, and that any number of deaths wouldn't truly be a surprise.

A year before *Harry Potter and the Deathly Hallows* was released, on an appearance on Channel 4's *Richard and Judy*, Jo Rowling made a simple statement about how the writing was going. She revealed: "I've actually killed two people I didn't intend to, and one person has gotten a reprieve."

And we were off to the races, in some cases literally. Every Web site, television station, news organization, newspaper, and news outlet in this country and many others carried the story. By this time I knew how to gauge the shock level of a particular story by how often my phone was ringing. Now that we were so close to the end of the publication of the series, many reporters had my number in their Potter files, and I was becoming a go-to person for articles and commentary, as were the webmasters of all the big Harry Potter sites. On any given day, Emerson Spartz and I were quoted in different newspapers about the same topic. Reporters couldn't get the author or publishers to comment while a book was under embargo, so I was becoming a good substitute, and it felt fraudulent, like I had taken to calling myself Dr. Melissa on a talk show or something. A story had to reach a certain threshold for those kinds of calls to start, and for a really hot story I probably received two or three calls throughout one day. The day after this story broke I had to turn my cell phone off to get anything reasonable accomplished at work.

The one phone call I took at lunch was from MSNBC. Within

hours I was sitting in the studio, with a plug in my ear and a fake backdrop of New York City beside me, about to start talking to a host I couldn't see but who I was imagining lived right behind the camera. I had a flash to my first-ever interview, the phone call to BBC during the Get a Clue auction, and how I'd stammered my way through half of it and sped-talked through the rest.

The first thing this reporter did was ask me how to pronounce Jo Rowling's name.

"It's Rowling like bowling," I blurted out, thrilled to finally set the record straight, and then went on to explain how two deaths in Harry Potter weren't that big of a deal, that Jo Rowling had promised and was probably going to deliver a bloodbath. "It's like a trilogy, in film," I said. "It's war; people die."

As amazed as I'd been initially that this was a story at all, it made sense with a little reflection: it had been almost a full year since there was any tangible Potter news—Jo Rowling hadn't yet announced that she was finished writing book seven and had given absolutely no other information out about it, not even the title. The starvation led to a feast over an ultimately insignificant detail. And as I said on the show, this was like the end of a trilogy: anyone could die. No one was necessary for the next book. Even Harry could die.

That was the big question, of course. Would Harry live or die? Early on, before Jo Rowling became the literary equivalent of Brad Pitt, she would laugh the question off. When asked if she would ever go on to write more than seven books, she'd say she wanted to stop before we got to *Harry Potter and the Midlife Crisis*. But she eventually switched tactics, in line with the growth of the phenomenon. Somewhere around 2000, all her answers became, "You seem certain that he's not going to die," or, if asked about Harry's future children, "How do you know he will have children?"

I couldn't find enough willful ignorance to throw at this question.

I had taken a tack just slightly more dignified than sticking my fingers in my ears and shouting "Lalalalalalalalalalala!" whenever anyone suggested Harry would die, and certainly when a reporter suggested it. By mid-June I must have answered the question, "Will Harry die?" sixty times, with several variations of admonitions and shock that anyone would ever suggest such a thing. It got to the point on tour that when my phone rang, my friends would roll their eyes and mentally count how long it would be until they heard something from me like, "No, certainly not, this story is about love, and triumph, and if Jo Rowling wanted to kill him and still achieve those goals she certainly could, but she won't. I don't know why, but she won't."

We were starting to get nervous, though, about book leaks. We were close, too close, to the release of the book; in May, right about the time the books went to print, I put up a note on Leaky urging fans not to engage in the ruthless swapping of Potter secrets on the Internet.

Harry and the Potters had also taken to recording public-service announcements and playing them during our show. They recorded them in the van, which was obvious from the staticky hum of rolling tires in the background track.

"Hi, this is Harry Potter, from Harry and the Potters," one said. "Pizza is a wonderful food, but don't go near it in England. They don't know what they're doing!" Or, "Hey, Muggles! Science is rad! Keep up the good work!"

There were about nine of them, but the one that took first prize was their last.

"Hi, I'm Harry Potter," said Paul.

"And I'm Harry Potter," said Joe.

"And we're Harry and the Potters, with a special-service announcement for all you PotterCast listeners."

"You know when Voldemort killed my mom?"

"And my dad?"

"That wasn't a very nice thing to do."

"Neither is spoiling a book for millions of people."

"This July, keep your MOUTH SHUT!"

CHAPTER FOURTEEN

On the (Internet) Radio

t was almost July before I cracked. We were finishing up lunch at a Chinese-Mexican fusion restaurant in Phoenix, Arizona. The food was just about as difficult to digest as its category was to remember, and we were antsy and tired when someone from a newspaper a few states away called me. We went through the rote interview questions—why is Harry so popular, what's in store for the site and for us when the series is done, etc.—while John, Sue, and Bre (John's girlfriend, who was traveling with us) sniggered harder and harder with each of my answers, because I (and they) had taken to making faces while I talked. They could guess which questions were coming by now and recite the answers, and the whole exercise was starting to look as ludicrous as it sometimes felt. By the time the reporter got to the end of his list I was as punchy and desperate for a joke as they were, so I wasn't totally in my right mind when he asked, "So, Harry, will he live, or will he die?"

"Oh, come on, Harry is going to live, and if you don't believe me, you can just bite me."

I stopped, and looked around at my friends, who wore identical expressions of blank shock.

"Melissa!" Sue mouthed, and I had to stuff a napkin in my mouth to stop from laughing.

"Please don't print that," I begged, and was happy to find the reporter was laughing, too. "We're just very tired out here."

That was the truest statement I'd ever made. After only a few days into the PotterCast tour we understood why we weren't rock stars (as if that had ever been in question). We tired out after a few hours of driving, we were late to shows, and we sometimes let the weariness we felt bleed into our performances on the podcast. Yet the crowds were huge and enthusiastic, and at times their predictions were hilarious. One attendee in Albuquerque suggested that Snape didn't really exist in the books—he had simply been McGonagall the whole time.

"So who was McGonagall when she was talking to Snape?" asked Sue.

The boy paused a second, and then threw his hands wide. "An illusion!"

Harry Potter podcasts didn't truly exist until a month after the sixth Potter book. Leaky had been working on the concept since the previous February, and was just getting back around to planning and implementing it when MuggleNet released its "MuggleCast" on iTunes. The response was shocking—it hit the top five spots in iTunes' chart within its first week of release, and almost instantly a new medium for Potter analysis was born. MuggleNet would never stop teasing us that we only created a podcast because they had done

one. They were wrong, of course, and there was proof in that we had bought and registered PotterCast.com in March, a full five months before MuggleCast had been released, but they didn't care. Following my and Emerson's controversial interview together, the boys from MuggleNet and I started to share a very siblinglike relationship, complete with shared affection, lighthearted taunting, and vicious bickering.

Our shows weren't much different; both had book discussion and news segments and, as we learned early on, depended on the personalities of the presenters to maintain an audience. In our first show, I did all the introductory segments and most of the interviews; I recorded it into a microphone at my roommate's dining room table at three in the morning, feeling like a complete fool. The next week, Sue, who'd had personal responsibilities to deal with the week before, took over the news segments. But the show didn't really gain its most loyal following until about week six, when John Noe joined me for a discussion segment.

John had wanted to produce, not be part of, the podcast, but one night, thinking we needed to record some sort of discussion around our news, I pulled him in. I'd known John to be a very passionate and hardworking guy, but I'd never known he was funny. Suddenly he was playing the fool almost perfectly and didn't seem to mind at all.

John: "I can produce any name [from the Potter books] on cue."

"Oh yeah?" I said.

"Yeah, dare you."

"Tom Riddle's mother."

"Tom Riddle's mother . . . umm . . . I dunno . . . I dunno the damn book six stuff yet!"

"You said any name!"

"Any from the first five, please!"

"You know, we are eventually going to compete [in trivia] against the MuggleNet boys and you are not on my team."

"I'll be on their team and handicap them."

The response was instantaneous and clamorous, and took the weird fame that Emerson and I had been granted after the Jo Rowling interview to a different level. Suddenly there were fan groups and Web sites; mine was called M.A.F.I.A., or Melissa Anelli's Fans in Action, a slight joke at my Italian heritage. The club consisted of a handful of very sweet girls who collected smart or funny things I'd said on the show. Sue's was S.Q.U.E.E., after the sound she made whenever she was excited; John's was I Noe John, a play on his name. Soon everyone on each podcast had fan clubs, and we were mostly just baffled—but definitely flattered—by them. If I thought about it, I could see how a podcast was a form of entertainment that could gather its own fans, and that made more sense to me (and felt different) than being a Big Name Fan. The latter had long-ingrained fandom connotations of fanfiction and Web sites, and a slight air of elitism; this new wave of fans-of-fans seemed to me to have a sweeter attitude and seemed genuinely focused on the entertainment value each person brought to the podcast. John's humor made him our biggest star, instantly.

In November, to celebrate the release of the fourth movie and since we were all going to be in New York together anyway, we planned our first live joint show with the MuggleNet crew. We figured we'd just sit at a Starbucks somewhere, and a few fans might show up to enjoy recording with us. We were much too naïve to realize what our forty-thousand-plus listeners meant: as soon as we floated the idea, we were inundated with e-mails from fans promising to attend. When we hit one hundred, I told Andrew Sims of MuggleCast that I'd look into a bookstore to hold us. When the list hit four hundred, the Barnes & Noble in Columbus Circle was deemed too small by management and they searched for another option. When five hundred people e-mailed to say they were excited to see our joint show, Barnes & Noble decided to host our first-ever live podcast at the Union Square flagship store.

The morning of the show I was picking up our sound guy from the Bronx when Emerson called me from the B&N. It was not even noon, and more than seventy people were lined up outside the building to wait for the 7:00 p.m. show. I shut the phone off, dazed, finally starting to realize what this podcast thing meant, and called Cheryl at her Scholastic office, my breath starting to come in short bursts like it did when I had a panic attack. She spent fifteen minutes calming me down, reminding me that I had interviewed Jo Rowling and this should be a cakewalk.

I'd been in fandom situations before; I'd been asked to sign autographs at conferences before. It was more like being a member of student council, I thought, than anything else. I signed someone's Harry Potter book (always with silent apologies to Jo) the way I'd sign a friend's yearbook. This was much, much different. It was the night of the New York premiere of the film version of *Goblet of Fire*, which was why so many fans were in town and able to come to the show. I reported from the red carpet for Leaky but, unlike everyone else from our site and MuggleNet, didn't go to the screening; I ran back to the bookstore to get things set up. Fans were sitting in every aisle of the top floor of the bookstore; they clogged the escalator on every floor; the security guard told me they had to rope people off. By five o'clock, the *New York Post* had shown up to interview me; documentary filmmakers Gerald Lewis and Josh Koury had done the same for their film, *We Are Wizards*. More than seven hundred people were on three separate floors, some forced to watch via videofeed. I paced like an anxious hen waiting for the rest of the podcasters to get back from the screening. The MuggleNet guys were first, but Sue and John couldn't get a cab and we had to start the show without them. Andrew and I, the main hosts of our respective shows, came out to start the show together. The roar that greeted us made me so nervous I shook for the entire thing, even when Sue and John came running in to join the proceedings.

An hour and a half later we'd exhausted ourselves on discussion of the film, so we said good night. As soon as we did, it seemed as though everyone in the room pushed themselves toward the stage; the staff at Barnes & Noble were trying valiantly to organize things, but fans were just grouping around each podcaster in hopes of a picture and an autograph. I saw Emerson sign a fan's jeans, and I saw a girl ask him to sign her chest; the rest of the MuggleNet boys garnered similar screechy adoration. Sue and I got more hugs and notes of appreciation for providing fans with weekly entertainment. It took an extra hour to clear the place out and when we were done and had gathered at a restaurant for dinner, we looked around at one another like we'd just scaled Everest. The teenage boys could never expect such a reaction from their schoolchums; Ben Schoen, a bearish teen from Kansas, told me he'd get made fun of without restraint if he wore his MuggleNet shirt to school. Andrew was a twerpy video geek. I could almost see their postures straighten, their confidence grow, after such a warm reception. We all shared one thought: we have to do that *again*.

Meanwhile Potter podcasts were proliferating, growing into the hundreds; soon there was Snapecast, devoted to everyone's loved/hated Potions professor. Some podcasts focused on the Weasleys, some on the movies, and some even on MuggleCast and PotterCast (but mostly MuggleCast: the teen boys would always gather an exponentially higher level of hysteria than the "older" show ever could).

That spring, Kris Moran from Scholastic called me to ask more about the podcasts and live events we'd been hosting. Soon, she called again to discuss one of the most flattering ideas ever offered to me: Scholastic wanted to send me, Cheryl, and Emerson on a national speaking tour to discuss the books, record the talks as podcasts, and celebrate the release of the paperback of *Half-Blood Prince*. We worked the tour around Lumos 2006, the fan conference in Las Vegas, Nevada, where our next Leaky Mug (the new name for our joint MuggleCast/PotterCast ventures) would be held. We spent the summer traveling, meeting hordes of Potter fans in Chicago, Los Angeles, Las Vegas, and New York, and then capped the experience with another huge Leaky Mug at the Union Square Barnes & Noble, on the occasion of Jo Rowling's Radio City Music Hall reading on August 2. She was appearing in New York as part of "An Evening with Harry, Carrie and Garp," a series of readings that served as a benefit for Doctors Without Borders and the Haven Foundation, which also featured fellow novelists Stephen King and John Irving.

At this point, I was taking a lot of time off work. I'd garnered enough vacation time to handle it, but the *Advance* was holding less promise for me than it once had. One of my favorite editors had left and the assignments were getting repetitive, but worse, I was no longer working to overcome that drudgery, the way I had in the beginning. My day job was starting to feel more like my hobby; my real reporting work lay with the Harry Potter fandom. I was even daydreaming about writing a book about the phenomenon.

Like all Jo Rowling question-and-answer sessions, the Radio City Music Hall shows provided some excellent topics for discussion at our Leaky Mug, and the show went much like the previous one, except that even larger crowds and louder pandemonium ensued afterward. The PotterCast and MuggleCast crew spent the rest of our time together in New York doing tourist things, like riding the Circle Line, which I hadn't done in years. The last night, I sat cross-legged on the floor, in deep discussion with Emerson; it had been a year since we'd first been seen as entertainers by our fans, and I was just starting to really come to terms and appreciate what it meant. These events were fun, but I was even happier at what had started to happen behind the scenes: I'd started getting letters from young girls, some who wanted to be journalists and asked for advice, and others who just thought I sounded like someone they could talk to. One girl poured her heart out to me in an eight-page missive, admitting she had low self-esteem and an unhealthy body image. I nearly tripped over myself going to my desk to write her back. As fleeting and contrived as Harry Potter–induced fame felt, I couldn't deny that I liked it.

"Look at us," I told Emerson, and he looked around. Andrew was showing John funny YouTube videos, his spiky hair glowing from the screen; Ben and Kevin were locked in a discussion about the virtues and pitfalls of Windows Vista. "Geeks! Pimply, schlubby"—I pointed to myself—"chubby nerds, and somehow they like us for it."

"I know," Emerson said, and high-fived me, as a slow grin dawned on his face. "We win."

CHAPTER FIFTEEN

Spoiled

e were on tour in San Francisco on July 4, 2007, and luckily, so was Cheryl Klein. She was on a much-needed vacation with her boyfriend, James, and we maneuvered to meet for dinner and watch the Independence Day fireworks together.

"I'm so glad Cheryl is here," John said, clapping his hands a few times and sitting up straighter in his booth, "because I have some theories."

Sue, James, Cheryl, Bre, and I let out identical groans.

"No, no, no, listen, I want to tell Cheryl my theories now so that on July twenty-first she can call me up and tell me how right I was. I want to state them for the record."

I rolled my eyes, but was interested; so was Cheryl.

"First of all, that dragon is, like, in the basement of Hogwarts or something. And I think on the cover, Harry's holding out his arm for Fawkes. And, ooh, ooh, wouldn't it be amazing if—this came up during our show last week—if the suits of armor, the knights, in Hogwarts, came to life and fought for the school? Someone just shoots a spell at them and *bam,* they go clanking down the hall?"

Cheryl said nothing but "Hm," told John she had recorded his thoughts properly, and suggested we hurry to the waterfront for the fireworks.

It was a superquick visit and then we were back in the car, shoved into our seats as though we were Harry and the Potters, with our luggage, boxes of T-shirts, half-eaten bags of chips, cameras, notebooks, and computer cords all around us. The Potters had split with us when we traveled to London to cover the film's release, and we were touring on our own now.

We had now done more than twenty live shows and had traversed the country twice, and despite so many nights in dirty motels or driving through mountains fighting over which set of directions was accurate, and so many hours stuffed in our seats in the van that we were starting to share thoughts and finish each other's sentences, July 21 was like a mirage that was constantly out of reach. But the shows were still fun, and we hadn't yet killed each other, so we entered a Borders in high spirits in the second week of July. I could hear the fans as we entered the store—the approach of the book was making everything buzz, everything festive. We were almost skipping as we approached the back of the store, where we could put our bags in the general manager's office.

We were happily having coffee a fan had left for us there, when Sue, who had been reading e-mail on her phone, groaned.

"What?"

"Nothing. It's . . . nothing." She waved her hands around but I saw anguish on her face. "Nothing."

"It is so not nothing—what?"

"I think I've just been spoiled. Dammit." She checked her phone again. "Yeah. Yeah. That's real."

For most fans, getting "spoiled" on Harry Potter is a tragedy. Spoiled means you have seen a detail about the upcoming book, usually a big one. You always knew when one was real. A real piece of

Potter information had a resonance to it, like a correctly struck note. Sue definitely looked as though she'd been struck.

I dialed Kris Moran, the Scholastic publicist.

"Kris, I'm so sorry to call you at home, it's Melissa."

Kris's voice immediately lowered. "What's happening?"

"We think it's a real spoiler this time."

Kris must have already been dialing a second phone, because the next time she talked it wasn't to me. I heard the name "Mark," and knew she was on the phone with Mark Seidenfeld, the main lawyer at Scholastic who dealt in Harry Potter issues—America's answer to Neil Blair. We gave Kris the e-mail address where the spoiler had originated, and properly ruined her Friday night.

For the previous week, low-level, obviously fake spoilers for *Deathly Hallows* had started to circulate on the Internet. These supposed book excerpts never looked real; most often it was clearly a fanfic, or mislabeled as Harry Potter just to encourage people to open it and visit an unrelated site. Still, I had stopped reading any e-mail that didn't come from a trusted source. When forced to open it I'd squint down hard with my eyes, forcing everything blurry, and carefully read, word-by-word, in as slow a manner as I possibly could, the first few lines of the e-mail to be sure it wasn't a spoiler. Sometimes Sue, sitting with me as I scrolled through my mail, would hold her hand up to the screen for me in a two-person effort to avoid details about a book we were both dying to read.

If it looked like it even might, possibly, in the smallest of circumstances, resemble a spoiler, I hit forward and sent it off to Jo Rowling's lawyers, agents, and editors.

Thus far, the spoilage had been relatively minimal. I had made a post two months earlier on Leaky, called "Spoil Us Not, Sneaks!" that reinforced Leaky's antispoiler policy—not only would we not be willing to post the information you had sent us, we made it very clear that anyone who tried to do so would be dealing with Jo Rowling's lawyers next.

"If Harry dies, we don't want to know about it until Jo Rowling decides to tell us. And if you decide to tell us before that you'll incur the wrath of a staff of almost 200, most of whom have been waiting almost 10 years for these final revelations and can NEVER get back the moment you rob by spoiling them. That's some wrath, right there. We own pitchforks, hot wax, and feathers. And we're not afraid to use them."

The post had been heralded, most notably by Jo Rowling, who mentioned it on her Web site, ensuring that reporters everywhere quoted my original story—but only insomuch as they took the quote about pitchforks and feathers way out of context and killed the tongue-in-cheekiness of it. I looked like a total loon, everywhere. It was wonderful.

A half hour after Sue was spoiled, I was on camera, speaking to a reporter from CBS on site. She had walked right into our conversation about the spoiler and so started to ask me about it on the record. I said, as I always did, that we weren't sure it was real—that unless Scholastic said it was a real spoiler (and they never would), all we had were suspicions. The associate producer who had come along asked me why we didn't want to read the spoiler—weren't we, as fans, desperate to get any information we could?

"It's our job to act as sentinels," I said, trying to hide the way I was internally bristling at the implication that fans had no ability to control themselves. "We as fans have to protect her work."

A great part of the joy of Harry Potter reading is what happens next, the revelation of the next piece of the elaborate seven-book puzzle. For a lot of die-hard fans, getting spoiled was the equivalent of having a dog shred your book to pieces while you watched.

The first Harry Potter spoiler was actually Jo Rowling and her publishers' fault. They had intended not to even reveal the title of the fourth Harry Potter book until it was released. The press then frequently referred to the book as a "cloak-and-dagger operation," or "under wraps," or "shrouded in mystery," the lattermost of which still makes Jo laugh.

"It became inadvertently one of the best marketing campaigns in history," she said. "I said to [my publishers], 'Could we not give this out, just yet? I don't know yet, I don't think this is going to be it.' " The working title was *Harry Potter and the Doomspell Tournament*, and she only gave that to her publishers on assurances that it would only appear in a trade catalog. Fat chance; it leaked widely, and was corrected on June 27, 2000. For *Phoenix*, Jo gave out the title herself when a cute child asked her the question during a television appearance. Immediately someone bought the Internet domain associated with the name, and demanded millions of dollars from the Christopher Little Agency to get it back. From then on Jo and Warner Bros. had decided to engage in a disinformation campaign: they registered a company called Seabottom Productions Limited and began protecting a litany of fake titles such as *Harry Potter and the Mudblood Revolt, Harry Potter and the Quest of the Centaur,* and my personal favorite, *Harry Potter and the Green Flame Torch.* (Fan myth became that the torch was an item that killed all evil and protected the bearer.) She would send her representatives lists of titles to register and protect, and by the time she decided to announce a real one, Seabottom had already secured it for her.

"Now it's over, thank Christ, I can say it," she said, folding over herself in relief. "I think we had several fronts. We just needed to keep a little bit of confusion going for those last few hours until we got it out there."

I tried not to look too mutinous, but Seabottom had caused me a lot of rough days battling an in-box full of rumors. I even said once, right on Leaky, that if anyone registered a domain name for Harry Potter "it will be JKR or her camp before WB, or we will hear about it far before WB (and certainly a company called Seabottom) registers it."

Those fake Harry titles, however, absolutely paled in comparison to what started coming out of the Republic of China in 2002, when publishing houses, unsatisfied with the long wait for *Order of the Phoenix*, started producing their own Potter novels. *Harry Potter and Leopard-Walk-Up-to-Dragon* and *Harry Potter and the Golden Turtle*, and those like it, were never big commercial hits—Jo and her lawyers sued them and forced the publishers to apologize as well as pay fines, winning a copyright victory in an area of the world where this was hard to protect—but they were, to Westerners, at least, entertaining.

"Harry doesn't know how long it will take to wash the sticky cake off his face," reads the opening paragraph of *Harry Potter and Leopard-Walk-Up-to-Dragon*. *"For a civilized young man, it is disgusting to have dirt on any part of his body. He lies in the elegant bathtub, keeps wiping his face, and thinks about Dudley's face, which is as fat as Aunt Petunia's bottom."* In the story, Harry is transformed into a plump dwarf whose magical powers are taken away.

By 2007, the market had expanded there again, and the *New York Times* ran the story, "Chinese Market Awash in Fake Potter Books." Now there wasn't just a fake *Deathly Hallows*, but *Harry Potter and the Hiking Dragon, Harry Potter and the Chinese Empire,* and *Harry Potter and the Big Funnel.*

On August 10, 2007, the *New York Times* published eight excerpts of the Chinese rip-offs. In one, called *Harry Potter and the Waterproof Pearl,* Harry, Gandalf (from *Lord of the Rings,* naturally), and the Little Warriors (from . . . somewhere?) find a sea city in a desert, travel through a keyhole to a foreign shore, obtain gold armor, and kill the bad guy. Then Harry and friends find a waterproof pearl, which is somehow helpful in saving Hermione from the Dragon King.

I almost wanted these books to be published legitimately in English.

The concept of a spoiler as it related to Harry Potter before the publication of *Deathly Hallows* is different from how it's usually defined. A spoiler is any fact about a piece of media, be it book or film or television show or anything else, that gives something away before the readers/watchers/participants have had a chance to experience the entire thing for themselves. It's like walking into a room where everyone has just sat down to play Clue and shouting, "It was Colonel Mustard in the conservatory with a knife!" During that time for Harry Potter, it would be like saying this before those who intend to find out on their own have had the chance.

Harry Potter spoilers existed for years. Every time Jo Rowling gave a chat, every time some piece of canon gave way to a fan's irrefutable conclusion, every time there was an interview, there was almost inevitably a spoiler. But small ones. Parallel ones. Things that clarified and provided further information. Nothing that ruined the plot of future books—only things that magnified the cat-and-author game the fans were playing as we desperately scrabbled to piece together all the parts of her puzzle. It was the biggest real-life mystery game of all time and it went on for years, in hundreds of countries.

Spoilers became pernicious when they didn't come from Jo Rowling: they were a sign of disrespect to the author, and the information revealed could ruin your enjoyment of the books. They weren't part of the game.

With each progressive book release, the antics of would-be spoilers became more and more creative. The people who did the spoiling weren't usually fans. They were usually people who held no regard for the series, who would sell their ill-gotten copies for money or fame.

We had a strict policy at Leaky: information about the books would come from Jo Rowling or her publishers, and no one else. We were fans, not thieves. We would protect our favorite author.

Before book five came out, we had almost no information about it; the only bona fide information to come through about the book had happened in such a Deep-Throat manner I half expected it to occur in a parking garage. That was partly because it was April Fool's, a day of complete hysterics in Harry Potter fandom. There's no sense to it, no reason why April Fool's should even be mentioned—we didn't even find out until 2006 that it's the Weasley twins' birthday, and it's never mentioned in the books. But the pranks in the Potter fandom to celebrate the day were elaborate. That year the Sugar Quill was "taken over" by Draco Malfoy. He turned the site green and spent the day on message boards, terrorizing the guests. I was busy laughing about that when I got an e-mail from someone I'd never heard from before, nicknamed Rosalind.

She claimed she had a copy of a summary of *Harry Potter and the Order of the Phoenix* that had appeared in a Scholastic catalog for summer and fall 2003, a catalog mostly read by teachers and book distributors. She had typed up the entire passage, which said that Harry's Defense Against the Dark Arts teacher had a personality like poisoned honey, and there was some sort of venomous, disgruntled house-elf in the picture, and that Harry was dreaming of doors and hallways, and that Ron was doing terribly at Quidditch. It was all believable enough—I took considerable pause at the phrase "poisoned honey" as sounding very JKR-esque, but I hadn't enough experience with spoilers yet to sort out the real gems, and it was April Fool's Day, after all. And if there really was a summary for this book available in a free and widely distributed catalog, surely we would have had readers e-mailing us every other day about it. Surely the most anticipated book in history, the one with the tightest security, the one about which there was the least amount of precious information, was not fully described in a book sale catalog. I e-mailed Scholastic just in case, and they told me no summary existed.

"Tsk, tsk, Rosalind, we've got your number now!" I crowed. "Thought you could get us, didn't you?"

Rosalind swore she was telling me the truth and said she'd send me a copy. I was sure I'd never hear from her again, but I gave her my address anyway.

A few days later my mother called me at my job at MTV and told me that a large package had arrived for me with no return address. Intrigued, I told her to open it.

"It's a Scholastic book catalog," she told me. "And there's a little blue sticky note coming out the top."

"Go on, open it, open it," I whispered, to stop myself from screaming.

I could have recited with her the summary as she started reading it to me. The rest of the day passed more slowly than if I had been asked to refile all of Denise's credit card receipts, and I spent the bus ride tapping my fingers and foot impatiently. I nearly ran through the door, barely said hello to my family, and stared down at the thing like it would vanish if I didn't hold it very still. The little blue sticky said, "Ahem . . ."

"I . . . need the scanner," I told my mother.

This wasn't a spoiler, it wasn't illegal, it wasn't even unofficial. It was in a catalog bearing Scholastic's name. It had been written and approved and published *by* Scholastic. It was a public book, mostly read by teachers but certainly not meant to be kept secret from anyone. It was information that was meant to be consumed. As soon as

I could see it was real I came down with a case of classic reporter-itis. In minutes, just like I'd done with the old *Vanity Fair* pictures, it had been scanned and put up on Leaky, with heavy spoiler warnings, watermarked to show that the images originated from our site, and "humblest[sic], most abject apologies," offered to Rosalind, our mysterious benefactor.

The response was instant and clamorous. Some doubted it was real, just like I had when I had first read it, which was why the scans had been essential in pointing out that the image was Scholastic's. I'd made attempts to get the description verified through Scholastic but they were mum, and I hadn't been working with them long enough to know what that meant. After the catalog copy went live, everything else went pretty silent.

That is, until the book was found in a field.

In early May 2003, the tabloid the *Sun* ran a banner "exclusive" headline crowing that they had read a copy of *Order of the Phoenix*, and it was wonderful, and weren't we sad we hadn't read it? They claimed someone had found two copies in a field next to a publishing plant and sent them to the paper.

Everyone was skeptical about the story, and still is. The culprits were found out by private detectives to be teenage boys; they were prosecuted and publicly apologized, but still maintain they found the books in the purported field. Jo Rowling rolls her eyes at this, as does Neil Blair.

"As everyone would have done, [the person who found the book] decided to send it to the *Sun*, not go to the printers and say, 'This might be yours,' or phone the police or Bloomsbury or us, but take it to the *Sun* newspaper," Blair said.

The Christopher Little Agency, which was often put in the position of acting as legal mavericks since the Harry Potter books had the annoying habit of getting into legal gray areas, had been arguing up until then that they should be able to use John Doe orders in Britain the way they're used in America: that is, they should be able to take legal action against someone whose name they don't yet know, on grounds of potential future harm. This case got them their wish: the law was changed to allow action against John Does, enabling injunctions against any person who might try and spoil the books by publishing content within them. The John Doe order is now colloquially referred to as the Harry Potter order. I asked Neil why he didn't demand that people call it the Voldemort order.

He laughed. "I'm saving that for something really nasty."

There was another odd incident involving book five: June 15, 2003, at about 10:30 p.m. Greenwich time, a truck containing more than 7,600 copies of *Harry Potter and the Order of the Phoenix* went missing from Newton-le-Willows near Manchester, and reappeared the next afternoon eighteen miles away, halfway to Liverpool. When the truck reappeared, however, it was empty. No one ever found the books.

"I think somebody's probably still got them, thought they were cigarettes or something," said Neil Blair.

"More likely," said Christopher Little, leaning forward in his chair and already laughing, "somebody opened it and said, 'My God, this was supposed to be whiskey!' "

Only once in the lead-up to book five did genuine information leak, and how it did was somewhat understandable. By June there were tens of millions of copies in print, and by that time and by law they had to get to their sellers' locations before the embargo ended. No complicated legal maneuver, well-laid plan, or threat of penalty has ever been enough to ensure against the actions of the uninformed or uncaring. Some people will inevitably put the books on sale before they're supposed to, and not-so-inevitably the address of one of those places will catch the ear of someone who knows a reporter, who will call that reporter, and next thing you know the New York *Daily News* has a copy of *Harry Potter and the Order of the Phoenix*.

The headline was "Hocus-Pocus! We Got Harry," and the ensuing four-hundred-word piece started: "Holy Hogwarts!" and detailed the story of a Brooklyn, New York, health-food-store owner promptly displaying four copies of the big blue book a full five days prior to publication. He had put them out on his shelves as though they were vitamins or wheat germ.

The *Daily News* reprinted two full pages of the text, as well as many juicy details, including the name of the new Defense Against the Dark Arts teacher and the name of a house-elf. Those two bare facts were all I knew, because I refused to read the article or, in fact, any of my e-mail. I had started to realize the only way I could successfully read my e-mail, without being spoiled, was by squinting at it and tilting my head, and by doing so allowing myself to focus on one word at a time instead of gulping the whole page in a glance the way I was used to doing. It made me look as though I were eighty years old and in search of my bifocals, but I did it anyway, despite the weird looks I got from colleagues and the vague pain I felt behind my eyes each time I tried. I was trying to simultaneously be the fandom's reporter and the least informed megafan alive, and it was giving me a crimp in the neck.

The *Daily News* story seemed to have vague underpinnings of truth, but I wasn't risking finding out and didn't know how I'd do so anyway. Jo Rowling and her lawyers immediately rushed to action, filing a suit for $100 million that claimed the *Daily News* had violated Jo Rowling's copyright. It all seemed like it might, perhaps, go away, if it hadn't been for Ain't It Cool News.

Ain't It Cool News, a movie gossip and review site run by film-fan-cum-Web-czar Harry Knowles, was a site we rarely linked to on

Leaky. Sometimes it picked up an interesting bit of casting news, or posted an interview with a director or actor from Harry Potter, but generally we avoided linking to the site because of the mature content often posted by its users. On June 18, 2003, AICN posted all the spoilers from the *Daily News*. They were quickly ordered to take them down, and apparently did so within a day, but not before half the online world and I succumbed. So far all I'd known about the book was what I had read in the summary, and the brief overview of what had been in the *Daily News* story. I opened Ain't It Cool with that same sense of dreadful apprehension, as though it were pulling me in by an invisible string. Yet as I allowed one eye to open and focus, one word became clear against the background blur, as though under a magnifying glass. *Umbridge.* In a flash the words, *Defense Against the Dark Arts Teacher with a personality like poisoned honey* played in my head. Umbridge. Umbrage. Taking umbrage. As you would against sweet but secretly malicious statements. As surely as if Jo Rowling had told me herself, I knew the spoilers were real. A tuning fork had been struck. I closed the browser window so fast it was as though I'd been looking at porn.

Mostly, the spoiling never got very far, and didn't hurt anyone—once, thieves threw a bunch of books off of a train during a robbery in California, likely never realizing what they were. The girl who found them in her garden sold them around her school. It's possible no one would have ever found out—except that the girl's father was a lawyer, and the lawyer friend he called to discuss the situation with happened to be working with Christopher Little to determine who had thrown the books off the truck. The man visited his daughter's school, delivered a lecture on copyright infringement, and got every copy back.

That changed before book six was published, when there was a gun shootout over unsold copies of the books. *Sun* reporter John

Askill got a phone call from someone who said he had the book and would sell it for £50,000. Askill went to the meeting, but brought police, intending to recover the book before it was leaked. The man with the book, Aaron Lambert, a security guard for a regional printing plant, got spooked and fired his gun. Askill would call it the most frightening moment in his then twenty-eight-year career; having been to Afghanistan and Kosovo, he realized he was about to be "shot for the sake of a Harry Potter novel."

Luckily for Askill, the gun was loaded with blanks, and Aaron Lambert was sentenced to four and a half years in prison.

When Jo Rowling heard about the shooting, she wanted to publish the book early.

"Just that fact that you've produced something that people want to steal, to put on the Internet is, for me, very uncomfortable," said Jo. "And when a gun gets involved, the joke's gone out the window. Completely out the window.

"Nearly always, it had nothing to do with the fandom. It had to do with people's own desire for either money, or notoriety, or I suppose excitement in some way."

After the first spoiler for book seven was revealed on the Internet, all kinds of spoilery hell broke loose. Scans of at least three different *Deathly Hallows* were circulating online, and people were bragging that they had read the whole book, while some weren't sure if they had read the real book or a fake one. Books started to appear in stores willy-nilly, and fans started wearing buttons that said, "I've been spoiled! Let's talk about *Deathly Hallows*!" or "I'm not spoiled, Shh!"

• • •

By the time we hit Wichita, our last stop on the tour before the book release, John and I were barely able to keep our heads up. Sue, a single mom, had gone home for a while to Columbus to see her son, but would reunite with us in Chicago. We had one day off between this show and our final ones in Illinois, and couldn't be happier about it if it were the end of a two-hour aerobics class.

I hadn't any high hopes for Wichita. It was intentionally a small show in a more intimate setting before the craziness that would precede the release of the book—a bit of a breather while we traveled backward across the country.

A smattering of fairly quiet and polite fans greeted us inside, and the store had left out water and grapes for us to eat. And though eating and drinking is a distinct no-no in the world of podcasting, we ate them as though they were our last meal, and shared them with the ten-to-fifteen-person crowd.

"We are fifty-three hours away!" I tried to say with gusto as we started the show, but it came out like I had just won sixth place in my local beauty pageant. John looked just as drained. I realized it'd been weeks since I'd seen some of my closest friends or my family. Everyone in fandom seemed to be coming to closure and readiness, and something felt off. And as soon as I realized what was wrong, I knew where I was headed. I'd been living so immersed in the phenomenon for so many weeks that I couldn't see the surface anymore; it was show after city after show after city, and it was threatening to allow the arrival of *Deathly Hallows* to come, for me, with all the exuberance of a wheat harvest.

I'd spent so much time—not just on this tour, but over the past six years—wrapped up inside this phenomenon, and now the biggest day, the day all of us had looked toward for years, had almost arrived, and here I was approaching it like any other day at work. Sue was with her son, and John had his girlfriend with him on tour. As July 21 approached, I remembered my life before Potter, and had a sudden urge to see my mother, to dance with abandon at a wizard rock show, to just revel in the series and not be "Melissa from Leaky" to a crowd of strangers. Just for one day. The release of *Deathly Hallows* had huge emotional importance for me and I couldn't feel any of that anymore. I couldn't let that happen. I had to go home.

CHAPTER SIXTEEN

One Day More

42 Hours

ohn dropped me off at the Kansas City, Missouri, airport at 3:00 a.m., looking thoroughly confused.

"I still don't get what you're doing."

"I just need to go home. I have this interview. I'll meet you in Chicago."

I did have an interview, but it wasn't why I was going home. I had agreed to the ABC interview *because* I was spending the day in New York, not the other way around.

At 4:00 a.m., there was no one in the airport—not a janitor, not a coffee-cart guy, no one. I sighed and sat on the floor, and rubbed at my eyes futilely. If I did things right I could stay awake just long enough to make my plane and fall asleep there.

At 5:00 a.m., Kris Moran called to get a phone number, and was followed shortly by Kyle Good, another Scholastic publicist.

"Do you all ever sleep?" I wondered. "What is it, the Scholastic Slumber Party '07 over there?"

"Something like that . . ."

There had been more spoilers over the week, because some stores had illegally displayed copies, which led to people buying them and publishing reviews. Last night the whopper of them all occurred: The *New York Times* published a spoilerific review of the series. Michiko Kakutani, the paper's star critic, had run a review that was full of exactly the kind of small details we had been trying to avoid. It was a highly complimentary, front-page, everything-you-could-wish-for review, but still an unauthorized, before-July-21 write-up. The paper said it got its book at a store that had put the book out early, and everyone from every corner of the Potter firmament was angry about it, except one person, the same who had just put a note on her site that said she was disappointed in the newspaper for ruining the plots for children.

"Everyone [was] up in arms about it, lawyers [were] calling me," Jo said, shaking her head at the memory. "I'll tell you this, though, and this really is the true story of Harry Potter." An apologetic spasm crossed her face. "You know, all I gave a damn about—" She stopped, went back, tried to explain better. "I had to put out a response saying, 'We're disappointed,' because fans really didn't want to know. But all I wanted to know—" Again she stopped, seeming to hope she'd explained it thoroughly.

"I'm a writer! *Was it a good review?* No one told me! As an author— and she's a good critic—I want to know. Did she like it?"

One of Jo's publicists would call her while she was on the train on the way to London for the launch and deliver the good news that it was a positive review.

"And I said, 'I love you.' No one said anything! For all I knew, it was a terrible review. With leaks."

36 Hours

My mother met me at my apartment and drove with me to do some errands. She hadn't needed to, at all, but something in my voice must have made it obvious how badly I wanted to see her, and forty-five minutes later she was in front of my door.

After I'd picked up some cold medicine to ward off whatever virus I'd picked up on the road, she pushed the car into park and sat back in her seat.

"So, you ready, baby?"

She asked with such inherent understanding—such a strong hint at the hugeness of the occasion—that I started. We hadn't had any real conversations about what the release of the book meant to me, yet I was sure she was asking more than whether I was ready to find out the plot of the remainder of the series. Now that I thought about it, no one else in the world witnessed, so closely, what Harry Potter had done to me, and how it had taken me from a scared, self-conscious twenty-one-year-old, whose first job frequently reduced her to tears, to a twenty-seven-year-old reporter who led a global Web site and was part of a fan community, and, because of it, was about to publish a book on the Harry Potter phenomenon. Suddenly I knew my mom understood all of that.

"Yeah. I think I am."

35 Hours

Samantha, a friend I'd made through Leaky, called my cell phone.

"Are you spoiled yet?" she asked almost immediately.

"No, thank goodness! You?"

"Kind of. I read a fake epilogue where, get this, Harry and Ginny name their kids James, Lily, and *Albus Severus*."

I snorted with laughter.

"Albus Severus, yeah, right."

33 Hours

The interview took place at the Scholastic store; the broadcasters had already interviewed Cheryl and were having me walk around the store and fondle Harry Potter–related merchandise for background footage. The clip that aired showed me trying on a Sorting Hat, and then cut to a three-year-old I hadn't seen who had been standing next to me, doing the same thing. Implied immaturity always made my day so much better.

The clip also showed Cheryl and me as friends, and finally said, point-blank, on ABC: "The two are now friends, joined by Harry Potter." We joked that we were finally out of the closet, once and for all.

28 Hours

I arrived at the Bohemian Hall & Beer Garden in Astoria, Queens, with Cheryl and a few more friends, and almost as soon as I made it inside Paul DeGeorge came running at me like a bowling ball, crushing me in a hug. The Potters were playing a show here, and it felt like everything had been heightened, scrubbed raw. We weren't just happy to see each other—we were desperate to see each other, and the show was like a reunion, with three Potter bands and people I'd seen previously at PotterCast shows (one of whom gave me a very puzzled look, as if to say, *Aren't you supposed to be in Kansas?*) and Emily doing her merch and little Darius of the Hungarian Horntails still screaming and running around and his mother Tina carrying the newborn baby Violet in a papoose.

I didn't even bother teasing Cheryl about the book and what she knew, or what the *Deathly Hallows* were. We were both past the joke. But she did, at one point, grow pensive and tapped my hand, so I leaned in to hear what she had to say. I wondered if she'd been thinking hard about it.

"You know, people have had fun. They've had fun with their theories. It's been fun, but now it's time for J. K. Rowling to finish her story her way. I just hope everyone can let go of everything they expected to happen, and go with it, and love this book. And make sure John calls me when he's done."

At least six hundred people showed up, and the show was epic. Halfway through the Potters' set a horn section joined them; the bubble machine that hardly ever worked now spewed translucent spheres onto the crowd, who riotously demanded an encore.

Though I'd been dancing on a picnic bench, I had to jump down to dance with Cheryl for "These Days Are Dark," the light, poppy melody that ended their first-ever album:

> "These days are dark
> but we won't fall
> we'll stick together
> through it all
> these days are dark
> but we won't fall-all-all."

And my favorite part:

> "And the world is beautiful
> Just look around
> And the world is beautiful
> Just look at all your friends."

People were openly sobbing, holding on to each other, while others were standing on tables and benches, pumping fists, and in the many, many Harry and the Potters shows I'd seen lately, this was the most emotional. Paul and Joe launched themselves into the crowd and showed no sign they'd ever return.

"Melissa, I just hope you love this book," Cheryl said seriously, as we said our good-byes.

She made me promise to call her while reading the book—"when he comes back," she said. Whatever that meant.

"And make sure John calls me when he's done," she said again.

Heavy with exhaustion from all the travel, but exhilarated and free, I left with the Potters, the Malfoys, and the Hungarian Horntails. We went back to a mutual friend's Williamsburg apartment, where I sat down to fix a thread on my shoe and woke up fifteen minutes later, Paul laughing at me because I had been snoring. Before I left, we each grabbed a beer, and clinked our bottles together. To Harry.

20 Hours

I took a long, luxurious shower in my apartment. After a month of touring, of the van, of noise, of air trips and car trips, the constant presence of other people, and the endless ring of crowds, everything seemed quiet, palatial. I emerged feeling as though I'd scrubbed several layers of life off my body, and wrapped myself in two towels. I huddled in the space between my bedroom and my bathroom, closed my eyes, and just stood there, too tired to sleep, enjoying the quiet, and, at last, feeling the thrill of the impending book start to course through me again. It skittered under my skin and made me dance on the spot, as though I'd been tickled.

I packed a lighter bag and left for the airport.

CHAPTER SEVENTEEN

Deathly Hallows

t least five Leaky staff members awaited me when I got to Naperville, all grinning outside the Tivoli Theater, an old movie house where we'd have our first podcast of the day. We got coffee and caught up, amazed that the day was finally here, that in about fifteen hours we'd never again be able to say we were in a time when Harry's fate was unknown.

Throughout the day, I was calling friends and friends were calling me, but we weren't sure what to say to each other. Good-bye? It's been fun? Is our friendship over now? We usually settled for something like, "See you on the other side!"

Cheryl and Arthur were party-hopping in New York, like the victors of a presidential race. When Cheryl called, I could hear the Scholastic street fair going on in the background, and Arthur was chattering with an ebullience I'd never heard from him before.

"It's wonderful here!" I told Cheryl, and it was the truth. Naperville was like an all-day carnival: magicians, street performers, games everywhere. The bookstores were calling themselves Scrivenshafts and Flourish & Blotts, after similar stores from Harry Potter; the eateries, of course, were the Leaky Cauldron or the Hog's Head. Even better, Anderson's was at the center of it, filled all day long with people in cloaks and hats. We judged a costume contest at the end of a lane, and drank Butterbeer-esque concoctions in coffee shops. Police said that about seventy thousand people showed up. It was the biggest party Naperville had ever seen.

At Harvard Square, in Cambridge, Paul and Joe were trying to shake out their nerves before going onstage, a rare event for them. Joe said he felt like a slingshot about to burst. They had been planning for three thousand to five thousand people, and for the first time in his life, Paul's spreadsheets had failed him. More than ten thousand people were crammed into the square by early evening; estimates would later range from fifteen thousand to twenty thousand. They single-handedly held up traffic on the Massachusetts Turnpike.

A radio reporter cornered Paul, and asked him if he and his brother weren't just like "a pair of skateboarders who've grabbed onto the fender of a passing car, that's speeding to the bank?"

Paul bristled, trying not to let such a mean-spirited comment eat into the day. He said he hoped to use the books as a gateway to music for kids, and got out of the interview as fast as he could.

The boys changed into their costumes behind a tree, their shirts finally crisp, white, and new. Just before storming the stage, Joe squeezed Paul's arm and said, "This is it!"

They bounded onto the stage promising to "burn this place down!" and were met with raucous cheers from the sea of people in front of them. For the first time ever for them, gates had to stand between them and the audience. Joe led the crowd in a pledge of allegiance.

"I pledge allegiance / to not spoil the book / that millions of kids are counting on / To read every page / with love in our hearts / and the power of rock!"

Paul told the crowd that he was honored to spend the night with them.

"We're Harry Potter. This is our way of fighting evil. The power of music to bring people together—it's awesome, it's wonderful. Like in *Bill and Ted's Excellent Adventure*. They may not have been the best band, but they loved doing it, you know?"

Laura Mallory didn't know the book was coming out. She claimed.

There had never been a bookstore line like this one in Israel; it was 2:00 a.m. on a Saturday, and this was against the law. Businesses were supposed to be closed for Shabbat, and any store that opened faced strict fines from the minister for industry, trade, and labor.

But come nightfall they were lined up anyway, hundreds of them, around a Steimatzky chain store in the Tel Aviv Port, despite the book only being available in English. The managers of the store would say they were part of one massive party everywhere in the world. Fans waited in line for hours, queuing up from 11:00 p.m., and had reached halfway around the pier by the time the book went on sale: promptly at 1:57 a.m., four minutes before the international trade embargo expired. No one minded.

• • •

Jo was trying to keep her emotions in check. It'd been six months and nine days since she finished writing *Deathly Hallows*, buried in the Balmoral Hotel in Edinburgh, wearing jeans and no makeup and her eyeglasses, amid crumpled chewing-gum wrappers and lipstick-smeared coffee cups.

Now, she was sitting on a throne in front of two thousand shining young faces, the London Natural History Museum's vast atrium awash in deep blue, pink, and yellow light. For weeks, she'd been mourning Harry, and the loss of what he had meant to her life. She'd mourn until her birthday on the thirty-first, when she'd cry as she'd never cried before, except the night her mother died. For now, the mourning had abated somewhat, and she donned a shiny gold jacket to greet the crowd. She answered questions about the series before the cameras started to roll, and thought, *This is it. This is the last time.*

At 11:30 p.m., we descended from the stage, full of adrenaline. We had just addressed our largest crowd ever; we couldn't even venture a guess as to how many thousands of people had been in front of us. It had been dizzying. I handed back my microphone and started toward our T-shirt table, but the next minute I was running at full speed right into the two people who had come out of nowhere but whom I'd been waiting for all night.

David and Kathleen screamed and jumped with me and now, *now* it was time to go to the bookstore.

"Just gotta do one thing," I said, balancing my computer on a trembling hand. David caught it and used his foot for me to prop it against. I sprawled myself on the street and started typing a post onto Leaky.

"The Beginning."

The signing was well under way, and kids had buried their heads in their books while they waited for their autographs. After a while they started walking up to Jo and whispering, "It's good. It's really good." One marched up to the table and shouted, "Hedwig!" while others said, "What? What? What about Hedwig?"

When a couple approached wearing Lupin and Tonks costumes, Jo could barely look at them.

We ready to go?"

Standing in front of me, my staff, and my friends, in sweats and a Cubs cap, was Sarah Walsh, my old *Hoya* friend. She was taking us to her lake house, so that we could all read together, and she beamed with an excitement I hadn't seen on her since our first-ever Potter discussion.

David read the whole way to Sarah's house. I wasn't driving this time, but I kept my word, not daring to open my book. Kathleen drove, David read, and David's sister, Rachel, sat next to me in the backseat. I put my head back and listened.

Sarah's house was on the lake, and had enough nooks to make sure that all thirteen of us were spread comfortably. John and his girlfriend, Bre, went downstairs; Sue read on her own, on a chaise; some read on couches or on the floor. Sarah's parents made us pizza and snacks, and David and Kathleen and I holed up in a back bedroom. We kept at each other's pace, taking measured naps and making sure no one person was too far ahead. I was only halfway through the book when Sue knocked on the door and came in, eyes sparkling, smiling. She was done, but that's all that she would say.

"Oh yeah, that's right, Harry's gonna live," I muttered. "Uh-HUH!"

The signing was over; it had only taken Jo about six hours to go through all two thousand kids, and her shoulder was tired, but she was elated. On the way out she noticed through her car window that a group from Brazil, representing Potterish.com, was standing outside the museum with a big sign and flags, just in case she came by. She rolled down the window and did one last signing before letting *Deathly Hallows* go.

At a vineyard in Virginia, Meg was walking with her boyfriend, Devin, who wanted to show her the place where he had finished the book. It was warm, and gently lit. The path widened around a small copse of trees, and Devin showed her a spot against them.

"Here's where I read the end," he said.

Meg thought it had been perfect, and told him so.

"Then let's make it doubly perfect."

And he knelt, then brought forth a glinting ring, and asked her to marry him. Meg would later say the moment lasted several sunlit days.

We read through the night, sometimes napping. We had a confessional set up the way we had for book five but hardly anyone used it; one of the only times I'd done so was when Ron leaves Harry and Hermione in the woods.

"Not cool," I said belligerently. "Not cool at all." And I left, slamming the door behind me.

David, Kathleen, and almost everyone else was done with the book when I finished. I'd been hunched over, paging swiftly as the final showdown happened at Hogwarts, but unlike everyone else in the house I hadn't lost it when Harry sacrificed himself. It was only when Neville stood in the no-man's-land between all the fighters and Voldemort that I broke. I remembered him striding forward to finish off a boggart in book three, and something uncorked, the thing that I'd been holding back throughout the entire summer, since I'd learned the book was coming out. It was like something, or someone, was trying to drag a concrete block through my rib cage. Everything tightened, and my vision blurred, and Neville's act of extreme friendship recalled seven years of friendship and love and community that had given me a second family, that had shown me first that I was going to be all right, that had been a constant friend while everything else in life was wavering . . . I read the rest of the book sniveling and hiccupping. It only got worse at the epilogue, when I discovered that Harry had become, simply, an average nearly middle-aged man with a family and a nine-to-five job. We not only wouldn't be reading about him anymore; we didn't need to. His adventures were over, and when the Hogwarts Express left *without us*, and there were no more pages to turn, I left the room to find David and Kathleen standing outside it, knowing I had finished. We gripped each other and they let me cry.

A half hour later I lay on my back on the wooden pier outside Sarah's, having finally stopped crying, and started laughing. I felt drained. We had called Cheryl but we couldn't say much, because people—including John, who didn't yet know that his Knights of Hogwarts theory had been so dead-bang on—were still reading. We were outside going over our favorite bits—the fight with Ron and Hermione in the woods, Ron's musings on Death's flapping cloak, and any and all things involving Professor McGonagall.

Sarah's family had a boat, so while the rest of the stragglers finished up their books, we piled in and sat together on the water. It was near sunset, and we powered around the little lake slowly, talking about the past ten years and how it had changed us.

"Sarah doesn't know this," I admitted, "but she was the *cool* kid at *The Hoya*. I was so excited to make friends with her, you have no idea." Everyone laughed, and we continued going over our favorite bits from the books, and our favorite stories from our Harry-related lives. David sneaked a bottle out of his pocket and I laughed heartily: Ginevra, the searing liquor from Amsterdam that he'd forced on me in Edinburgh two years ago.

The sunset made the lake glint like green glass, and as we started toasting—to Molly Weasley! To George! To Fred! To Molly Weasley again, because she is that cool!—the boat circled leisurely.

Two days later, Jo Rowling and her family were cowering in a pub at King's Cross in London. They were supposed to be taking the train back up to Edinburgh, but it had been canceled, and a comfortable first-class journey now looked like a staggering nightmare in which, two days after launching twenty-five million books onto the world, she would spend six hours sitting on her suitcases and attempting to corral three children. Fiddy was trying to arrange alternate travel plans, while the family sat quietly so as not to be too noticed.

And all around, brightly colored books were emerging from people's bags. She looked around to find herself surrounded by her creation, at the same train station where she had imagined one scrawny, lonely boy's magical journey would have begun.

One woman in particular was reading nearby and looked to be about Jo's age. Jo, on a post-publication high, giddy with relief that she was not tick-tocking her way up the British Isle at that moment, tapped the woman on the shoulder.

"Would you like me to sign that for you?"

"*Augh!*"

The woman threw the book in the air, and Jo Rowling's cover was blown. She didn't care, and it was no big deal anyway, if she had to spend the rest of the day signing autographs. But she didn't. People just waved at her happily and left for their trains, more content with their books than an audience with the famous J. K. Rowling, and that was how she liked it.

I returned to normal life on the Tuesday following the release. I clicked on my iPod and shifted my backpack as I waited for the train, in my own world and on a bit of a post-publication high myself.

All the rush and business of the past few days was gone and—except the surfeit of excellent memories and a calm feeling of accomplishment—felt as if it had never happened. The Q train was packed, but I didn't mind: I was on my way to meet a friend and had a Web site to run and, now, a book to write. I'd been researching and writing for most of the year, having quit my job at *The Staten Island Advance* once I realized that I couldn't run the Web site, write this book, and also have a daily reporting job. When I laid the three responsibilities out, the newspaper job stuck out as the one I could stand to lose—even if it meant moving back in with my parents. I was planning on doing exactly that until the eve of my last day at the paper, when I was informed that my book had sold and, at least for a while, I could call myself a full-time writer.

I leaned against the metal pole of the subway car as we started chugging into the heart of New York City. If my music hadn't stopped playing I might never have noticed—one, two, three, four, at least ten people were holding up their giant orange books. Some were halfway through, some nearly all the way through. Some propped it on their legs, and a few more had taken off the jacket so as to be inconspicuous. They spanned all ages, and were all engrossed.

One young woman, not much younger than me, sat near the end of my eye line; she was reading, too, her colorful backpack on her lap and her arms circling it, her book acting as a buckle to hold it in place. I traveled to the next pole down to get a surreptitious closer look; she wasn't reading *Deathly Hallows* at all. Her book wasn't orange but rose and water and sand, and featured a kid on a broomstick and a white unicorn. *Harry Potter and the Sorcerer's Stone*. She didn't notice me staring at her.

Oh, I envy you, I thought, but was smiling for her. She had just begun.

Epilogue

he cabdriver knew where I was going as soon as I told him the address. I saw his graying brow rise like a questioning finger, and the eye I could see through the rearview mirror seemed to play between respect and suspicion. Maybe he was concerned that he was delivering a crazed woman to the gate, who would throw herself at it and stick like a starfish against a fish tank. I looked away, comfortable and pleasantly warm in my jeans and flat boots.

"She's a rich lady," he finally said.

"Mmm-hm."

"You come to Edinburgh to see her?"

I nodded. I had come directly, the first moment I knew I could. A huge picture of Jo, smiling and waving after getting an honorary degree from the University of Edinburgh, greeted me at the airport, as cheerily as though she were the city's official mascot, and I laughed and waved back at it.

"I've been here before. We've talked before. I'm writing a book."

He looked back at me as quickly as he could without losing control of the wheel. "Oh yeah?" I nodded. "What's it about?"

"Oh . . . everything."

He laughed.

"No, it's about Harry Potter. About what she made, about the past ten years in the real world."

"Oh yeah?" He turned down a street I'd seen once before. "You know about that?"

"Yep. I run a Web site," I said clearly. "It's called the Leaky Cauldron."

I paid him and got out, and this time, without hesitating, hit the buzzer and let myself through the iron gate. It was very early, but I'd come early on purpose, to have some coffee time with Fiddy. We sat in the office's main room, at the table where I'd sat for an interview two years previous, dressed up and twitching. The table had been cleared, then; now it was piled high with paperwork regarding invitations for a charity gala for *The Tales of Beedle the Bard*, Jo's newest book. The short volume of fables had been referenced in *Deathly Hallows*, and Jo was in the process of writing them out by hand in pocket-sized leather jackets, the covers set with chased silver and semiprecious gems. She would pen seven copies and hand them out to several people who had been instrumental in Harry Potter's growth throughout the years.

Now that I had some time to do so, I walked around the saffron-colored room, gazing at all the international covers of Harry Potter; unlike last time, there seemed to be no further room for them. They spilled out of boxes; Fiddy hastened to show me the Japanese versions of *Half-Blood Prince*. She remembered they had been some of my favorite covers when I'd seen them on the Net. While I pored over that, she produced the Ukrainian cover, which featured a highly stylized and almost photo-real depiction of the trio, and very literal illustrations of everything else (its version of Shell Cottage was a house with a giant shell on top). Harry, Ron, and Hermione looked like windblown sportswear models on it, and I spent some time rif-fling through the incomprehensible pages.

We had coffee and caught up while Fiddy expertly juggled piles of mail—correspondence, legal letters, and the standard fan mail—sorting it in what appeared to be order of importance for Jo. Being in this room now was like visiting a declassified spy station. Everyone seemed more casual about letting me know what they had been working on. Yet it was still the nucleus of what had become the Harry Potter operation; by now Fiddy had two assistants working for her who sorted the 1,500 letters that still came in weekly. Each one got cataloged, entered in the database, and replies were recorded; the excess went into a vault somewhere. Jo said, one day, when she's feeling down, she might go roll around in them. Paraphernalia and minutiae filled out the rest of the room, making up a story of the past decade like a movie reel: the picture of the plastic cow (the original of which was now at Jo's second home); rows and rows of drawers that seemed to disappear into one wall; a large Golden Snitch, and, I realized with delight, two framed photographs from the Edinburgh release, one of Fiddy and me at the Provost's Headquarters and one of Jo, Emerson, and me right after the 2005 interview. I had sent them along as Christmas presents that year.

Fiddy and I were joking and laughing about being survivors of a long war, when Jo came in, wearing a thick white coat and im-mensely cool boots. Her finger was stuck in a Dorothy Sayers book, and she looked pink in the face, like she'd been walking briskly. I waved from my seat, then got up so we could hug.

"Right, we're going to go over to the house," she said, and I tried to look unexcited about that fact. As we tramped across the backyard, she apologized. "Be careful! I have two dogs; I can make no promises for the status of this lawn!"

One of those dogs, Butchie, a Jack Russell terrier, started barking with abandon as soon as he saw me; I put a hand out to calm and pet him, but he was having none of it.

"No, Butchie, no, no, we like Melissa, don't we, don't we, Butchie?" Butchie gave me a curious look and kept barking, but also let me pet him.

It had been four months since the release of *Deathly Hallows*, and it felt like a blink. I'd mostly been working on this book, which was now taking up most of my time.

As it turned out, John had been wrong about Prophecy, the fan convention we'd gone to in August. Instead of sadness and moping that the series was over, it had been full of celebrations and dance parties. Hardly anyone cried, or acted like we were at the end of anything. We'd had a formal ball, and an after party that went on so long and so loudly we were amazed not to have gotten kicked out of the hotel. So we termed the room it was in, room 514, the Room of Requirement. It was at that party, still in our ball attire, that my staffers decided they wanted to throw our own conference: Leaky-Con in 2009. A few months later we were in the throes of planning.

Jo had gone on tour in North America, doing signings and question-and-answer sessions in three cities in the United States and one in Canada, dispensing post–*Deathly Hallows* information in a way she had never been able to before. Partly to thank us for our role helping tamp down spoilers about the seventh book, she had invited five Leaky staffers, including me, to see her at Carnegie Hall. John, Sue, Nick, Alex, and I paced backstage for a full forty-five minutes before we were let into her dressing room, where Sue and John set upon her for an at-last answer about whether Helga Hufflepuff had enslaved the house-elves.

"I would say she gave them refuge," Jo said, and Sue cheered, "but that's like saying she's a kind plantation owner, isn't it?" John bellowed in triumph. I groaned. I was hoping Jo would end the argument. They're still fighting about it today, this time each armed with quotes from Jo.

I stood on my foot for half the meeting, too happy that my Leaky fellows were getting a chance to converse with Jo to say much to interrupt it. Before we had left, Jo and her daughter Jessica mock-bowed to us—in a very *Wayne's World* fashion—for being kings of the Internet scene. We'd laughed, but later John kept saying, "They bowed, they bowed, they effing bowed!" The picture we took with Jo, in which it seems everyone is shining with happiness, now sits in pride of place on my desk.

Jo admitted to us that she was nervous about the reading, and asked us to scream at "totally inappropriate moments," to help bring the proceedings to a more suitably ridiculous level than usually befitted a Carnegie Hall event. We said we'd try, but it turned out to be completely unnecessary. She was greeted with a standing ovation that took minutes to die down, and the look of gratitude on her face, and feeling of completion and homecoming, left people swiping at their eyes. After years of cagey interviews and spoiler-sensitive statements, it was as if, finally, the real Jo Rowling could come out to play; she teased some of the questioners and gave ponderous answers about love, about why Molly Weasley had to kill Bellatrix, and, early on—possibly setting the triumphant tone for the evening—she announced that Dumbledore was gay.

When she said it, there was a breath of pause, as though everyone were shaking water out of their ears, and then the place erupted. My hand grabbed John's shoulder as if to prove that he was there and could validate what I'd just heard. It wasn't that I was shocked Dumbledore was gay, but I couldn't believe I was present for his glamorous coming-out party. Arthur Levine, one box over, was whooping and hollering along with everyone else for what seemed to go on for ages.

"If I'd have known it was going to make you this happy I would have told you ages ago!" Jo said and, buoyed by the response, let loose with some of the funniest insights she'd ever given.

"Dumbledore's past love life never, ever came up as a question before while I was on a stage," she told me later. "Occasionally a fan would say to me, 'I love Dumbledore,' and ask me a little something about him. I was asked once before by a female, adult fan, something about Dumbledore and I said—and I cannot remember what she asked me to elicit the information, but I said, 'I've always seen Dumbledore as gay.' She didn't seem to particularly like that answer, but she didn't go on the Internet and put it there, so . . . I had told people in conversation that I saw him that way but it was really never a big deal to me. And it still isn't, and I don't think it's the most interesting thing about Dumbledore.

"One guy came out in Carnegie Hall that night, on the back of that information. So for that reason alone, I think it's a very good reason to have said it."

Immediately after the event, Laura Mallory was talking about how the gayness proved her point, and the Christian right chimed in, and so did anti-gay groups and hate groups, but they didn't matter, because on Facebook there were suddenly groups like Dumbledore's Army: The New Gay-Straight Alliance. At the next Gay Pride Parade, Harry Potter fans will likely be wearing T-shirts with Dumbledore's picture on them.

The reaction to the news had created the most popular news day on Leaky *ever*. It had been applauded and decried, reactions of all stripes filled my in-box, and I'd been giving commentary to television stations and newspapers for weeks. As soon as we had settled down with our coffee on Jo's green-diamond-patterned couch, I asked her about the announcement, and whether homosexuality had the same taboo in her world that it did in the Muggle one. (David, in particular, wanted to know that one.)

"Insomuch as it's something else someone like Malfoy would use against you," Jo explained, and we were off, neck-deep in canon. In a matter of seconds we were talking about Dumbledore's relationship with Grindelwald, his former object of affection, and if Dumbledore had ever gotten over the heartbreak of losing him. She explained that he just turned inward and remained isolated and academic the rest of his life. "Does that mean he was a one-hundred-fifty-year-old virgin? I don't know," she said softly, peering into her coffee cup as though it held an answer.

I'd worked up my courage to ask for this interview only a short while before, and I never thought she'd say yes. After all, she'd once turned down Oprah, and just about everyone else in the world. I'd been worried to ask, like it was overstepping bounds, but I'd looked at the ring on my left hand, gathered myself, and sent the letter. Cheryl as well as a few other wise friends had insisted, telling me with such authority that I'd needed to send it that it gave me the final push. A few weeks after she got the letter Jo told me yes, and soon after that I was on a plane.

And now we were at the second half of what had turned into a two-day, eight-hour meeting. We had to struggle to stay on topic, because we both wanted so badly to veer into discussions on Harry Potter canon that we would just keep talking about the books instead of the phenomenon. She told me that Hedwig was originally supposed to open the Snitch at the end of the seventh book, and so had originally caught Harry's first Snitch in book one. She told me about George's marriage to Angelina, his twin's ex-girlfriend and what it meant for how he was coping with life without his brother. She described how she had fallen apart while editing the epilogue with her British editor. We talked about wand lore, and soon were on Teddy Lupin, and we realized we have to stop.

"Right, sorry! Now ask me about the phenomenon of Harry Potter!"

It's a struggle; we can't help derailing. We talk about love, and weight, and social consciousness, and the HP Alliance, my favorite new cause, the group that my friend Andrew Slack had started in order to help people use their love of Harry to pursue agendas for social change. Andrew, an impassioned and impressive public speaker, came across my radar via a former staffer, who told me how he was using messages from the Potter books—the way Harry stands up to the Ministry, the principles of self-defense and moral rectitude behind Dumbledore's Army—and applying them to real-world situations. He had already mobilized hundreds of young people to form chapters of the HP Alliance at their schools, and he was making great strides organizing fund-raisers and awareness campaigns to aid the victims of the genocide in Darfur. After a few in-person conversations that lasted hours, Andrew asked me to serve as a board member for the organization; it felt like a perfect outlet for whatever fandom credibility I had earned.

This wasn't even the interview I had once dreamed of having with Jo; it was more like we had been on opposite sides of a wall for years and were finally allowed to visit each other (with an interview thrown in). She showed me the den where Mackenzie made a plaything out of a life-sized Dobby, and the printed-out Outstanding grade Jessica got on the W.O.M.B.A.T. test from jkrowling.com, and her stunning wedding pictures, and a copy of *The Tales of Beedle the*

Bard, Arthur Levine's to be exact, which she was halfway through writing. I held it as though I were handling finely spun crystal, and there is a small chance I drooled on it.

Jo could talk for hours about her characters; information about them fell out of her mouth whenever our interview hit a lull, and I wouldn't dream of stopping her, work be damned. Every five minutes, it seemed, over two days, we had to stop ourselves, and swerve back on topic. Three times she talked about Albus Severus Potter, Harry's son from the *Deathly Hallows* epilogue, and how intriguing he was as a character.

"That's quite a name you gave him," I said. The shock that I'd been spoiled after all for the epilogue had worn off quickly. Though some fans felt the ending to the series turned out sappy, I thought it a fitting and touching tribute in light of the events of the book.

"I know. Albus Severus, could you imagine?"

"And Potter!"

"And Potter! The triple-whammy of notoriety. Poor boy." She got a far-off look. "He interests me most."

I raised an eyebrow, wondering if she had written about him, but stayed silent.

"Imagine having to go to Hogwarts bearing that name. Imagine that—even if your family calls you Al. Imagine having to walk to the headmaster's office and seeing those two portraits. Ha. Nothing to live up to—yeah, he's the one that really—but anyway."

A minute later she's off again, talking about the family trees of the survivors, and how hard she cried to Emma, her editor, just because she had mentioned Teddy Lupin.

"I just burst into tears. First time I've ever done it. I had to show Teddy Lupin was okay. I hated killing Lupin and Tonks. Hated it. Hated it. But I was writing about war. That's what war does. It leaves little, newborn babies who never know . . ." She trails off. "So, it hap-

329

pened to Harry, and it happened again. They let it happen again; they didn't want to believe Harry. So I had to show that evil all over again." She seemed to come back to herself and notice me again. "Sorry! Let's get back on subject!"

I couldn't stop laughing, because this was a Jo I'd never seen, not even in all her post–*Deathly Hallows* interviews. She was unspooled, just throwing information out there as though it had built up over seventeen years and this was payback time. It was wonderful, and so free, that the air around us both seemed to lighten, despite the serious fictional subject matter.

She said she was writing again, and such a look of joy crossed her face when she said so that I couldn't help smiling back. We were only supposed to have spoken for an hour today; it's well after the third, and Fiddy is about to beat me up with a stapler for stealing Jo for so long. Around lunch, we wrap up. Jo piles her arms heavy with catalogs, legal documents, charity invitations, and the other trappings of a life that's no longer simply that of a writer, that is now the symbol of the ten years we've all spent in an unbelievable era. I have one last question: What does she hope people will take with them about this time?

She pauses, but then the answer is right on her tongue.

"When all the fuss and hoopla dies away, and when all the press commentary dies away, I think it will be seen that this phenomenon was generated, in the first instance, by kids loving a book. A book went on shelves, and a few people loved it. When all of the smoke and lights die away, that's what you'll be left with.

"And that's the most wonderful thought for an author."

ACKNOWLEDGMENTS

Many people have helped bring this book from concept to covers. I can never thank them enough, but let's try anyway:

Aimée and Richard Carter were the first people I ever spoke with about this book, what seems like a hundred years ago. They said, out of the blue, that it was a book I should write, and had no way of knowing that the kernel of an idea was already rattling around in my brain. Their immediate support and enthusiasm were crucial.

Rebecca Sherman, my agent and friend, nudged this idea into the real world, and held on tight until it grew. She helped me move the concept from a formless idea to a true outline, and has been honest, supportive, and helpful at every stage of this process.

Jennifer Heddle, my wonderfully blunt editor, provided insight and honest feedback that has made every page of the book, and the book as a whole, incalculably better.

Jo Rowling has been an incredible supporter, on more levels than it is possible to name or of which she could possibly know. Her trust in my reporting and her unwavering belief in a person's right to create—even when their creation concerns her—has given me great pride and confidence.

Jo Metivier, or, as we joke, "other Jo," came into this project for a few months before my first deadline to help me research bits and manage my life. Her enthusiasm for Potter, her patience and kindness, her extraordinary fact-finding abilities, and her friendship are all over this book.

Lizzie Keiper, who has helped me manage a monstrous to-do list every day for more than two years, has been another constant source of help and encouragement.

The following people from "Team Potter" have been unswervingly gracious and helpful to me throughout this process: Fiddy Henderson, a great pen pal, confidante, and friend; Neil Blair, who I can't believe I ever thought scary; Christopher Little, who still scares me a bit; Arthur Levine; Cheryl Klein; Kris Moran; Rachel Coun; Mark Seidenfeld; David Heyman; Barry Cunningham; Barbara Marcus; Tim Ditlow; Rosamund de la Hey; Diane Nelson; Vanessa Davies; Jules Bearman; Emma Schlesinger; Emma Matthewson; Sarah Odedina; Lucy Holden; and Emma Bradshaw.

Thank you to the following people for allowing me to interview them and talk about their lives: Paul and Joe DeGeorge, Megan Morrison, Devin Smither, Julie Just, Eden Lipson, Jennie Levine, Valerie Lewis, Alex Carpenter, Lizo Mzimba, Bradley Mehlenbacher, Brian Ross, Heather Lawver, Laura Mallory, Tom Goodman, Lindsey Benge, John Inniss, Jamie Waylett, Theresa Waylett, Alex Milne-White of Hungerford's Bookshop, Jan Dundon of Anderson's Bookshop, Alan Alger of Blue Square, Rupert Adams of William Hill, and Shirley Comer.

Thank you, Matthew Maggiacomo, a.k.a. the Whomping Willow, who provided great help distilling hundreds of pages of research (and made me laugh often while doing so).

Thank you to Erin Byrne and Judith Krug of the American Library Association, Cindy Loe of the Georgia public schools system,

Jeff Guillaume of HPANA ("It's an acronym!"), Heidi Tandy and Cassandra Claire for helping me locate some specific and helpful bits of information.

Thank you to the following people for helping transcribe interviews: Kyrane Thomas (who transcribed nearly all of a twelve-hour Harry and the Potters interview and a large chunk of the eight-hour Jo Rowling one), Delana Gray, Corena van Leuveren, and Sarah Hatter.

Reporting from Massachusetts for the *Deathly Hallows* chapter was contributed by Elisabeth Donnelly; reporting from New York was contributed by Angela Montefinise. These ladies are both fine journalists and friends.

The following friends provided priceless moral support at important moments: David Carpman and Kathleen Sheehy, who are always there when it matters most; Sue Upton, my friend and confidante, whom I love dearly; John Noe, who tends to make life a lot funnier; Cheryl Klein, the compassionate and brilliant secretkeeper; Megan Morrison, who understands the beauty of celebratory capital letters; Samantha Friedman (who, with John, helped keep me in fresh coffee, good food, and a clean apartment as I reached deadline); Josh Wittge, for chocolate and *Project Runway*; Ben, Kirky, and William DeLong; Gerald Lewis, Josh Koury, Gaia Cornwall, and all the *We Are Wizards* crew; George Beahm; Anthony Rapp; Andrew Sims; Ben Schoen; Emerson Spartz; Rebecca Anderson; Emily Wahlee; Evanna Lynch; and my brother-in-law Elliot Kathreptis.

My entire Leaky staff, especially my senior staff: John Noe, Nick Poulden, Sue Upton, Alex Robbin, Doris Herrman, Nick Rhein, Kristin Brown, and Ben DeLong. Everyone who works with as large a group of volunteers as I do says that they have the best staff in the world. Everyone besides me is wrong. The two hundred plus people who now work on Leaky, and everyone who has come and gone in the past seven years, are some of the brightest, strongest-minded, most passionate and dignified people with whom I have ever had the honor to interact. Every single one of them is part of this book, and of my heart. Thank you. *This cauldron's got a hole in it! It's where the news leaks out!*

Special thanks go to Ben DeLong for encouraging my hire at Leaky in the first place. My life would have been remarkably different without you.

Thank you to the following Web sites for general use and help throughout this process: SugarQuill.net; Harry Potter for Grown Ups (hpfgu.org.uk); FictionAlley.org; Fandomwankcom; Wizrocklopedia .com; Accio-Quote.org.

Thank you to the *Staten Island Advance*, and all my comrades there, for great and formative experiences.

Thank you to Nonna, who is a rock, and Nanny, who, I am sure, knew this would happen.

And last, but certainly always first: Mom, Dad, and Stephanie. I love you so much. You are why good things happen in my life, and your love and patience are more responsible for this book than anything else. I hope you liked it.

NOTES

Most of the reporting in *Harry, A History*, comes from my own research and interviews, but I have definitely relied on others' research as well. I claim all responsibility for errors, however. Cited below are the books, journals, Web site postings, articles, and other sources I have mentioned or used throughout this book. Facts, stories, and quotes not cited come from my research and interviews.

Two: The Beginning and the End

16 "Harry . . . Take my body back to my parents": J. K. Rowling, *Harry Potter and the Goblet of Fire* (New York: Scholastic Press, 2000), 668.

Three: Near Misses

18 *Rowling's brain for seventeen . . . two hundred territories:* This has been widely reported, but was provided to me by representatives for Jo Rowling at the time of writing.

quarter of the top twenty grossing films: "All Time Box Office," Box Office Mojo. www.boxofficemojo.com/alltime

18 *Harry Potter . . . worth $15 billion:* "Harry Potter, the $15 Billion Man," *Advertising Age,* July 16, 2007.

"*Harry Potter is actually about the Holy Grail*": Dan Brown, *The Da Vinci Code* (Doubleday, 2003), 164.

19 *It might have all been different:* Jo's lack of a pen has been reported various times, but she repeated it for me in an interview.

20 *U.K. publishers would excise . . . bodily functions:* Carolyn Hart, "Children are obscene but not heard; Farts are stifled, knicker-less Nicola wears jeans, and cars drive in the middle of the road. The author Carolyn Hart introduces the squeaky-clean world of children's publishing." *The Independent,* March 8, 1995.

21 *ponies for girls . . . Enid Blyton:* Christina Hardyment, "Poltergeist versus pony tales; Christina Hardyment examines books that sell—the big end of the book industry," *The Independent,* November 17, 1990.

Nestlé Smarties Book Prize: Consumer Help Web, http://book.consumerhelpweb.com/awards/nestle/smarties.htm. The official Web site for the Smarties prize is www.booktrusted.co.uk/nestle.

Whitbread Children's Book of the Year: Costa Book Awards, www.costabookawards.com/awards/previous_winners.aspx.

"*Parents and godparents . . . eco-home*": Christina Hardyment, "Poltergeist versus pony tales," *The Independent,* November 17, 1990.

22 "*There are none of the swings*" . . . "*loyal readers for long,*" Ibid.

22 *Children's book publishers saw more lucrative results:* Emily Bell, "Marketing is Child's Play," *The Guardian*, September 12, 1994.

Stine . . . The Girlfriend: R.L. Stine, official Web site. www .rlstine.com/#nav/rlstine.

sixty-two Goosebumps books between 1992 and 1997: Various sources contributed to and confirmed this number: the first Goosebumps book was published in 1992 (and says so on www .rlstine.com); book number 62, *Monster Blood IV,* came out in 1997, according to the book itself.

two board games: These were called Terror in the Graveyard and Escape from Horrorland.

three comic books: R. L. Stine, *Creepy Creatures,* Graphix, September 1, 2006; R. L. Stine, *Terror Trips,* Graphix, March 1, 2007; R. L. Stine, R. L. *Scary Summer,* Graphix, July 1, 2007.

a video game: PC Game: *R. L. Stine Goosebumps: Escape from Horrorland,* Dreamworks, November 15, 2001.

direct-to-video movies: Say Cheese and Die, Night of the Living Dummy, and *It Came from Beneath the Sink.*

television series: Goosebumps, the TV series, ran from 1995 to 1998 on Fox Kids and Cartoon Network. www.imdb.com/ title/tt0111987/.

Stine had reaped $41 million: Robert La Franco, "The Forbes Top 40," *Forbes,* September 22, 1997.

"instant horror or romance": Nicholas Tucker, "Children's Books: Earwigs in pirate's boots; Nicholas Tucker survives pagan rites, rampaging bears and creeping suburbanites in a selec-

tion of the best new books for teenagers," *The Independent*, March 30, 1996.

23 *eight thousand books published:* Joanna Carey, "Children's Books: 'How Can Children Enjoy Reading When They First Have to Wade Through Mountains of Nonsense?' Award-winning author Anne Fine sounds off to Joanna Carey about the low status of children's writing today." *The Guardian Education Page*, June 24, 1997.

Picture books . . . "if published now": Hilary Macaskill, "Hilary Macaskill on hype and piracy in children's publishing," *The Independent*, March 29, 1997.

28 "Mr. and Mrs. Dursley . . . very much": J. K. Rowling, *Harry Potter and the Sorcerer's Stone* (New York: Scholastic Press, 1998), 1.

29 *"ARE YOU A WITCH OR NOT?":* Ibid, 278.

Four: Public Assistance

41 *top of the Amazon.com best-seller list:* Sue Upton, "Pre-Orders of 'Deathly Hallows' Set Records." The Leaky Cauldron, February 2, 2007, www.the-leaky-cauldron.org/2007/2/2/pre-orders-of-deathly-hallows-set-records.

100,000 pre-orders: "Amazon lifts sales targets," (Liverpool) *Daily Post*, April 26, 2007.

45 *Barry had a business and marketing background . . . Random House:* Nick Curtis, "The two who really discovered JK (but never made a penny from Harry Potter . . .)," *Evening Standard*, July 23, 2007.

48 There are some things . . . one of them: J. K. Rowling, *Harry Potter and the Sorcerer's Stone* (New York: Scholastic Press, 1998), 179.

50 *grabbing distance of $1 billion*: Leah Rosch, "Magic School Buzz," *Chief Executive*, March 1, 1997.

$80 million to Scholastic: "Happiness Express granted license to produce a line of back-to-school products based on GOOSE-BUMPS, the popular children's book series," *Business Wire*, November 30, 1995.

supermarkets were returning their unsold copies: "Scholastic's 3rd Quarter Loss Linked to Slump in Popular Kids Book Series." Selling to Kids. March 19, 1997.

"the most successful children's book series of all time": "Scholastic Hopes Literacy Place Will Help Offset Declining Trade Business," *Educational Marketer*, March 3, 1997. (It also bears pointing out that before Goosebumps, Scholastic controlled another "most successful children's books series of all time"—The Baby-sitters Club.)

"ridiculously high": About Arthur A. Levine, www.arthuralevinebooks.com/arthur.asp.

52 *"There are several reasons . . . film interest"*: Arthur was kind enough to read this and a few other notes he had written at the time aloud to me during an interview.

55 *"Three years ago . . . manuscript under the other"*: Anne Johnstone, "Happy ending, and that's for beginners," *The Herald* (Glasgow), June 24, 1997.

"Tales from a Single Mother": Eddie Gibb, "Tales from a Single Mother," *Sunday Times* (London), June 29, 1997.

55 *"$100,000 Success . . . Mother"*: Nigel Reynolds, "$100,000 Success Story for Penniless Mother," *The Telegraph* (London), July 7, 2007. Accessed via Accio-Quote.org: www.accio-quote.org/articles/1997/spring97-telegraph-reynolds.htm.

56 *about £65,625*: This figure was derived from GBP/US exchange rates: www.taxfreegold.co.uk/1997forexrates.html.

57 *hit the top of a best-seller list*: "Smaller Company Accounts: Bloomsbury Publishing," *Investor's Chronicle*, July 31, 1998.

58 *"a gripping story" . . . "put it down"*: Anne Johnstone, "Paging 1977," *The Herald* (Glasgow), December 11, 1997.

   that has about thirteen million listeners: Ron LaBrecque and Joe Holley, "For NPR, freedom in variety," *Columbia Journalism Review*. May/June 1997.

   "thinks it's a book about philosophy": "Interview with Arthur Levine, Co-Editor of Harry Potter," www.the-leaky-cauldron-org/features/interviews/levine2.

59 *she thought was truly significant about the galley*: This galley was the object of one of many mini grail quests I went on while researching this book. I knew what Arthur said in the opening, but only anecdotally. I was determined to find someone with a copy, so I could quote it. Kris Moran at Scholastic pointed me toward Margot Adler, and I got a two-for-one out of the deal: a glance at that treasured book and a great story about one of Harry Potter's influential early adopters. I know few people who get the same light in their eyes when discussing the Harry narrative as Margot, though I confess to blanching when seeing the book was protected by a zip-lock bag.

60 *in September of that year:* The official U.S. publication date is October 1998, but the book was being reviewed by the beginning of September. Publication dates for Potter didn't mean then what they do now.

"hugely enjoyable": "Harry Potter and the Sorcerer's Stone," *Kirkus Reviews*, September 1, 1998.

"brilliantly imagined and beautifully written": Michael Cart, "Harry Potter and the Sorcerer's Stone; Review." *Booklist*, September 15, 1998.

ten-year-old . . . television: Nancy Gilson, "Sorcerer's Stone Looks Like a Real Page-Turner," *Columbus Dispatch*, September 17, 1998.

62 *Margot's piece:* Margot Adler, "All Things Considered: Harry Potter." National Public Radio, December 3, 1998. You can still listen to this excellent piece here: www.npr.org/templates/story/story.php?storyId=1032154. You can also hear a follow-up interview with Arthur Levine about his prideful words here: www.npr.org/templates/story/story.php?storyId=11935611.

number of books in print had doubled: "U.K.'s Number One Best-Seller, 'Harry Potter and the Sorcerer's Stone,' Tops Best-Seller Charts in U.S." *Business Wire*, December 7, 1998.

63 New York Times *Best Seller List:* "Best Sellers," *New York Times*, December 27, 1998.

determined by sales . . . retailers: These statistics can be read at the bottom of any *New York Times* best-seller list.

Jamie Lee Curtis . . . Moore: "Best Sellers," *New York Times*, December 27, 1998.

63 *E. B. White's . . . done so well:* Doreen Carvajal, "Children's Book Casts a Spell Over Adults; Young Wizard Is a Best Seller and Copyright Challenge," *New York Times*, April 1, 1999.

so desperate for the second book . . . how to get the book themselves: Ibid.

64 *a small fraction—less than a twentieth—of what they are now:* This figure came from e-commerce reporting for 1998 and 2007: Zbar, Jeffery. "Internet Commerce: No Longer a Novelty." *Credit Card Management.* March 1, 1999. "Submission for OMB Review." *Commerce Department Documents and Publications.* March 27, 2008.

$250 million mark: "Briefs," *Infotech Weekly*, July 26, 1999.

68 *Scholastic was bending its schedule . . . in Britain:* Cecilia Goodnow, "Wild About 'Harry': Phenomenal popularity of children's series has buyers—and booksellers—scrambling," *Seattle Post-Intelligencer*, June 24, 1999.

69 *three quarters of a million sales:* "Children Spellbound by Harry Potter's Magical Adventures," *The Journal* (Newcastle), August 20, 1999.

70 *upped to 157,000:* Anthony Barnes, "Truancy Fears Delay Book," *The Mirror*, June 21, 1999.

71 *Tatnuck Bookseller . . . event:* Rosemary Herbert, " 'Harry Potter' author causes stir," *Boston Herald*, October 11, 1999.

as if the Beatles had come to town: Carol Beggy and Beth Carney, "Publishing Wizardry," *The Boston Globe*, October 12, 1999.

73 *And Harry Potter was hogging it:* One of the most surprising things I learned while researching was that *Sorcerer's Stone* did not hit number one on the *New York Times* best-seller list until subsequent publications in the series propelled it there.

74 *into eight pieces:* Dinita Smith, "The Times Plans a Children's Best-Seller List," *New York Times*, June 24, 2000.

Five: Spinning the Web

87 *12 million copies in the United States:* Sue Upton, "12 Million First Print Copies of 'Harry Potter and the Deathly Hallows' Due from Scholastic," the Leaky Cauldron, March 14, 2007. www .the-leaky-cauldron.org/2007/3/14/12-million-first-print-copies -of-harry-potter-and-the-deathly-hallows-due-from-scholastic.

approaching one million: Susan Flockhart, "Bookshops braced for Pottermania," *Sunday Herald*, June 27, 1999.

7.5 million total copies: Renee Tawa, "Area Book Buyers Wild About Latest 'Harry,' " *Los Angeles Times*, September 9, 1999.

World Internet Project: The UCLA Internet Report, "Surveying the Digital Future," UCLA Center for Communication Policy, October 1, 2000, www.worldinternetproject.net.

88 *Mosaic . . . 1993:* Marc Andreessen, "Mosaic—The First Global Web Browser," www.livinginternet.com/w/wi_mosaic.

About three years later . . . Spain: The UCLA Internet Report, 10.

89 *three quarters of people were checking their e-mail:* The UCLA Internet Report, 6–7.

89 *$50,000 or more per year:* The UCLA Internet Project, 87.

91 *40 percent of users:* "Livejournal Statistics," www.livejournal.com/ stats.bml. Retrieved through the Internet Archive: web.archive .org/web/20000925051658/http://www.livejournal.com/stats.bml.

 win the award three times: http://book.consumerhelpweb.com/ awards/nestle/smarties.htm.

92 *Anne Rice . . . the author said on her Web site:* Anne Rice, "Anne's Messages to Fans," *Anne Rice Readers Interaction,* http://annerice .com/ReaderInteraction-MessagesToFans.html. Date confirmed via several Internet postings including: "Anne Rice Biography and List of Works." www.biblio.com/authors/574/Anne_Rice_ Biography.html.

95 *The Brit tabloid . . . feature story on Field* Ian Key, "Give Up Potter Website, Film Giant Tells Girl, 15; We'll Pay You £9.99 For It'," *The Mirror,* December 8, 2000.

96 *Alastair Alexander . . . Potterwar.org.uk:* Accessed through the Internet Archive: http://web.archive.org/web/*/http://potter war.org.uk.

97 *told* Entertainment Rewired *magazine:* Ryan Buell, "Fans Call for War; Warner Bros. Claims Misunderstanding!" *Entertainment Rewired,* January 27, 2001, http://web.archive.org/web/20010 302022348/www.entertainment-rewired.com/fan_apology.htm.

 vibrating Harry Potter broom . . . play with this!": The original Amazon listing was at www.amazon.com/exec/obidos/ASIN/ B00005NEBW. It was deleted from the database but not before many sites recorded the associated reviews. Some of them may be seen at: http://everything2.com/index.pl?node_id=1355704;

Nine: Banned and Burned

179 Harry Potter: Witchcraft Repackaged: Caryl Matrisciana, "Harry Potter: Witchcraft Repackaged," *Loyal*, 2002.

182 *Georgia Superior Court:* Ben Smith, "It's Round 5 of Mallory vs. Potter; Loganville mom wants Superior Court to ban series," *Atlanta Journal-Constitution*, May 29, 2007.

town of Loganville: Loganville is mostly in Walton County but overlaps a little into Gwinnett; Laura Mallory is from the Gwinnett area and her children go to school there.

six-square-mile . . . seventy times bigger: American Fact Finder. U.S. Census Bureau, www.census.gov/popest/counties/CO-EST2004-09.html.

largest school system in the state: Gwinnett County Public Schools, www.gwinnett.k12.ga.us/.

population boom of 50 percent since the year 2000; among the fastest-growing; 85 percent of residents: American Fact Finder, U.S. Census Bureau, www.census.gov/popest/counties/CO-EST 2004-09.html.

184 *The appeal . . . magic:* Laura Diamond, "Hearing draws Potter foes, fans; Battle lines are drawn as mom fights to ban books," *Atlanta Journal-Constitution*, April 21, 2006.

Censorship Destroys Education: Ibid.

By the 2000s . . . school and library shelves: Hillel Italie, "Harry Potter, Huckleberry Finn, among controversial library books," Associated Press, September 13, 2000.

www.enuze.com/archive/index.php/vibrator-for-children-t32 52p1.html; www.charchaa.com/mattels_vibrating_harry_potter _broomstick_big_hit_among_girls_mattel_pulls_toy_off_the _shelves.

99 *Dercum Society:* Heather Lawver, The Dercum Society, Dercumsociety.org (accessed February 25, 2008).

100 *Claire's site, HarryPotterGuide.co.uk:* Claire Field, "About the Site," The Boy Who Lived, www.btinternet.com/~harry potterguide/aboutsite.html.

"unofficial Harry Potter site . . . enter." Claire Field, Harry PotterGuide.co.uk, (accessed April 20, 2008).

Six: Rocking at Hogwarts

106 *Celine Dion . . . "My Heart Will Go On":* Fred Schuster, "Her Heart Will Go On; Switchblade Kittens Generate 'Titanic' Interest," *Daily News of Los Angeles*, January 29, 1999.

"I can't help . . . Colin Creevey": This song was an Internet download and the band's only Potter-centric song until the Kittens released *The Weird Sisters*, a full wizard rock album, in 2006. Switchblade Kittens, "Ode to Harry," *The Weird Sisters*, 2006. Lyrics reproduced with permission.

end of 2000 . . . three million times: Switchblade Kittens, www .switchbladekittens.com/harrypotter/.

111 *Lansdowne Street . . . Clear Channel:* Maureen Dezell, "Is Bigger Better? In the Entertainment Business Clear Channel is Everywhere, and Critics Say That is the Problem," *Boston Globe*, January 27, 2002.

113 *"The bus . . . the train"*: Harry and the Potters, "Platform 9 and 3/4," *Harry and the Potters*, 2002. Lyrics reproduced with permission.

115 *"These days are dark . . . fall-all-all"*: Harry and the Potters, "These Days are Dark," *Harry and the Potters*, 2002. Lyrics reproduced with permission.

119 Am I . . . really: This post is no longer available to the public, but Cassandra Claire unlocked it so I could use it, for which I am very grateful. Cassandra Claire. http://epicyclical.livejournal.com/158214.html.

120 *"and we won't let . . . PMRC"*: Harry and the Potters, "Voldemort Can't Stop the Rock," *Voldemort Can't Stop the Rock*, 2004. Lyrics reproduced with permission.

124 "My Dad's always there . . . dead.": Draco and the Malfoys, "My Dad is Rich," *Draco and the Malfoys*, 2005.

125 *By 2005 . . . users daily*: Stephen Humphries, "Heard it through the Web grapevine," *Christian Science Monitor*, October 8, 2004.

127 *found themselves in the* Boston Globe: Rachel Strutt, "Band of Brothers," *Boston Globe*, June 19, 2005; *U.S. News & World Report*: Vicky Hallett, "Siriusly, Potter Rocks!" *U.S. News & World Report*, July 16, 2005; Forbes.com.: Lacey Rose, "Wizard Rock," Forbes.com, July 13, 2005, www.forbes.com/2005/07/13/rowling-potter-band-cx_lr_0713harryband.html.

132 *"The Decemberists . . . lit-rock like this"*: Amy Phillips and Ryan Dombal, "2005 Comments & Lists: Top Live Shows and Music Videos," December 12, 2005, www.pitchforkmedia.com/article/

feature/10349-staff-list-2005-comments-lists-top-live-sh[ ]-music-videos.

134 *"The weapon we have is . . . love"*: Harry and the Potters, Weapon," *Voldemort Can't Stop the Rock*, 2004.

Eight: Getting a Clue

150 *truly desperate for news*: Jo was mostly accused of writer's bloc[ ] when the public realized there would be no Potter book in 2001; she spent most of 2002 denying, in interviews and through publicists and others, that she had the affliction. Hundreds of stories were written about it, not all of which I'll list here. This *Scotsman* article started all the speculation: Paul Gallagher, "Has Harry Finally Lost His Magic for J K Rowling?" *The Scotsman*, August 8, 2001.

151 *falsified to make Stouffer's case*: Scholastic, Inc., J. K. Rowling, and Time Warner Entertainment Company, L.P. vs. Nancy Stouffer. United States District Court for the Southern District of New York, 2002.

159 *released a report*: "New Study Reveals the Reading Habits a[ ] Attitudes of Children and Families in American Hom[ ] Today." www.scholastic.com/aboutscholastic/news/readi[ ]report06.htm.

167 *"Hi Arthur, Cheryl"*: Arthur Levine was kind enough to re[ ] me these e-mails, as I had a computer crash and lost them[ ]

184 *472 cumulative challenges:* "Harry Potter series again tops list of most challenged books," American Library Association, press release, January 2001.

185 *646 challenges:* Ibid.

how many other children: www.kidspeakonline.org/kidspeakis .html.

186 *by the Ministry of Education in the United Arab Emirates:* "Emirates ban Potter book," BBC News, February 12, 2002.

Greek and Bulgarian Orthodox churches: "Church: Harry Potter Film a Font of Evil," *Kathimerini*, January 14, 2003. Clive Leviev-Sawyer, "Bulgarian Church Warns Against the Spell of Harry Potter," *Ecumenica News International*, June 28, 2004.

"I read stories": Kimberley Blair. "PotterCast #55: The Return of Fiddy-Five: Fan Interview," http://pottercast.the-leaky-cauldron.org/transcript/show/74?ordernum=4.

"first encyclical": Pope Benedict XVI, "To the Bishops, Priest and Deacons, Men and Women Religious, and All the Lay Faithful on Christian Love," December 25, 2005, www.vatican.va/holy_ father/benedict_xvi/encyclicals/documents/hf_ben-xvi_enc_ 20051225_deus-caritas-est_en.html.

a prefect of the congregation for the Doctrine of Faith: The Holy See: www.vatican.va/roman_curia/congregations/cfaith/index .htm.

189 *in which tragic school shootings occur:* "Ban 'Harry Potter' or face more high school shootings," *Daily Mail*, October 4, 2006.

189 *Rachel Joy Scott . . . God is what we need!*: "Testimony of Darrell Scott, Father of Two Victims at Columbine High School," www.garnertedarmstrong.org/WWArchives/vol24.htm.

190 *Dan Mauser . . . shot in the face*: Various sources: for example, www.acolumbinesite.com/victim/danm.html.

194 *"We think" . . . "self-sacrifice"*: "Editorial: Why we like Harry Potter," *Christianity Today*, January 10, 2000.

198 *between 1990 and 2004*: "Top Ten Challenged Authors, 1990–2004," American Library Association, www.ala.org/ala/oif/bannedbooksweek/bbwlinks/authors19902004.cfm.

199 *Cedarville . . . restricted list*: "Parents sue over school library's special measures on Harry Potter," the Associated Press, July 6, 2002.

200 *quickly decided*: Beverly Goldberg, "Judge smites Harry Potter restrictions," *American Libraries*, June 1, 2003.

201 *On May 29*: Harry R. Weber, "U.S. judge upholds schools' decision to keep Harry Potter books," Associated Press Worldstream, May 29, 2007.

Ten: High Seas

211 *Between . . . 4,000 people*: Harry Potter for Grownups: A History. www.hpfgu.org.uk/faq/history.html#2.

215 *"H/H and why it's just wrong" . . . "shunted aside"*: Harry Potter for Grownups, http://groups.yahoo.com/group/HPforGrownups/message/2236.

216 *Zsenya appeared:* Harry Potter for Grownups, http://groups
.yahoo.com/group/HPforGrownups/message/5235.

219 *Sugar Quill's Purpose of Existence on the Web:* The Sugar Quill,
www.sugarquill.com, retrieved through Archive.org, February
23, 2001 entry: http://web.archive.orgweb/20010224063058/
www.sugarquill.com/spew.html.

220 *"ridiculous impossibility":* Ibid.

sign her posts with Captain of the Cruiseliner H/H: Harry Potter
for Grownups. http://groups.yahoo.com/group/HPforGrown
ups/message/11323.

222 *Restrictedsection.org:* www.restrictedsection.org.

cease-and-desist letter: ChillingEffects.org, www.chillingeffects
.org/fanfic/notice.cgi?NoticeID=522.

224 *"Do you know who the voice of my conscience is":* The Nimbus-
2003 Programming Team, Edmund Kern, and Roger High-
field, "Selected Papers from Nimbus-2003 Compendium: We
Solemnly Swear These Papers Were Worth the Wait" (Houston: HP Education Fanon, Inc., 2005), p. 274.

"and pretty": Ibid, p. 271.

Eleven: Access

232 *$70 million:* Box Office Mojo, http://boxofficemojo.com/
movies/?id=goldencompass.htm.

Emma . . . class: "Daniel Radcliffe, Rupert Grint and Emma
Watson Bring Harry, Ron and Hermione to Life for Warner

Bros. Pictures' Harry Potter and the Sorcerer's Stone," *Business Wire*, August 21, 2000.

Thirteen: Independence

268 *between 40 and 50 percent:* Cari Tuna, "The Book That Shall Not Make Big Money," *Star-Tribune* (Minneapolis), July 20, 2007.

Goblet of Fire . . . *loss leader:* Various sources including: Fritz Lanham, "Harry rises again; Fifth book about young wizard casts a spell on booksellers, fans," *Houston Chronicle*, June 18, 2003.

269 *Net Book Agreement:* The Booksellers Association, www.book sellers.org.uk/industry/display_report.asp?id=1164http://www .booksellers.org.uk/industry/display_report.asp?id=1164.

anticompetitive in 1997: Nigel Reynolds, "Court ruling opens new chapter for bookshops," *The Telegraph*, March 14, 1997.

271 *first recorded instance:* Joanna Carey, "Who hasn't met Harry?" *Guardian Unlimited*, February 16, 1999.

272 *Bungay . . . destruction:* Bungay Suffolk Town Guide, www .bungay-suffolk.co.uk.

Fifteen: Spoiled

290 *"If Harry dies . . . use them":* "Spoil Us Not, Sneaks!" the Leaky Cauldron, April 28, 2007.

by Jo Rowling . . . Web site: Melissa Anelli, "J. K. Rowling Updates Diary Regarding Spoilers," the Leaky Cauldron, May 14, 2007.

291 *on June 27, 2000:* Elizabeth Manus and Ted Diskant, "The Secret of Harry Potter IV? It Almost Blew Deadline," *New York Observer*, July 3, 2000.

292 *"it will be JKR . . . registers it":* Melissa Anelli, "Regarding Seabottom and HP6/HP7 Titles," the Leaky Cauldron, September 9, 2003.

Republic of China . . . Golden Turtle: "A Memo to the Dept. of Magical Copyright Enforcement," *New York Times*, August 10, 2007.

sued them and . . . fines: Tim Greening, "But there is a fifth 'Potter' novel . . .", *Shreveport Times*, November 12, 2002.

"Harry doesn't know" . . . "Aunt Petunia's Bottom": "Harry Potter and Leopard-Walk-Up-to-Dragon," *New York Times*, August 10, 2007.

On August 10 . . . Dragon King: Ibid.

297 *June 15, 2003 . . . Manchester:* Mark Rice-Oxley, "Harry Potter and the disappearing books," *Christian Science Monitor*, June 19, 2003.

reappeared the next afternoon: Helen Carter, "The plot thickens in Harry Potter lorry theft: Security operation in chaos as bogus driver makes off with more than 7,000 copies days before launch of boy wizard's latest adventure," *The Guardian* (London), June 18, 2003.

298 *headline was "Hocus-Pocus":* Tamer El-Ghobashy, "Hocus-Pocus! We Got Harry," New York *Daily News*, June 18, 2003.

299 *That changed before book six . . . "novel":* John Askill, "The Prisoner of Askill Bang," *The Sun,* June 7, 2005.

300 *Luckily for Askill . . . prison:* John Askill, "Judge: Potter Thug Set for Spell in Jail," *The Sun,* December 21, 2005.

Sixteen: One Day More

304 *Michiko Kakutani . . . review:* Michiko Kakutani, "An Epic Showdown as Harry Potter is Initiated into Adulthood," *New York Times,* July 19, 2007.

Seventeen: *Deathly Hallows*

316 *several sunlit days:* J. K. Rowling, *Harry Potter and the Half-Blood Prince* (New York: Scholastic Press, 2005), p. 533.

Epilogue

326 *"If I'd have known . . . ages ago":* Edward Drogos, "J. K. Rowling at Carnegie Hall Reveals Dumbledore is Gay; Neville Marries Hannah Abbott, and Much More," the Leaky Cauldron, October 19, 2007.

Laura Mallory . . . point: Phil Kloer, "Dumbledore's Gay? A cauldron of reactions," *Atlanta Journal-Constitution,* October 23, 2007.

BIBLIOGRAPHY

The following are books and other materials I referenced or found helpful in forming thoughts and opinions while writing. Most direct sources may be found in the end notes, though I recommend these books.

Granger, John. *Looking for God in Harry Potter: Is there Christian meaning hidden in the bestselling books?* Carol Stream, Ill.: Tyndale, 2004.

Granger, John. *Unlocking Harry Potter: Five Keys for the Serious Reader.* Allentown, Penn.: Zossima Press, 2007.

Hafner, Katie and Matthew Lyon. *Where Wizards Stay Up Late: The Origins of the Internet.* New York: Simon & Schuster, 1998.

Morris, Tom. *If Harry Potter Ran General Electric: Leadership Wisdom from the World of the Wizards.* New York: Doubleday Business, 2006.

Neal, Connie. *The Gospel According to Harry Potter.* Louisville, Ky.: Westminster John Knox Press, 2002.

Neal, Connie. *Wizards, Wardrobes and Wookiees: Navigating Good and Evil in Harry Potter, Narnia and Star Wars.* Downers Grove, Ill.: InterVarsity Press, 2007.

Nimbus-2003 Programming Team, Edmund Kern, and Roger High-field. *Selected Papers From Nimbus-2003 Compendium: We Solemnly Swear These Papers Were Worth the Wait.* Houston: HP Education Fanon, Inc., 2005.

Okin, J. R. *The Internet Revolution: The Not-For-Dummies Guide to the History, Technology and Use of the Internet.* Winter Harbor, Maine: Ironbound Press, 2005.

Rowling, J. K. *Harry Potter and the Sorcerer's Stone.* New York: Scholastic Press, 1998.

———. *Harry Potter and the Chamber of Secrets.* New York: Scholastic Press, 1999.

———. *Harry Potter and the Prisoner of Azkaban.* New York: Scholastic Press, 1999.

———. *Harry Potter and the Goblet of Fire.* New York: Scholastic Press, 2000.

———. *Harry Potter and the Order of the Phoenix.* New York: Scholastic Press, 2003.

———. *Harry Potter and the Half-Blood Prince.* New York: Scholastic Press, 2005.

———. *Harry Potter and the Deathly Hallows.* New York: Scholastic Press, 2007.

Tapscott, Don and Anthony D. Williams. *Wikinomics: How Mass Collaboration Changes Everything.* New York: Portfolio Hardcover, 2006.

www.enuze.com/archive/index.php/vibrator-for-children-t32
52p1.html; www.charchaa.com/mattels_vibrating_harry_potter
_broomstick_big_hit_among_girls_mattel_pulls_toy_off_the
_shelves.

99 *Dercum Society:* Heather Lawver, The Dercum Society,
Dercumsociety.org (accessed February 25, 2008).

100 *Claire's site, HarryPotterGuide.co.uk:* Claire Field, "About the
Site," The Boy Who Lived, www.btinternet.com/~harry
potterguide/aboutsite.html.

"unofficial Harry Potter site . . . enter." Claire Field, Harry
PotterGuide.co.uk, (accessed April 20, 2008).

Six: Rocking at Hogwarts

106 *Celine Dion . . . "My Heart Will Go On":* Fred Schuster, "Her
Heart Will Go On; Switchblade Kittens Generate 'Titanic' Interest," *Daily News of Los Angeles,* January 29, 1999.

"I can't help . . . Colin Creevey": This song was an Internet download and the band's only Potter-centric song until the Kittens
released *The Weird Sisters,* a full wizard rock album, in 2006.
Switchblade Kittens, "Ode to Harry," *The Weird Sisters,* 2006.
Lyrics reproduced with permission.

end of 2000 . . . three million times: Switchblade Kittens, www
.switchbladekittens.com/harrypotter/.

111 *Lansdowne Street . . . Clear Channel:* Maureen Dezell, "Is Bigger
Better? In the Entertainment Business Clear Channel is Everywhere, and Critics Say That is the Problem," *Boston Globe,* January 27, 2002.

113 *"The bus . . . the train"*: Harry and the Potters, "Platform 9 and 3/4," *Harry and the Potters*, 2002. Lyrics reproduced with permission.

115 *"These days are dark . . . fall-all-all"*: Harry and the Potters, "These Days are Dark," *Harry and the Potters*, 2002. Lyrics reproduced with permission.

119 Am I . . . really: This post is no longer available to the public, but Cassandra Claire unlocked it so I could use it, for which I am very grateful. Cassandra Claire. http://epicyclical.live journal.com/158214.html.

120 *"and we won't let . . . PMRC"*: Harry and the Potters, "Voldemort Can't Stop the Rock," *Voldemort Can't Stop the Rock*, 2004. Lyrics reproduced with permission.

124 "My Dad's always there . . . dead.": Draco and the Malfoys, "My Dad is Rich," *Draco and the Malfoys*, 2005.

125 *By 2005 . . . users daily*: Stephen Humphries, "Heard it through the Web grapevine," *Christian Science Monitor*, October 8, 2004.

127 *found themselves in the* Boston Globe: Rachel Strutt, "Band of Brothers," *Boston Globe*, June 19, 2005; *U.S. News & World Report*: Vicky Hallett, "Siriusly, Potter Rocks!" *U.S. News & World Report*, July 16, 2005; Forbes.com.: Lacey Rose, "Wizard Rock," Forbes.com, July 13, 2005, www.forbes.com/2005/07/13/rowling-potter-band-cx_lr_0713harryband.html.

132 *"The Decemberists . . . lit-rock like this"*: Amy Phillips and Ryan Dombal, "2005 Comments & Lists: Top Live Shows and Music Videos," December 12, 2005, www.pitchforkmedia.com/article/

feature/10349-staff-list-2005-comments-lists-top-live-shows-and -music-videos.

134 *"The weapon we have is . . . love"*: Harry and the Potters, "The Weapon," *Voldemort Can't Stop the Rock*, 2004.

Eight: Getting a Clue

150 *truly desperate for news:* Jo was mostly accused of writer's block when the public realized there would be no Potter book in 2001; she spent most of 2002 denying, in interviews and through publicists and others, that she had the affliction. Hundreds of stories were written about it, not all of which I'll list here. This *Scotsman* article started all the speculation: Paul Gallagher, "Has Harry Finally Lost His Magic for J K Rowling?" *The Scotsman*, August 8, 2001.

151 *falsified to make Stouffer's case:* Scholastic, Inc., J. K. Rowling, and Time Warner Entertainment Company, L.P. vs. Nancy Stouffer. United States District Court for the Southern District of New York, 2002.

159 *released a report:* "New Study Reveals the Reading Habits and Attitudes of Children and Families in American Homes Today." www.scholastic.com/aboutscholastic/news/reading report06.htm.

167 *"Hi Arthur, Cheryl"*: Arthur Levine was kind enough to resend me these e-mails, as I had a computer crash and lost them.

Nine: Banned and Burned

179 Harry Potter: Witchcraft Repackaged: Caryl Matrisciana, "Harry Potter: Witchcraft Repackaged," *Loyal*, 2002.

182 *Georgia Superior Court:* Ben Smith, "It's Round 5 of Mallory vs. Potter; Loganville mom wants Superior Court to ban series," *Atlanta Journal-Constitution*, May 29, 2007.

town of Loganville: Loganville is mostly in Walton County but overlaps a little into Gwinnett; Laura Mallory is from the Gwinnett area and her children go to school there.

six-square-mile . . . seventy times bigger: American Fact Finder. U.S. Census Bureau, www.census.gov/popest/counties/CO -EST2004-09.html.

largest school system in the state: Gwinnett County Public Schools, www.gwinnett.k12.ga.us/.

population boom of 50 percent since the year 2000; among the fastest-growing; 85 percent of residents: American Fact Finder, U.S. Census Bureau, www.census.gov/popest/counties/CO-EST 2004-09.html.

184 *The appeal . . . magic:* Laura Diamond, "Hearing draws Potter foes, fans; Battle lines are drawn as mom fights to ban books," *Atlanta Journal-Constitution*, April 21, 2006.

Censorship Destroys Education: Ibid.

By the 2000s . . . school and library shelves: Hillel Italie, "Harry Potter, Huckleberry Finn, among controversial library books," Associated Press, September 13, 2000.

184 *472 cumulative challenges:* "Harry Potter series again tops list of most challenged books," American Library Association, press release, January 2001.

185 *646 challenges:* Ibid.

how many other children: www.kidspeakonline.org/kidspeakis .html.

186 *by the Ministry of Education in the United Arab Emirates:* "Emirates ban Potter book," BBC News, February 12, 2002.

Greek and Bulgarian Orthodox churches: "Church: Harry Potter Film a Font of Evil," *Kathimerini,* January 14, 2003. Clive Leviev-Sawyer, "Bulgarian Church Warns Against the Spell of Harry Potter," *Ecumenica News International,* June 28, 2004.

"I read stories": Kimberley Blair. "PotterCast #55: The Return of Fiddy-Five: Fan Interview," http://pottercast.the-leaky-cauldron.org/transcript/show/74?ordernum=4.

"first encyclical": Pope Benedict XVI, "To the Bishops, Priest and Deacons, Men and Women Religious, and All the Lay Faithful on Christian Love," December 25, 2005, www.vatican.va/holy_ father/benedict_xvi/encyclicals/documents/hf_ben-xvi_enc_ 20051225_deus-caritas-est_en.html.

a prefect of the congregation for the Doctrine of Faith: The Holy See: www.vatican.va/roman_curia/congregations/cfaith/index .htm.

189 *in which tragic school shootings occur:* "Ban 'Harry Potter' or face more high school shootings," *Daily Mail,* October 4, 2006.

189 *Rachel Joy Scott . . . God is what we need!*: "Testimony of Darrell Scott, Father of Two Victims at Columbine High School," www.garnertedarmstrong.org/WWArchives/vol24.htm.

190 *Dan Mauser . . . shot in the face:* Various sources: for example, www.acolumbinesite.com/victim/danm.html.

194 *"We think" . . . "self-sacrifice":* "Editorial: Why we like Harry Potter," *Christianity Today*, January 10, 2000.

198 *between 1990 and 2004:* "Top Ten Challenged Authors, 1990–2004," American Library Association, www.ala.org/ala/oif/bannedbooksweek/bbwlinks/authors19902004.cfm.

199 *Cedarville . . . restricted list:* "Parents sue over school library's special measures on Harry Potter," the Associated Press, July 6, 2002.

200 *quickly decided:* Beverly Goldberg, "Judge smites Harry Potter restrictions," *American Libraries*, June 1, 2003.

201 *On May 29:* Harry R. Weber, "U.S. judge upholds schools' decision to keep Harry Potter books," Associated Press Worldstream, May 29, 2007.

Ten: High Seas

211 *Between . . . 4,000 people:* Harry Potter for Grownups: A History. www.hpfgu.org.uk/faq/history.html#2.

215 *"H/H and why it's just wrong" . . . "shunted aside":* Harry Potter for Grownups, http://groups.yahoo.com/group/HPforGrownups/message/2236.

216 *Zsenya appeared:* Harry Potter for Grownups, http://groups .yahoo.com/group/HPforGrownups/message/5235.

219 *Sugar Quill's Purpose of Existence on the Web:* The Sugar Quill, www.sugarquill.com, retrieved through Archive.org, February 23, 2001 entry: http://web.archive.orgweb/20010224063058/ www.sugarquill.com/spew.html.

220 *"ridiculous impossibility":* Ibid.

sign her posts with Captain of the Cruiseliner H/H: Harry Potter for Grownups. http://groups.yahoo.com/group/HPforGrown ups/message/11323.

222 *Restrictedsection.org:* www.restrictedsection.org.

cease-and-desist letter: ChillingEffects.org, www.chillingeffects .org/fanfic/notice.cgi?NoticeID=522.

224 *"Do you know who the voice of my conscience is":* The Nimbus-2003 Programming Team, Edmund Kern, and Roger High-field, "Selected Papers from Nimbus-2003 Compendium: We Solemnly Swear These Papers Were Worth the Wait" (Houston: HP Education Fanon, Inc., 2005), p. 274.

"and pretty": Ibid, p. 271.

Eleven: Access

232 *$70 million:* Box Office Mojo, http://boxofficemojo.com/ movies/?id=goldencompass.htm.

Emma . . . class: "Daniel Radcliffe, Rupert Grint and Emma Watson Bring Harry, Ron and Hermione to Life for Warner

Bros. Pictures' Harry Potter and the Sorcerer's Stone," *Business Wire*, August 21, 2000.

Thirteen: Independence

268 *between 40 and 50 percent:* Cari Tuna, "The Book That Shall Not Make Big Money," *Star-Tribune* (Minneapolis), July 20, 2007.

Goblet of Fire . . . *loss leader:* Various sources including: Fritz Lanham, "Harry rises again; Fifth book about young wizard casts a spell on booksellers, fans," *Houston Chronicle*, June 18, 2003.

269 *Net Book Agreement:* The Booksellers Association, www.book sellers.org.uk/industry/display_report.asp?id=1164http://www .booksellers.org.uk/industry/display_report.asp?id=1164.

anticompetitive in 1997: Nigel Reynolds, "Court ruling opens new chapter for bookshops," *The Telegraph*, March 14, 1997.

271 *first recorded instance:* Joanna Carey, "Who hasn't met Harry?" *Guardian Unlimited*, February 16, 1999.

272 *Bungay . . . destruction:* Bungay Suffolk Town Guide, www .bungay-suffolk.co.uk.

Fifteen: Spoiled

290 *"If Harry dies . . . use them":* "Spoil Us Not, Sneaks!" the Leaky Cauldron, April 28, 2007.

by Jo Rowling . . . Web site: Melissa Anelli, "J. K. Rowling Updates Diary Regarding Spoilers," the Leaky Cauldron, May 14, 2007.

291 *on June 27, 2000:* Elizabeth Manus and Ted Diskant, "The Secret of Harry Potter IV? It Almost Blew Deadline," *New York Observer,* July 3, 2000.

292 *"it will be JKR . . . registers it":* Melissa Anelli, "Regarding Seabottom and HP6/HP7 Titles," the Leaky Cauldron, September 9, 2003.

Republic of China . . . Golden Turtle: "A Memo to the Dept. of Magical Copyright Enforcement," *New York Times,* August 10, 2007.

sued them and . . . fines: Tim Greening, "But there is a fifth 'Potter' novel . . .", *Shreveport Times,* November 12, 2002.

"Harry doesn't know" . . . "Aunt Petunia's Bottom": "Harry Potter and Leopard-Walk-Up-to-Dragon," *New York Times,* August 10, 2007.

On August 10 . . . Dragon King: Ibid.

297 *June 15, 2003 . . . Manchester:* Mark Rice-Oxley, "Harry Potter and the disappearing books," *Christian Science Monitor,* June 19, 2003.

reappeared the next afternoon: Helen Carter, "The plot thickens in Harry Potter lorry theft: Security operation in chaos as bogus driver makes off with more than 7,000 copies days before launch of boy wizard's latest adventure," *The Guardian* (London), June 18, 2003.

298 *headline was "Hocus-Pocus":* Tamer El-Ghobashy, "Hocus-Pocus! We Got Harry," New York *Daily News,* June 18, 2003.

299 *That changed before book six . . . "novel":* John Askill, "The Prisoner of Askill Bang," *The Sun*, June 7, 2005.

300 *Luckily for Askill . . . prison:* John Askill, "Judge: Potter Thug Set for Spell in Jail," *The Sun*, December 21, 2005.

Sixteen: One Day More

304 *Michiko Kakutani . . . review:* Michiko Kakutani, "An Epic Showdown as Harry Potter is Initiated into Adulthood," *New York Times*, July 19, 2007.

Seventeen: *Deathly Hallows*

316 *several sunlit days:* J. K. Rowling, *Harry Potter and the Half-Blood Prince* (New York: Scholastic Press, 2005), p. 533.

Epilogue

326 *"If I'd have known . . . ages ago":* Edward Drogos, "J. K. Rowling at Carnegie Hall Reveals Dumbledore is Gay; Neville Marries Hannah Abbott, and Much More," the Leaky Cauldron, October 19, 2007.

  Laura Mallory . . . point: Phil Kloer, "Dumbledore's Gay? A cauldron of reactions," *Atlanta Journal-Constitution*, October 23, 2007.

BIBLIOGRAPHY

The following are books and other materials I referenced or found helpful in forming thoughts and opinions while writing. Most direct sources may be found in the end notes, though I recommend these books.

Granger, John. *Looking for God in Harry Potter: Is there Christian meaning hidden in the bestselling books?* Carol Stream, Ill.: Tyndale, 2004.

Granger, John. *Unlocking Harry Potter: Five Keys for the Serious Reader.* Allentown, Penn.: Zossima Press, 2007.

Hafner, Katie and Matthew Lyon. *Where Wizards Stay Up Late: The Origins of the Internet.* New York: Simon & Schuster, 1998.

Morris, Tom. *If Harry Potter Ran General Electric: Leadership Wisdom from the World of the Wizards.* New York: Doubleday Business, 2006.

Neal, Connie. *The Gospel According to Harry Potter.* Louisville, Ky.: Westminster John Knox Press, 2002.

Neal, Connie. *Wizards, Wardrobes and Wookiees: Navigating Good and Evil in Harry Potter, Narnia and Star Wars.* Downers Grove, Ill.: InterVarsity Press, 2007.

Nimbus-2003 Programming Team, Edmund Kern, and Roger Highfield. *Selected Papers From Nimbus-2003 Compendium: We Solemnly Swear These Papers Were Worth the Wait.* Houston: HP Education Fanon, Inc., 2005.

Okin, J. R. *The Internet Revolution: The Not-For-Dummies Guide to the History, Technology and Use of the Internet.* Winter Harbor, Maine: Ironbound Press, 2005.

Rowling, J. K. *Harry Potter and the Sorcerer's Stone.* New York: Scholastic Press, 1998.

———. *Harry Potter and the Chamber of Secrets.* New York: Scholastic Press, 1999.

———. *Harry Potter and the Prisoner of Azkaban.* New York: Scholastic Press, 1999.

———. *Harry Potter and the Goblet of Fire.* New York: Scholastic Press, 2000.

———. *Harry Potter and the Order of the Phoenix.* New York: Scholastic Press, 2003.

———. *Harry Potter and the Half-Blood Prince.* New York: Scholastic Press, 2005.

———. *Harry Potter and the Deathly Hallows.* New York: Scholastic Press, 2007.

Tapscott, Don and Anthony D. Williams. *Wikinomics: How Mass Collaboration Changes Everything.* New York: Portfolio Hardcover, 2006.